T0229840

Web Technology

Web Technology

Theory and Practice

Dr. Akshi Kumar

CRC Press
Taylor & Francis Group
Boca Raton London New York

CRC Press is an imprint of the
Taylor & Francis Group, an **informa** business

A CHAPMAN & HALL BOOK

CRC Press
Taylor & Francis Group
6000 Broken Sound Parkway NW, Suite 300
Boca Raton, FL 33487-2742

© 2019 by Taylor & Francis Group, LLC
CRC Press is an imprint of Taylor & Francis Group, an Informa business

No claim to original U.S. Government works

International Standard Book Number-13: 978-1-1385-5043-8 (Hardback)

This book contains information obtained from authentic and highly regarded sources. Reasonable efforts have been made to publish reliable data and information, but the author and publisher cannot assume responsibility for the validity of all materials or the consequences of their use. The authors and publishers have attempted to trace the copyright holders of all material reproduced in this publication and apologize to copyright holders if permission to publish in this form has not been obtained. If any copyright material has not been acknowledged please write and let us know so we may rectify in any future reprint.

Except as permitted under U.S. Copyright Law, no part of this book may be reprinted, reproduced, transmitted, or utilized in any form by any electronic, mechanical, or other means, now known or hereafter invented, including photocopying, microfilming, and recording, or in any information storage or retrieval system, without written permission from the publishers.

For permission to photocopy or use material electronically from this work, please access www.copyright.com (http://www.copyright.com/) or contact the Copyright Clearance Center, Inc. (CCC), 222 Rosewood Drive, Danvers, MA 01923, 978-750-8400. CCC is a not-for-profit organization that provides licenses and registration for a variety of users. For organizations that have been granted a photocopy license by the CCC, a separate system of payment has been arranged.

Trademark Notice: Product or corporate names may be trademarks or registered trademarks, and are used only for identification and explanation without intent to infringe.

Library of Congress Cataloging-in-Publication Data

Names: Kumar, Akshi, author.
Title: Web technology : theory and practice / Akshi Kumar.
Description: Boca Raton : Taylor & Francis, a CRC title, part of the Taylor & Francis imprint, a member of the Taylor & Francis Group, the academic division of T&F Informa, plc, 2019. | Includes bibliographical references and index.
Identifiers: LCCN 2018014613| ISBN 9781138550438 (hardback   ) | ISBN 9781351029902 (ebook)
Subjects: LCSH: World Wide Web.
Classification: LCC TK5105.888 .K86 2019 | DDC 025.042--dc23
LC record available at https://lccn.loc.gov/2018014613

Visit the Taylor & Francis Web site at
http://www.taylorandfrancis.com

and the CRC Press Web site at
http://www.crcpress.com

I dedicate this book to my parents, Shri Prem Parkash Kumar and Shrimati Krishna Kumar, for their infinite love, understanding, and support. Without them none of my success would have been possible and I would not be who I am today.

Thank you Mom and Dad!

Contents

Section I   Internet Computing

Section II   Web Theory

Section III   Web Development

Section IV   Web Research

List of Figures

List of Tables

List of Acronyms

AC	Accuracy
ACID	Atomicity, Consistency, Isolation, Durability.
AJAX	Asynchronous JavaScript and XML
API	Application Program Interface
APRANET	Advanced Research Projects Agency Network
AS Number	Assigned Number
ASP	Active Server Pages
AQE	Automatic Query Expansion
BOOTP	Bootstrap Protocol
CERN	European Organization for Nuclear Research
CGI	Common Gateway Interface
CIR	Contextual Information Retrieval
CMS	Content Management System
CRUD	Create, Retrieve, Update, Delete
CSS	Cascading Style Sheets
CSV	Comma Separated Values
DBMS	Database Management System
DDP	Distributed Data Protocol
DOM	Document Object Model
DRY	Don't Repeat Yourself
DSL	Digital Subscriber Line
DSS	Digital Satellite Systems
DTD	Document Type Definition
DTL	Django Template Language
ERb	Embedded Ruby
FN	False Negative
FP	False Positive
FTP	File Transfer Protocol
HITS	Hyperlink-Induced Topic Search
HTML	Hypertext Markup Language
HTTP	Hyper Text Transfer Protocol
HTTPS	Hyper Text Transfer Protocol Secure
IAB	Internet Architecture Board
IANA	Internet Assigned Numbers Authority
ICANN	Internet Corporation for Assigned Names and Numbers
ICMP	Internet Control Message Protocol
IE	Information Extraction
IESG	Internet Engineering Steering Group
IETF	Internet Engineering Task Force
IGMP	Internet Group Management Protocol

IMAP	Internet Message Access Protocol
IP	Internet Protocol
IR	Information Retrieval
IRC	Internet Relay Chat
IRSG	Internet Research Steering Group
IRTF	Internet Research Task Force
ISDN	Integrated Services Digital Network
ISOC	Internet Society
ISP	Internet Service Provider
IQE	Interactive Query Expansion
JDBC	Java Database Connectivity
JS	JavaScript
JSON	JavaScript Object Notation
JSP	Java Server Pages
KDD	Knowledge Discovery in Databases
KDT	Knowledge Discovery in Textual Database
LAMP	Linux, Apache, MySQL, Px (Perl, PHP, Python)
LAN	Local Area Network
MAN	Metropolitan Area Network
MDA	Mail Delivery Agent
MIME	Multipurpose Internet Mail Extensions
MTA	Message Transfer Agent
MVC	Model View Controller
MVT	Model View Template
MVW	Model View Whatever
NAP	Network Access Point
NER	Named Entity Recognizer
NLP	Natural Language Processing
NNTP	Network News Transfer Protocol
NSP	Network Service Provider
NVT	Network Virtual Terminal
ODBC	Open Database Connectivity
OGM	Neo4j Object Graph Mapping
ORM	Object-Relational Mapping
OSI	Open System Interconnection
OWL	Web Ontology Language
P	Precision
P2P	Peer-to-Peer
PC	Personal Computer
PDA	Personal Digital Assistant
PGP	Pretty Good Privacy
PHP	Personal Home Pages/Hypertext Pre-processor
POP	Post Office Protocol
PPP	Point-to-Point Protocol

PR	PageRank™
PTP	Point-to-Point
QoS	Quality of Service
R	Recall
RDBMS	Relational Database Management System
RDF/RDFS	Resource Description Framework/RDF Schema
RegEx	Regular Expression
REST	Representational State Transfer
RIR	Regional Internet Registries
ROR	Ruby on Rails
RSS	Rich Site Summary/RDF Site Summary/Really Simple Syndication
RTP	Real-time Transport Protocol
RTT	Round Trip Time
SMTP	Simple Mail Transfer Protocol
SNMP	Simple Network Management Protocol
SONET	Synchronous Optical Networking
SPARQL	Simple Protocol and RDF Query Language
SQL	Structured Query Language
SSL/TLS	Secure Socket Layer/Transport Layer Security
TCP	Transmission Control Protocol
TDM	Text Data Mining
tf-idf	Term Frequency-Inverse Document Frequency
TFTP	Trivial File Transfer Protocol
TLD	Top Level Domain
TN	True Negative
TP	True Positive
TTT	Total Transmission Time
UDP	User Datagram Protocol
UI	User Interface
URI	Uniform Resource Identifier
URL	Uniform Resource Locator
URN	Uniform Resource Name
VoIP	Voice over Internet Protocol
VSM	Vector Space Model
WAMP	Windows, Apache, MySQL, Px (Perl, PHP, Python)
WAN	Wide Area Network
WWW	World Wide Web
XAMPP	Cross-Platform (X), Apache (A), MariaDB (M), PHP (P), Perl (P)
XML	eXtensible Markup Language

Preface

With the transformation of the Web into a ubiquitous tool for e-activities, such as e-commerce, e-learning, e-governance, and e-science, its use has pervaded to the realms of day-to-day work, information retrieval, and business management. Moreover, much progress has been made in terms of technological innovations to match the tech-savvy, socially mindful Gen-Y. This growing popularity has fostered the need to include studies in this field as a part of the core curriculum. Many universities are now offering a full course on web technology for undergraduate, postgraduate, and doctoral students in the disciplines of computer science engineering, information technology, and computer applications. This book is intended to be a complete reference book for a course on Web Technology. It includes a clear description of relevant concepts of the Web. The significant feature of this book is that it explicates the developments and approaches in the field of the Web from three perspectives: Web in Theory, Web in Practice, and Web in Research.

This book is organized into 12 chapters. The topics are intelligibly explained with examples and real-life case studies, making it suitable for a course on Web Technology. At the end of each chapter, self-review questions have been given to reinforce the concepts covered within the text.

This book content has been divided into four sections: Internet Computing, Web Theory, Web Development, and Web Research. Section I (Chapters 1 and 2) focuses on the Internet Computing for highlighting the difference and relationship between the terms "Internet" and "Web." They are two discrete but correlated concepts. This section of the book proffers a pre-requisite primer on the What, How, Who, and Why of the Internet. It expounds the details pertaining to the architecture and applications of the Internet.

Section II (Chapters 3 through 6) of this book offers the theoretical concepts of the World Wide Web with a detailed discussion on the underlying application layer protocol, HTTP, which makes the Web work. Much progress has been made regarding the Web and related technologies in the past two decades. Thus, the evolution of the Web is witnessed to understand the state-of-the-art for Web generations from its advent. Search engines have assumed a central role in the World Wide Web's infrastructure as its scale and impact have escalated and so a complete illustration on their architecture and working is presented in this section.

Section III (Chapters 7 through 11) expounds on web development. The development of the Web involves multiple concepts, tools, and technologies that help developers build complex yet fascinating web sites that are dynamic and interactive. It explains browsers, client-side and server-side programming languages, frameworks, and databases. The discussion includes foundational technologies like HTML, CSS, JavaScript, and PHP and is extended to the current industry trends Bootstrap, AngularJS, Node.js, Django, and Ruby on Rails.

Section IV (Chapter 12) describes web research. It is a primer on recent research trends, such as web mining, contextual retrieval, and sentiment analysis. With the rapid development of the Web, it is imperative to provide users with tools for efficient and effective resource and knowledge discovery, thus making research studies in this field highly active and dynamic.

Lastly, Appendixes A and B have been added for reference and hands-on practice, which includes examples using HTML and a case study project using Django and Neo4j, respectively.

The end of this book includes several bibliographic notes for further reading.

It is my pleasure in presenting this book to you and hope that it will serve as a course textbook to undergraduate and postgraduate students, as well as a reference guide for faculty, research scholars, and professionals. Readers are welcome to send suggestions and constructive criticism, which may help to improve the contents of the book and motivate me to continue working hard.

As the adage says: "You are your only limit"

Akshi Kumar
Delhi Technological University, India.

Acknowledgments

I am most thankful to my family for constantly encouraging me and giving me time and unconditional support while writing this book.

I am extremely grateful to MPS Bhatia, Professor, Netaji Subhas Institute of Technology, Delhi, India for being a constant source of inspiration throughout my research and teaching career. I will always be indebted to him for his extensive support and guidance.

My heartfelt gratitude to Arunima Jaiswal, Asst. Professor, Indira Gandhi Delhi Technical University for Women, Delhi, Aditi Sharma, Divya Gupta, Saurabh Raj Sangwan, Dhiraj Kumar Gupta, research scholars, Delhi Technological University, Delhi, India who worked closely with me during the evolution of the book. My sincere thanks to all my undergraduate, postgraduate, and doctoral students in the Department of Computer Science & Engineering, Delhi Technological University, Delhi, India, for motivating me to work on this book. Their interest and queries within the field were intriguing and helped me defining the text of the book. A special thanks to Team Kitchen Ninja (Pranav, Pratiksha, Priyal, and Rachit) for working with me on the Django-Neo4j case study, presented in Appendix B. I am also grateful to Sonal Jetly, Quality Manager, NIIT Technologies, Gurugram, India for her opinions and suggestions on the industry trends in the field of web development.

Lastly, thank you my sonny boy Kiaan Kumar for being less cranky and demanding when I was working on the book. I love you!

Author

Akshi Kumar is a PhD in Computer Engineering from the University of Delhi, Delhi, India. She has received her MTech (Master of Technology) and BE (Bachelor of Engineering) degrees in Computer Engineering. She is currently working as an Assistant Professor in the Department of Computer Science & Engineering at the Delhi Technological University, Delhi, India. She was a teaching-cum-research fellow at Netaji Subhas Institute of Technology, University of Delhi, India.

Dr. Kumar's research interests are in the area of text mining, sentiment analysis, recommender systems, social and semantic web, and analytics of user-generated big-data. She has many publications in various international journals/conferences to her credit, she has authored books, and has co-authored book chapters within her domain of interest. She is actively involved in research activities as the editorial review board member for international journals, session chair and technical program committee member for international conferences, and providing research supervision at undergraduate, postgraduate, and doctorate levels. She has visited foreign universities like Imperial College, London and University of Cambridge, UK. She is a member of Institute of Electrical and Electronics Engineers (IEEE), IEEE Women in Engineering (WIE), and Association for Computing Machinery (ACM), a life member of Indian Society of Technical Engineers (ISTE) and Computer Society of India (CSI), India, a member of International Association of Computer Science and Information Technology (IACSIT), Singapore, a member of International Association of Engineers (IAENG), Hong Kong, and a member of the Internet Computing Community (ICC), AIRCC.

Dr. Kumar can be contacted via e-mail at akshi.kumar@gmail.com

Section I

Internet Computing

1

INTERconnected NETwork: Internet

1.1 Internet: The Giant Wide Area Network

The first sets of computers developed during the Second World War were innately expensive and isolated. Eventually, with their gradual decrease in price, researchers began to implement experiments to connect these computers. Consequently, sharing over these low-cost, remote computers appeared to be an interesting idea. An obvious intent to share resources, share information, and facilitate communication further motivated the researchers to realize networking as a key enabler. The pertinent literature published in the early 1960s substantiated the vision of building computer networks. As a meta-network, or network of networks, the Internet (acronym for INTERconnected NETwork) emerged to be a promising technology for providing ubiquitous access. In 1969, ARPANET started as a federally funded research project, which was initiated by the Advanced Research Project Agency (ARPA) and the US Department of Defense (DoD). The experiments initially linked researchers with remote computer centers allowing them to share hardware and software resources, such as computer disk space and databases. Later, it was renamed the Internet. This inter-network operated with a technique called packet switching where digital data is transmitted in small bundles called packets. These packets contain the information about the address, error control, and the sequence in which packets are to be sent. The network was designed to operate without centralized control. If a portion of the network failed, the remaining working portions would still route packets from senders to receivers over alternative paths. ARPANET used the Transmission Control Protocol (TCP) for communication. TCP ensured that messages were properly routed from sender to receiver. As the Internet evolved and added to the realms of intra-organization and inter-organization day-to-day e-activities, it became challenging to allow communication with different networks. ARPA solved the problem by developing the Internet Protocol (IP), which truly created the network of networks—the current architecture of Internet.

A network is a communication system for connecting end-systems (a.k.a. "hosts," PCs, workstations, dedicated computers, network components, nodes) and an *Internetwork* (INTERconnected NETwork or Internet) is an arbitrary collection of physical networks interconnected by routers to provide some sort of host-to-host packet delivery service. The Internet is defined as the globally distributed network of networks that consists of millions of private, public, academic, business, and government networks, which are linked by an extensive range of electronic, wireless, and optical networking technologies. The networks can primarily be classified either based on the transmission media used as wired (unshielded twisted-pair cables, shielded twisted-pair cables, coaxial cables, fiber-optic cables) or wireless; or on the basis of physical topology explicating the shape or layout of the network as point-to-point (PTP) or multi-access (ring, star, or bus); or on the basis of application-centric architecture as Peer-to-Peer or Client-Server depending on the role the networked computers play in the network's operation; or on the basis of the geographical area covered as Local Area Networks, Metropolitan Area Networks, or Wide Area Networks.

- A *Local Area Network* (*LAN*) is a network that is used for communicating among computer devices, usually within an office building or home. Though it is limited in size, typically spanning a few hundred meters and no more than a mile, it is fast, with speeds from 10 Mbps to 10 Gbps with minimal infrastructure requirements, low cost, and high security. LANs can be either wired or wireless. Nodes in a LAN are linked together with a certain topology.

- A *Metropolitan Area Network* (*MAN*) is optimized for a larger geographical area than a LAN, ranging from several blocks of buildings to entire cities, typically covering an area ranging from 5 to 50 km diametrically. As a high-speed network, MAN allows sharing of regional resources. It might be owned and operated by a single organization, but it is typically used by many individuals and organizations. Although the speeds achieved in a MAN are typically as high as in a LAN, it requires high-speed connections, such as fiber optics. The relative installation and operational costs of MANs is also high.

- A *Wide Area Network* (*WAN*) covers a large geographic area such as country, continent or even whole world. It is two or multiple LANs connected using devices such as bridges, routers, or gateways, which enable them to share resources. To cover great distances, WANs may transmit data over leased high-speed phone lines or wireless links such as satellites. Internet is the giant WAN, the world's most popular WAN in existence.

Another classification of networks focuses on the roles of the networked computers. The millions of connected computing devices (also called hosts or end-systems) that constitute the Internet, can be divided into two basic types relying on their role classifications for networks: the Peer-to-Peer networks (also known as a workgroup) and Server-based networks (also known as a Client/Server network). The difference between the two revolves around which computer is in charge of the network.

- *Client/server network*: In the client/server model, all end systems are divided into clients and servers, each designed for specific purposes. Clients have an active role and initiate a communication session by sending requests to servers. Clients must have knowledge of the available servers and the services they provide. Clients can communicate with servers only; they cannot see each other. A central computer, such as a workstation or server is a common source that provides shared services with other machines and manages resources in the network. Servers have a passive role and respond to their clients by acting on each request and returning results. One server generally supports numerous clients (Figure 1.1).

- *Peer-to-peer network* (*P2P*): In the P2P network architecture, all end systems have equivalent capabilities and responsibilities and either party can initiate a communication session. There is no central location for authenticating users, storing files, or accessing resources. The P2P model does not have the notion of clients or servers but only equal peers (a.k.a. servents, servent = SERVer + cliENT) that simultaneously function as both clients and servers. They are inexpensive, easy to install and extremely limited in scope. The accepted maximum number of peers that can operate on a peer-to-peer network is ten (Figure 1.2).

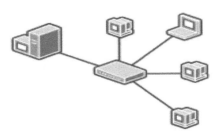

FIGURE 1.1
Client/server network.

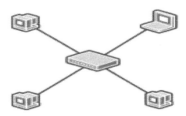

FIGURE 1.2
Peer-to-peer network.

There are two types of P2P networks: the Pure P2P Network and Hybrid P2P Network.

- *Pure P2P network*: A P2P system that has no central service of any kind i.e., the entire communication occurs among connected peers without any assistance from any server is referred to as a pure P2P Network. Examples: Workgroups in Microsoft Windows Network, Gnutella, Freenet.
- *Hybrid P2P network*: Pure P2P systems work well only in a small-scale environment. Hybrid P2P system depends partially on central servers or allocates selected functions to a subset of dedicated peers. Central servers act as central directories where either connected users or indexed content can be mapped to the current location. Dedicated peers directly control information among other peers. Thus, client/server and P2P systems are not mutually exclusive. Examples: Skype (voice-over-IP P2P application where the centralized server helps finding address of remote party and the real communication is a direct client-client connection not through server), BitTorrent.

FUN FACT: BitTorrent is a protocol, not a provider: People frequently say things like "I downloaded Season 6 of *Game of Thrones* from BitTorrent." It is incorrect to say this since BitTorrent is a protocol, not a service, and you can't download a file from a protocol. You can download a file *using* this protocol. No one downloads a file *from* BitTorrent – files are downloaded from other individuals, *using* BitTorrent.

Torrent ≠ Piracy: BitTorrent, the protocol, is used by some legal content distributors such as BitTorrent Inc. (for movies/music/TV) and Linux operating system developers (such as for Ubuntu and Fedora).

1.2 Communicating over the Internet

As per the statistics available on Internet Live Stats (www.InternetLiveStats.com) as on June 13, 2018, there are 3,943,215,816 global Internet Users (individuals who can access the Internet at home, via any device type and connection) (Figure 1.3).

Two popular models—the Open Systems Interconnection (OSI) reference model and the TCP/IP model—have been adopted as formal models which allow us to deal with various aspects of networks abstractly, based on the concept of layering. In 1984, OSI reference model was approved as an international standard for communications architecture. The term "open" denotes the ability to connect any two systems which conform to the reference model and associated standards. The OSI model was considered the primary architectural model for inter-computer communications and described how information or data made its way from application programs (such as spreadsheets) through a network medium (such as wire) to another application program located on another network. It divides the problem of moving information between computers over a network medium into *seven* smaller and more manageable layers (Figure 1.4).

The process of breaking up the functions or tasks of networking into layers reduces the complexity. Each layer provides a service to the layer above it in the protocol specification. Each layer communicates with the same layer's software or hardware on other computers.

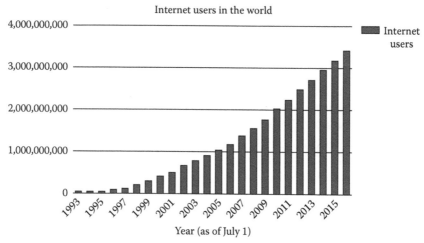

FIGURE 1.3
Statistical bar chart for available Internet users.

7. Application: Application programs using the network
6. Presentation: Data representation
5. Session: Inter-host communication
4. Transport: End-to-End connections; error detection and correction
3. Network: Handling of data grams-routing and congestion
2. Data link: Access to media
1. Physical: Binary transmission

FIGURE 1.4
OSI reference model.

OSI reference model	TCP/IP conceptual layers
7. Application (*DNS, FTP, HTTPS, POP3, SMTP, Telnet*)	4. Application
6. Presentation (*JPEG, MPEG, TIFF*)	
5. Session (*ZIP, SQL*)	
4. Transport (*TCP, UDP*)	3. Transport
3. Network (*ICMP, IGMP, IPSec, IPV4, IPV6*)	2. Internet (network)
2. Data link (*ATM, PPP, Frame relay*)	1. Network interface
1. Physical (*Bluetooth, Ethernet, DSL, ISDN, 802.11, Wi-Fi*)	

FIGURE 1.5
OSI versus TCP/IP model.

The lower four layers (transport, network, data link, and physical—Layers 4, 3, 2, and 1) are concerned with the flow of data from end to end through the network. The upper three layers of the OSI model (application, presentation, and session—Layers 7, 6, and 5) are oriented more toward services to the applications. The OSI model was a generic, protocol-independent standard. The TCP/IP Model was established to define protocol suite on which the Internet depended. Though, OSI reference model was a well-recognized model, the TCP/IP model provided an application viewpoint of the network. The OSI model conceptually defined the services, interfaces, and protocols; the TCP/IP (Internet) model provided its successful implementation (Figure 1.5).

FUN FACT: The TCP/IP model, which is realistically the Internet Model, came into existence about 10 years before the OSI model.

The following subsections expound the TCP/IP protocol suite and the addressing mechanism in the Internetworking environment.

1.2.1 Protocol Layering

To communicate using the Internet system, a host must implement the layered set of protocols comprising the Internet protocol suite (Figure 1.6).

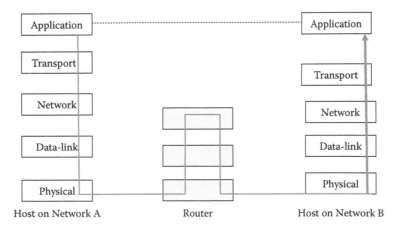

FIGURE 1.6
Internet working through router.

User application program (FTP, SMTP, HTTP, Telnet, DNS)
{Represents data to user and takes care of encoding}
Transmission control protocol (TCP)
{Supports communication between diverse devices across diverse networks}
Internet protocol (IP)
{Determines the best path through the network}
Network interface (Ethernet)
{Controls hardware devices and media that make up the network}
Hardware (Physical connection)

FIGURE 1.7
Internet protocol stack.

The protocol layers used in the Internet architecture are as follows (Figure 1.7).

The Internet Protocol stack (TCP/IP Protocol Suite) is based on the divide-and-conquer modus operandi to define and use the architecture entailing communication (Application, Transport), interconnection (Network, Link), and distance (Physical). The role of each layer is as follows:

- *Application layer*: The application layer of the Internet suite essentially combines the functions of the top two layers—Presentation and Application—of the OSI Reference Model. We distinguish two categories of application layer protocols: user protocols that provide service directly to users, and support protocols that provide common system functions. The most common Internet user protocols are: Telnet (remote login), FTP (file transfer), SMTP (electronic mail delivery), HTTP (web). Support protocols, used for host name mapping, booting, and management include Simple Network Management Protocol (SNMP), Bootstrap Protocol (BOOTP), Trivial File Transfer Protocol (TFTP), the Domain Name System (DNS) protocol, and a variety of routing protocols.

- *Transport layer*: The Transport Layer is responsible for reliable source-to-destination (end-to-end) delivery of the entire message. This layer is roughly equivalent to the Transport Layer in the OSI Reference as it provides end-to-end communication services. There are two primary Transport Layer protocols at present: TCP and User Datagram Protocol (UDP). TCP is a reliable connection-oriented protocol whereas UDP is a connectionless (datagram) protocol.

- *Internet layer*: All Internet transport protocols use the IP to carry data from source host to destination host. IP is a connectionless or datagram Internetwork service, providing no end-to-end delivery guarantees. IP datagrams may arrive at the destination host damaged, duplicated, out of order, or not at all. The Internet Control Message Protocol (ICMP) is a control protocol that is considered an integral part of IP, although it is architecturally layered upon IP—it uses IP to carry its data end-to-end. ICMP provides error reporting, congestion reporting, and first-hop router redirection. The Internet Group Management Protocol (IGMP) is an Internet layer protocol used for establishing dynamic host groups for IP multicasting.

- *Link layer (network interface)*: To communicate on a directly connected network, a host must implement the communication protocol used to interface to that network. The Link Layer protocol provides this interface. It specifies how to organize data into frames and how to deliver a frame over a network. Its responsibility is the correct delivery of messages.

- *Physical layer*: Provides physical interface for transmission of information. Defines rules by which bits are passed from one system to another on a physical communication medium. It covers all the mechanical, electrical, functional, and procedural aspects for physical communication.

IP is considered to be the most successful protocol ever developed. The "Hourglass Model" proposed by Dave Clark, shown in Figure 1.8, depicts IP as the waist of the hourglass of the Internet protocol architecture with multiple higher-layer protocols, multiple lower-layer protocols, and only one protocol at the network layer.

Curse of narrow waist: As the number of service interfaces doubles, changes are desired below and above the waist to avoid interoperability problems. Moreover, *below the waist bulge* is apparent too as the lower layers mostly seem to just make IP's job harder with cells, circuits, QoS, multicast, large clouds, opaque clouds. Many researchers have suggested a promising fitness goal to trim down from an hourglass to wineglass architecture.

1.2.2 Internet Addressing

An IP address is a unique global address for a network interface. It is 32-bit logical address, composed of four 8-bit fields, called octets. The address is represented in "dotted decimal notation" by grouping the four octets. Each octet represents a decimal number in the range 0–255 (since 255 is the maximum 8-bit binary number), i.e., the format of IP address is xxx.xxx.xxx.xxx, where each xxx is a number from 0 to 255. These are unique numbers and controlled by address registry. For example, 17.112.152.32 is the IP address for www.apple.com,

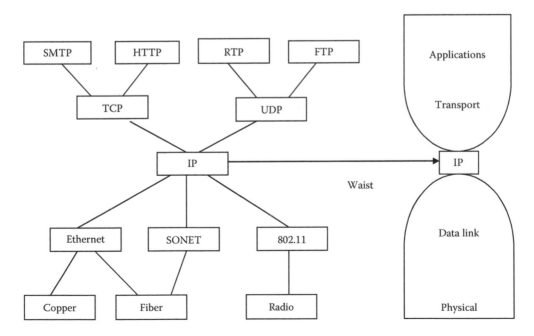

FIGURE 1.8
Hourglass architecture of the Internet.

for www.amazon.com it is 54.239.26.128 and that for www.dtu.ac.in is 122.160.182.54. IP address is divided into two parts: a prefix which identifies the physical network to which the host is attached and a suffix which identifies a specific computer (host/node) on the network. Each network on the Internet is assigned a unique network number and each computer on a given network is assigned a unique suffix. IP address scheme guarantees two properties that each computer is assigned a unique address, i.e., a single address is never assigned to more than one computer and the Network number (prefix) assignments must be coordinated globally whereas the suffixes are assigned locally without global coordination. Uniform Resource Locators (URL) specifies the Internet address of a file (any resource) stored on a host computer (server), connected to the Internet. URLs are translated into numeric addresses using a DNS. When we type a URL, this application-layer service called the DNS translates the human-friendly URL into the computer-friendly IP address. DNS performs this translation by consulting the databases maintained by the Domain Name Registrars. DNS is responsible for translating "www.apple.com" into "17.112.152.32" whenever we type that into a browser address bar. DNS is the "phone book" of the Internet: look up a name and find its number. A DNS refers to a network service that associates alphanumeric host names to their equivalent IP address. The domain name or IP address gives the destination location for the URL. The URLs are sensitive to correct spelling, additional spaces, and upper or lower-case letters.

A URL is made up of many parts.

The generic anatomy of a URL is:

protocol://domain name /path/filename

For example:

http://	www.dtu.ac.in/	Academics/	antiragging.php
protocol://	domain name	path (directory)	file name

- *Protocol*: It specifies the transfer protocol that will be used for retrieval of desired resource. Examples include Hypertext Transfer Protocol (http), HTTP Secure Protocol (https), and File Transfer Protocol (ftp).
- *Domain name*: The Domain name is also known as website name or host name. It is often divided into three parts: www (optional), second level name (e.g., dtu.ac in www.dtu.ac.in), and top level name (*Organizational*: 3-character code indicates the function of the organization, for example .com: commercial; .org: non-profit organization; .gov: government; .net: network resources; .edu: education; .ac: academic. *Geographical*: 2-character code indicates country or region codes for geographic sites, such as .in: India; .us: United States; .uk: United Kingdom; .au: Australia).
- *Path*: It is the directory or the folder on the server. It is the path used to specify and perhaps find the resource requested, i.e., a path to a file located on the web server.
- *File name*: The file name element of a URL is the file name within that directory with an extension such as htm, html, php, and so on.

The DNS is implemented as a distributed system and has a hierarchical structure, that is, the name hierarchy can be represented as a tree. Each node in the DNS tree represents a DNS name. Each branch below a node is a DNS domain. DNS domain can contain hosts or

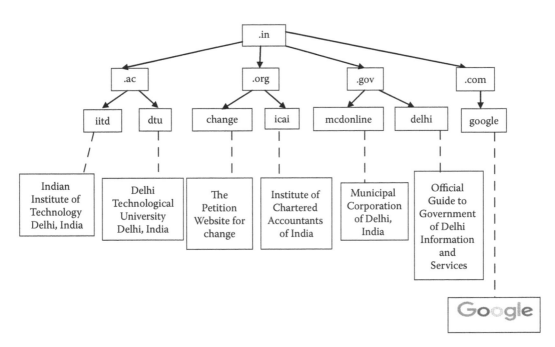

FIGURE 1.9
Sample DNS hierarchy.

other domains (sub-domains). The top-level domains are at the root of the tree followed by the top-down sub-domains. Figure 1.9 illustrates a sample DNS hierarchy.

More recently, a URL is now considered to be a subset of Uniform Resource Identifier (URI). A URI is a string of characters used to identify a name or a resource on the Internet and is recognized as a more general form of URL. It identifies a resource either by location, or a name, or both, i.e., a URI can be further classified as a locator, a name, or both. URL and URN (Uniform Resource Name) are two specializations of URI. Remember, every URL is a URI; every URN is a URI; URI and URL are NOT interchangeable—a URL is a URI, but a URI is not always a URL. We exemplify the three as follows:

- *URL*: Contains information about how to fetch a resource from its location. URLs always start with a protocol (http) and usually contain information such as the network host name (dtu.ac.in) and often a document path (/Academics/syllabus.php).

  For example: http://dtu.ac.in/Web/Academics/syllabus.php

  ftp://example.com/download.zip

- *URN*: Identifies a resource by a unique and persistent name. It usually starts with the prefix urn: URNs can be ideas and concepts. They are not restricted to identifying documents. When a URN does represent a document, it can be translated into a URL by a "resolver." The document can then be downloaded from the URL.

  For example: urn: isbn: 0451450523 to identify a book by its ISBN number.

- *URI*: The URI encompasses URLs, URNs, and other ways to identify a resource. In a simple real-world analogy, a URN is a globally unique name, like ISBN # for a book. A URI is the identifier representing the contents of the book, and a URL is the location of the book.

1.3 Accessing the Internet

Structurally, the Internet consists of millions of connected computing devices, known as hosts or end systems, which are connected together by communication links. The hosts are not usually directly attached to each other via a single communication link. Instead, they are indirectly connected to each other through intermediate switching devices called routers. The routers are responsible to forward chunks of data (packets). This architectural description is sometimes referred to as the "Nuts and Bolts" view of the Internet. The structural configuration of the Internet is discussed in Section 1.3.1.

1.3.1 Internet Configuration

Every computer connected to the Internet accesses the Internet through an Internet Service Provider (ISP). The ISP, in turn, may connect to a larger network such as a Network Service Provider (NSP) that provides backbone services to the Internet service provider. These connections are collectively known as Internet Backbone. The backbones carry Internet traffic around the world and meet at Network Access Points (NAPs). ISPs connect either directly to a backbone, or they connect to a larger ISP with a connection to a backbone. Thus, the basic building blocks of the Internet that allow the network communication and its successful implementation consist of:

- An *Internet backbone* is a collection of routers (nationwide or worldwide) connected by high-speed point-to-point networks.
- A *NAP* is a router that connects multiple backbones (sometimes referred to as *peers*).
- *Regional networks* are smaller backbones that cover smaller geographical areas (e.g., cities or states).
- A *point of presence (POP)* is a machine that is connected to the Internet.
- *ISPs* provide dial-up or direct access to POPs. Commercial organization with permanent connection to the Internet that sells temporary connections to subscribers. The computer first connects to the ISP and then to the Internet.

Thus, the Internet access structure is roughly hierarchical with "tier-1" ISPs that have national/international coverage, at the center, followed by the "Tier-2" ISPs, which are smaller (often regional) ISPs, finally connecting to the "Tier-3" ISPs and local ISPs which are the last hop ("access") network (closest to end systems).

Internet service provider (ISP) offers Internet accounts to configure the network connections either by using a dial-up access, high-speed access, or wireless access.

- *Dial-up access*: Dial-Up Connection works over an ordinary phone line, using analog modems establishing the Point-to-Point Protocol (PPP). As the personal computers are mostly equipped with analog modems, there is usually no additional money needed for hardware.
- *High-speed access*: A high-speed connection also known as the broadband connection comprises of divergent options such as Digital Subscriber Line (DSL), Integrated Services Digital Network (ISDN) Lines, leased line, and cable Internet connections. DSL is a family of all-digital, high-speed lines that use normal phone wires with special modems. ISDN lines, like DSL lines, are all-digital, high-speed phone lines that provide a faster way to connect to the Internet. To connect your

computer to an ISDN line, you need an ISDN adapter. DSL is most commonly used in the United States whereas ISDN is widely used in Europe. Similarly, a leased-line account can be opted which provides a point-to-point, high speed communication line that directly connects your computer to your ISP's network. It is suitable if an organization may need to transfer very large amounts of data or run Internet server software. More recently, major ISPs and online services, like EarthLink and AOL, had made deals with cable TV companies to provide cable Internet access. The cable modem allows the same network that brings you variety of TV channels get millions of websites. Finally, Digital Satellite Systems (DSS), or direct broadcast satellite is a method by which Internet content is downloaded to a satellite dish and then transmitted directly from the dish to the user's PC.

- *Wireless access*: Another way to connect to the Internet is via a Wireless access using Wi-Fi technology. A Wi-Fi enabled device, such as a PC, game console, cell phone, MP3 player, or personal data assistant (PDA), can connect to the Internet when its within range of a wireless network connected to the Internet.

1.3.2 Web Browser

A web browser is a software program that retrieves, presents, and traverses information resources on the Web. The primary function of a browser is to identify the URL and bring the information resource to user. To identify a web pages' exact location, a web browser relies on a URL. A URL, as described previously, is a four-part addressing scheme that tells the web browser:

- The transfer protocol to use for transporting the file
- The domain name of the computer on which the file resides
- The pathname of the folder or directory on the computer on which the file resides
- The name of the file

All major browsers allow users to access multiple information resources at the same time in different windows or in tabs. They also include pop up blockers to open windows with users' consent. Some of the well-known web browsers are Internet Explorer, Netscape Navigator, Mozilla Firefox, Opera, Google Chrome, Safari, and so on. The basic functions of a web browser include:

- Interpret HTML[1] markup and present documents visually.
- Support hyperlinks in HTML documents so that clicking on such a hyperlink can lead to the corresponding HTML file being downloaded from the same or another web server and presented.
- Use HTML form and the HTTP protocol to send requests and data to web applications and download HTML documents.
- Maintain cookies (name-value pairs) stored on client computers by a web application and send all cookies back to a website if they are stored by the web application at that website (cookies will be further discussed in Chapter 4).

---

[1] HTML is an acronym for HyperText Markup Language. It is the way Web pages are written so any computer can understand them and display them correctly with the help of web browser. The basics of HTML will be discussed in Chapter 3, with a detailed discussion on it in Chapter 8.

FUN FACT: The Mosaic was world's first graphical web browser and was developed by a team at University of Illinois' National Center for Supercomputing applications. The launch of Mosaic web browser in 1993 is today considered to be the turning point for the Web. Mosaic is today credited for making the Web popular.

1.4 Internet Organizations

No one actually owns the Internet, and no single person or organization controls the Internet in its entirety. The Internet is more of a concept than an actual tangible entity, and it relies on a physical infrastructure that connects networks to other networks. A number of loosely coupled organizations are concerned with governing the development of the Internet. There is no strict hierarchy in these organizations.

- *Internet Society (ISOC)*: ISOC is concerned with the long-term coordination of the Internet development.

- *Internet Engineering Task Force (IETF)*: IETF is an open international community of network professionals and experts. The mission of IETF is to produce high quality technical documents for improving the Internet's quality and performance.

- *Internet Corporation for Assigned Names and Numbers (ICANN)*: ICANN (formerly InterNIC) is an internationally organized non-profit organization under Californian rights. The responsibilities of ICANN are IP address space allocation, gTLD (generic Top-Level Domain) and ccTLD (country code TLD), DNS management (ICANN is the body that decides about the introduction of new TLDs), Root server system management, and Protocol identifier assignment.

- *Internet Assigned Numbers Authority (IANA)*: IANA is the predecessor organization of ICANN. It manages the different duties of ICANN: the TLD, protocol number, IP address and AS (Autonomous System) number management.

- *Internet Architecture Board (IAB)*: The IAB is responsible for the Internet architecture, as a whole, and protocol development oversight with respect to aspects like scalability, openness of standards and evolution of the Internet architecture.

- *Internet Engineering Steering Group (IESG)*: IESG carries out the technical management of IETF activities and the Internet standards process.

- *Internet Research Task Force (IRTF)*: IRTF conducts research on protocols, applications, architecture, and technology.

- *Internet Research Steering Group (IRSG)*: The IRSG is responsible for steering the IRTF and provides good conditions for research carried out by IRTF.

- *World Wide Web Consortium (W3C)*: W3C develops web technology standards. W3C is not directly related to IETF, IAB, or ISOC.

- *Regional Internet Registries (RIR)*: RIRs are responsible for the management and allocation of Internet number resources: IP addresses and AS numbers.

1.5 Cyber Ethics

Cyber Ethics refers to the code of responsible behavior on the Internet. It entails basic Internet etiquettes, also known as Netiquettes, which are the set of rules or guidelines for cyberspace behavior. The expected conduct must be ethical, and users must act within the laws of society and cyberspace. Mannerisms when using the Internet include a responsible human behavior, respecting privacy, and avoiding plagiarism. Netiquette varies from domain to domain. But one thing that remains same across domain is basic respect to other people's time and bandwidth, which implies strictly no to spamming, viruses, and hoaxes. A cyber-smart citizen is expected to commit to always acting safely, ethically, and responsibly while using the Internet. A good "cyber citizen" should practice the basic tenets of Cyber Ethics, which include:

- Communicating, sharing, and contributing to e-society in a positive manner
- To be respectful and courteous in communication (do not use rude or offensive language)
- Avoid harming others (do not spread pictures, viruses, gossip, information about others, do not use others' usernames and passwords, i.e., do not impersonate others and do not trespass in other's files)
- Sharing network resources, being honest and trustworthy
- Honor property rights and copyrights (do not download or take software, images, text that are copyrighted), and giving proper credit for intellectual property (do not plagiarize information, use citation properly)

The evolution of Internet into a transactional model with e-business, e-commerce, e-governance, and e-procurement etc. and with the rise in the number of Internet users, the need for cyber laws and their application has also gathered great momentum. Cyber law can also be described as that branch of law that deals with legal issues related to use of inter-networked information technology. In short, cyber law is the law governing computers and the Internet. As a gloomier face of technology, Cyber crime has been reported globally, and Cyber laws are the sole savior to combat cyber crime.

Review Questions

1. Answer the following:

   a. _____ network is optimized for a larger geographical area than a LAN, ranging from several blocks of buildings to entire cities, typically covering an area ranging from 5 to 50 km diametrically.

   b. In the Internet Protocol stack _____ layer is responsible for reliable source-to-destination delivery of the entire message.

   c. BitTorrent is an example of _____ network architecture.

   d. _____ is a 32-bit logical address, composed of four 8-bit fields, called octets.

    e.   _____ offers Internet accounts to configure the network connections either by using a dial-up access, high-speed access or wireless access.

    f.   _____ is a software program that retrieves, presents, and traverses information resources on the web.

    g. W3C is the acronym for _____.

    h. _____ refers to the code of responsible behavior on the Internet.

    i.   _____ develops standards for the Internet.

    j.   URL consists of three parts. They are _____, _____ and _____.

2. The terms "Internet" and "Web" are synonymous and can be used interchangeably. Comment.

3. What is the "Hourglass" Architecture of the Internet?

4. Differentiate between the following

    a. LAN, WAN, MAN

    b. Client/Server architecture and Peer-to-Peer architecture

    c. URI, URN, URL

5. How are the concepts of IP addressing, URL, and DNS associated?

6. In what ways can an Internet Service Provider (ISP) configure network connections?

7. What are the basic functions of a web browser? Name any four web browsers.

8. List a few Netiquettes that should be practiced in order to become a good "cyber citizen."

2

Internet Applications

2.1 Internet Services

The Internet can be viewed from two perspectives. One way is to describe the "nuts and bolts" of the Internet, and the other is the "Service" view of the Internet.

- *The nuts and bolts description*: In the world of the Internet, millions of devices are interconnected, and these devices are called hosts or end-systems that are connected by communication links. They are indirectly connected to each other through intermediate switching devices know as packet switches. Different links can transmit data at different rates, with the transmission rate of a link measured in bits/second. The path followed from the sender end-system to the receiver end-system is a sequence of communication links and packet switches traversed by a packet. End-systems, packet switches, and other pieces of the Internet run protocols that control the sending and receiving of information within the Internet. Transmission Control Protocol (TCP) and the Internet Protocol (IP) are two of the most important protocols in the Internet.
- *Service view description*: The Internet allows distributed applications, such as email, file transfer, real-time user communication, and web sites, running on its end-systems to exchange data with each other. It provides two services to its distributed applications: a connection-oriented reliable service and a connectionless unreliable service. The following sections discuss these distributed applications provided as services by the Internet.

2.2 Electronic Mail (Email)

Electronic mail, or email as its more commonly called, is a method of sending a message from a user at a computer to a recipient on another computer. Email systems are based on a *store-and-forward* model in which email computer server systems accept, forward, deliver, and store messages on behalf of users, who only need to connect to the email infrastructure, typically an email server, with a network enabled device for the duration of the message submission or retrieval. An email is a message that may contain text, files, images, or other attachments sent through a network to a specified individual or group of individuals. The first email was sent by Ray Tomlinson in 1971.

2.2.1 Working of an Email

Email is based around the use of electronic mailboxes. When an email is sent, the message is routed from server to server, all the way to the recipient's email server. More precisely, the message is sent to the mail server tasked with transporting emails (called the MTA, for Mail Transport Agent) to the recipient's MTA. On the Internet, MTAs communicate with one another using the Simple Mail Transfer Protocol (SMTP), and so are logically called SMTP servers (or sometimes *outgoing mail servers*). The recipient's MTA then delivers the email to the incoming mail server, called the Mail Delivery Agent (MDA), which stores the email as it waits for the user to accept it. There are two main protocols used for retrieving email on an MDA: Post Office Protocol (POP3) and Internet Message Access Protocol (IMAP). For this reason, incoming mail servers are called POP servers or IMAP servers, depending on which protocol is used. To use a real-world analogy, MTAs act as the post office (the sorting area and mail carrier, which handle message transportation), while MDAs act as mailboxes, which store messages (as much as their volume will allow) until the recipients check the box. This means that it is not necessary for recipients to be connected in order for them to be sent email. To keep everyone from checking other users' emails, MDA is protected by a username called a login and by a password. Retrieving mail is done using a software program called a Mail User Agent (MUA). When the MUA program is installed on the user's system, it is called an email client (such as Mozilla Thunderbird, Microsoft Outlook, Eudora Mail, or Lotus Notes). When it is a web interface used for interacting with the incoming mail server, it is called webmail (Gmail, Hotmail, Yahoo mail) (Figure 2.1).

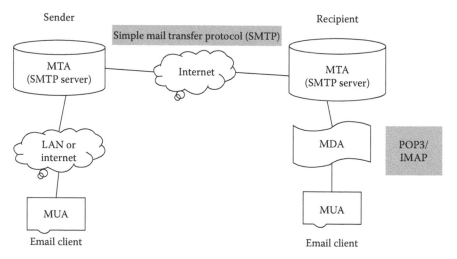

FIGURE 2.1
The store- and forward-model of email.

2.2.1.1 Email Protocols

The following protocols discussed are the most commonly used in the transfer of email:

2.2.1.1.1 Mail Transport Protocols: Simple Mail Transfer Protocol

Mail delivery from an originating server to the destination server is handled by the *Simple Mail Transfer Protocol (SMTP)*. The primary purpose of SMTP is to transfer email between mail servers. Some characteristics of SMTP are as follows:

- It is a client-server protocol where the client is the sending mail from an originating mail server to a receiving mail server.
- It allows reliable data transfer built on top of TCP (on port 25).
- It is a Push protocol where the sending server pushes the file to the receiving server rather than waiting for the receiver to request it.
- It is a Command/response interaction where commands are ASCII text and responses are three-digit status code and phrase.
- It is Synchronous as the sender awaits a response before issuing the next command.
- It has three phases of transfer: Handshaking, Transfer of messages, and Closure.

FUN FACT: SMTP protocol does not require authentication. This allows anyone on the Internet to send email to anyone else or even to large groups of people. It is this characteristic of SMTP that makes junk email or spam possible.

2.2.1.1.2 Mail Access Protocols: Post Office Protocol and Internet Message Access Protocol

There are two primary protocols used by email client applications to retrieve email from mail servers: the *Post Office Protocol (POP)* and the *Internet Message Access Protocol (IMAP)*.

- *POP*: When using a POP server, email messages are downloaded by email client applications. By default, most POP email clients are automatically configured to delete the message on the email server after it has been successfully transferred, however this setting usually can be changed. POP is fully compatible with important Internet messaging standards, such as *Multipurpose Internet Mail Extensions (MIME)*, which allows for email attachments. The most current version of the standard POP protocol is POP3. A few characteristics of POP are listed in the following:
  - It does not handle multiple mailboxes easily, and is designed to put user's incoming email into one folder.
  - It is poor in handling multiple-client access to a mailbox which is increasingly important as users have home PC, work PC, laptop, cyber café computer, friend's machine, etc.
  - It has high network bandwidth overhead, and it transfers all the email messages, often well before they are read (and they might not be read at all!).
- *IMAP*: When using an IMAP mail server, email messages remain on the server where users can read or delete them. IMAP also allows client applications to create, rename, or delete mail directories on the server to organize and store email. IMAP is particularly useful for those who access their email using multiple machines. The user also can delete messages without viewing or downloading

them on demand. IMAP, like POP, is fully compatible with important Internet messaging standards, such as MIME, which allow for email attachments. Some characteristics of IMAP are enlisted in the following:

- Multiple clients can connect to mailbox at once. It detects changes made to the mailbox by other clients and server keeps state about message (e.g., read, replied to).

- Allows access to MIME parts of messages and partial fetch as clients can retrieve individual parts separately, such as the text of a message without downloading attachments.

- Facilitates multiple mailboxes on the server where clients can create, rename, and delete mailboxes and can move messages from one folder to another.

- Enables server-side searches, i.e., search on server before downloading messages.

Thus, the main components of an email system that facilitate sending and receiving of emails on the Internet are an email client, an email server (SMTP server), and POP and IMAP servers.

Although email is a very practical tool for exchanging information, it is also vulnerable, and users can encounter problems such as interception, identity theft, and monitoring. One way to ensure confidentiality is by using and email client, such as Thunderbird, instead of webmail. Or, as an alternative, emails can use an encryption program which provides cryptographic privacy and authentication. Pretty Good Privacy (PGP) is one such protocol that encrypts the emails end-to-end and only the addressee can decrypt it, thus excluding any possibility of interception.

FUN FACT: Google didn't really come up with Gmail. Gmail.com was in fact a free email service offered by Garfield (the famous cartoon cat character). Google simply acquired Gmail.

2.3 File Transfer

To transfer files between two computers, an application layer protocol is used. File Transfer Protocol (FTP) is a standard, interactive, connection-oriented protocol based on client-server architecture that relies on TCP for transferring files.

So, what is "file transfer"? It does not really transfer, as in moving a file from one location to another. It is "file copying"—copying files from one computer to another. FTP, or rather SFTP if you are concerned about security, is the tool of choice for moving files. FTP is the standard mechanism provided by TCP/IP for copying a file from one host to another. Although transferring files from one system to another seems simple and straightforward, some problems must be dealt with first. For example, two systems may use different file name conventions. Two systems may have different ways to represent text and data. Two systems may have different directory structures. All these problems have been solved by FTP in a very simple and elegant approach. FTP addresses and resolves these problems related to heterogeneous systems that use

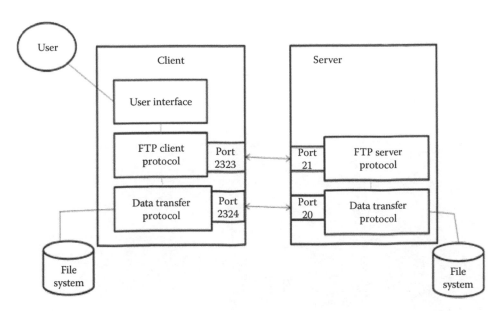

FIGURE 2.2
FTP model.

different operating systems, character sets, naming conventions, directory structures, file structures, and formats (Figure 2.2).

2.3.1 File Transfer Protocol Client Commands and Server Return Codes

To use FTP, you will need FTP client software and an FTP server. You also need to know the server address, the username, a password, and port number. The basic information desired for a successful login is as shown in Table 2.1.

Windows®, Mac OS® X, and Linux® operating systems have built-in command-line clients that can be used for establishing an FTP connection (Table 2.1). To initiate

TABLE 2.1

FTP Login

Login Information	Definition
site: **ftp.example.com**	This is the site address of the FTP server you're connecting to.
login: **abc.xyz**	Login or the USER command is the username used for logging into FTP.
pass: **P@ssworD**	PASS is the password.
port:**21**	PORT is the COMMAND port number you are using to connect to the server. The most common port number is port 21.

an FTP connection from Windows, type ftp at the command prompt, and press enter (Figures 2.3 and 2.4).

FTP server return codes always have three digits, and each digit has a special meaning. The first digit denotes whether the response is good, bad, or incomplete (Table 2.2).

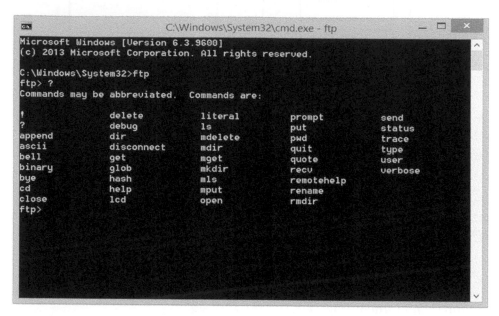

FIGURE 2.3
FTP commands for Windows.

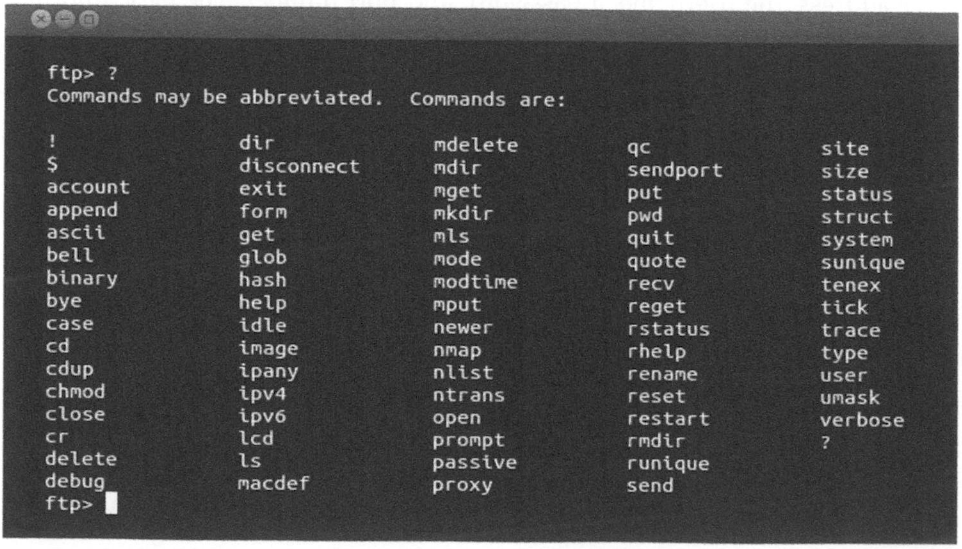

FIGURE 2.4
FTP commands for Linux.

TABLE 2.2

FTP Server Return Codes

Range	Purpose
1xx	**Positive Preliminary reply** The requested action is being initiated; expect another reply before proceeding with a new command. This type of reply can be used to indicate that the command was accepted, and the user-process may now pay attention to the data connections. The server-FTP process may send at most, one 1xx reply per command. For example, 150: File status is okay and about to open data connection.
2xx	**Positive Completion reply** The requested action has been successfully completed. A new request may be initiated. For example, 220: Service is ready for new user.
3xx	**Positive Intermediate reply** The command has been accepted, but the requested action is being held in abeyance, pending receipt of further information. The user should send another command specifying this information. This reply is used in command sequence groups. For example, 331: User name okay, need password.
4xx	**Transient Negative Completion reply** The command was not accepted, and the requested action did not take place, but the error condition is temporary and the action may be requested again. The user should return to the beginning of the command sequence, if any. It is difficult to assign a meaning to "transient," particularly when two distinct sites (Server- and User-processes) have to agree on the interpretation. Each reply in the 4xx category might have a slightly different time value, but the intent is that the user-process is encouraged to try again. A rule of thumb in determining if a reply fits into the 4xx or the 5xx (Permanent Negative) category is that replies are 4xx if the commands can be repeated without any change in command form or in properties of the User or Server (e.g., the command is spelled the same with the same arguments used; the user does not change his file access or user name; the server does not put up a new implementation.) For example, 430: Invalid username or password.
5xx	**Permanent Negative Completion reply** The command was not accepted, and the requested action did not take place. The User-process is discouraged from repeating the exact request (in the same sequence). Even some "permanent" error conditions can be corrected, so the human user may want to direct his User-process to reinitiate the command sequence by direct action at some point in the future (e.g., after the spelling has been changed, or the user has altered his directory status.) For example, 550: Request not taken, File unavailable (e.g., file not found, no access).
6xx	**Protected reply** The RFC 2228 (FTP standard by IETF) introduced the concept of protected replies to increase security over the FTP communications. For example, 631: Integrity protected reply.

2.3.2 File Transfer Protocol Connection Types

An important concept to remember is that FTP connects using two TCP ports for all communications between the server and user.

- *COMMAND Port*: This is the main TCP port created when a session is connected. It is used for passing commands and replies. Port 21 (unsecured) or 990 (secured) are the default command ports used.
- *DATA Port*: Each time when files or directories are transferred between server and client, a random TCP data connection is established, and data transfer commences over the connection. Once data transfer is complete, the connection is closed. Subsequent data connections are established and terminated as required. Data connections are never left open.

2.3.3 File Transfer Protocol Modes

- *Connection Modes—ASCII and Binary*

  FTP transfers files between systems by using one of these two modes—ASCII and binary. The mode is determined at the initial stage of all FTP transactions by the server. The FTP client will automatically switch to that mode. ASCII mode is used exclusively to transfer text and HTML. Binary mode transfers zip files, images or executable files in binary form. Binary files cannot be sent via ASCII mode and vice versa as corruptions will occur.

- *Transfer Modes—Passive and Active*

  Active and passive are the two modes that FTP can run in. FTP uses two channels between client and server, as described previously, the command channel, and the data channel. The command channel is for commands and responses; the data channel is for actually transferring files. During the address/port negotiation phase, the client should issue either the PORT command (when initiating Active Mode) or the PASV command (when initiating Passive Mode).

    - *Active Mode*—The client issues a PORT command to the server signaling that it will "actively" provide an IP and port number to open the Data Connection back to the client.
        - Client opens a command channel from client port 2000[1] to server port 21.[2]
        - Client sends PORT 2001[1] to server and server acknowledges on command channel.
        - Server opens a data channel from server port 20[2] to client port 2001.[1]
        - Client acknowledges on data channel.

    - *Passive Mode*—The client issues a PASV command to indicate that it will wait "passively" for the server to supply an IP and port number, after which the client will create a Data Connection to the server.
        - Client opens a command channel from client port 2000[1] to server port 21.[2]
        - Client sends PASV to server on command channel.
        - Server sends back (on command channel) PORT 1234[1] after starting to listen on that port.
        - Client opens a data channel from client 2001[1] to server port 1234.[1]
        - Server acknowledges on data channel.

  At this point, the command and data channels are both open.

FUN FACT: Archie (somehow short of "archive") was a simple pre-Web Internet search engine that would keep an index of file lists in all public FTP servers it could find. This way, users could find publicly available files and download them.

---

[1] The selection of ports on the client side is up to the client, as the selection of the server data channel port in passive mode is up to the server.

[2] Further note that the use of port 20 and 21 is only a convention (although a strong one). There's no absolute requirement that those ports be used although the client and server both have to agree on which ports are being used.

2.4 Real-Time User Communication

2.4.1 Internet Telephony: Voice/Video Communication over Internet

Internet Telephony is the service provided by the Internet that uses the Voice over Internet Protocol (VoIP) application layer protocol in the TCP/IP protocol stack to offer this service. It is the technology that is used to transmit voice over the Internet. The voice is first converted into digital data, which is then organized into small packets. These packets are stamped with the destination IP address and routed over the Internet. At the receiving end, the digital data is reconverted into voice and fed into the user's phone. VoIP is a form of communication that allows you to make phone calls over a broadband Internet connection instead of typical analog telephone lines. Basic VoIP access usually allows you to call others who are also receiving calls over the Internet. Some VoIP services require a computer or a dedicated VoIP phone, while others allow you to use your landline phone to place VoIP calls through a special adapter. Thus, for VoIP, you need a broadband Internet connection, plus a traditional phone and an adapter; a VoIP-enabled phone; or VoIP software on your computer. VoIP examples include Xbox Voice, Windows messenger, AOL Instant Messenger, Motorola Phone Adapter (Vonage), Cisco Phone, and Skype (Figure 2.5).

VoIP requires a connection to the Internet through an ISP, a VoIP service to extend the reach to traditional landlines, and VoIP software to place calls. It should be emphasized that there is no communication between user devices but between two user accounts registered on the Skype service, which includes registration, entering the username and password, and some basic, yet protected, personal information. Thus, Skype is used in a similar way as a Peer-to-Peer (P2P).

The basic VoIP components can include:

- *Phones*: End-point devices, including both analog and IP phones.
- *Gateways*: Allows a non-VoIP (analog) device to communicate with the VoIP network, or a VoIP device to communicate with an analog network.
- *Application servers*: Provides required applications to VoIP phones.
- *Gatekeepers*: Maps phone numbers to IP addresses, and grants permission for call setup.
- *Call agents*: Handles call routing and setup.

FIGURE 2.5
VoIP examples.

Digital Signal Processors (DSP's) are used by devices to perform analog-to-digital and digital-to-analog conversions. Both VoIP phones and gateways utilize DSP technology. The benefits of VoIP are considerable:

- *Better use of bandwidth*: Traditional voice requires a dedicated 64-Kbps circuit for each voice call, while VoIP calls use considerably less. Additionally, no bandwidth is consumed when calls are not being made.
- *Single form of cabling*: Reduces implementation and maintenance costs by having a standardized and consolidated cabling and equipment infrastructure.
- *Cost savings from integration into the data network*: Toll charges for inter-office voice communication can be avoided by routing voice traffic across existing data lines.
- Integration into devices beyond telephones.

FUN FACT: Some VoIP service providers allow you to check your voicemail via your email, while others allow you to attach voice messages to your emails.

2.4.2 Internet Relay Chat

Internet Relay Chat (IRC) is one of the most popular, text-based interactive service using TCP/IP on the Internet. An IRC client (program) gives a user the ability to exchange text messages interactively with other users around the world in real time. It is a multi-user, multi-channel teleconferencing system. This real-time, text-based chat process works on client/server architecture. IRC clients are computer programs that a user can install on their system. These clients communicate with chat servers to transfer messages to other clients. IRC clients and servers communicate by sending plain ASCII-formatted messages to each other over TCP. It is mainly designed for group communication in discussion forums, called channels, but also allows one-on-one communication via private messages as well as chat and data transfer, including file sharing. The only configuration allowed for IRC servers is that of a spanning tree where each server acts as a central node for the rest of the network it sees.

Let's consider a simple model of an IRC network: two servers and two clients. The servers are connected to each other, and each has a client (a user) connected to it. The structure would look like the example in Figure 2.6.

Say Client A wishes to send a message to Client B. Their machines don't connect directly but each connects to a server, which, in turn, is connected to the server to which the other user is connected. Therefore, Client A can make use of the indirect route that exists between

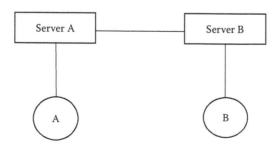

FIGURE 2.6
IRC network.

it and B. Client A sends server A the message to be transmitted. In this message, it tells server A the message's final destination (B) and its contents. Server A is aware of the existence of B, although it is not connected to it directly, and it knows that Client B is connected to server B. It therefore forwards—relays—the message to server B, which in turn sees that the recipient is one of its own clients and sends the message to B, who can then read it. Server A also adds the identity of the client sending it (A) before relaying it, so the recipient knows where it originated from. This transfer of information between the servers and its users typically happens within milliseconds, thus making the exchange of messages swift enough to match that of real conversation. For this reason, Client A does not need to connect directly to B to send his message. The IRC environment permits an almost unlimited number of recipients for the same message and can relay this message to all those users at the same time. IRC permits one-on-one communication, but its real advantage is the ability to communicate with large numbers of people by sharing a common channel of conversation. Thus, the actual text-exchange process involves three primary steps:

- *Locating client*: The two clients must be able to locate each other. Upon connecting to a server, a client registers using a label which is then used by other servers and clients to know where the client is located. Servers are responsible for keeping track of all the labels being used.

- *Relaying message*: The IRC protocol provides no mean for two clients to directly communicate, all communication between clients is relayed by the server(s).

- *Channel hosting and management*: IRC supports the creation of chat rooms (discussion forums) called channels. A channel is a named group of one or more users which will all receive messages addressed to that channel. Channels provide the means for a message to be sent to several clients. Servers host channels, providing the necessary message multiplexing. Server are also responsible for managing channels by keeping track of the channel members. The messages in an Internet Relay Chat may be delivered either using a one-to-one communication, one-to-many or one-to-all. The Architecture of a typical IRC server is shown in Figure 2.7.

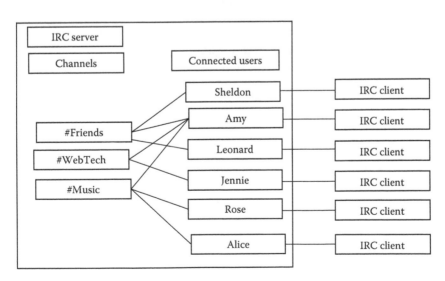

FIGURE 2.7
A sample IRC client-server.

TABLE 2.3

IRC Commands

Command	Description
/msg nickname message	Sends a private message to the user known by nickname Ex: /msg Amy Have a great holiday!
/me action	Sends a message to the channel describing an "action" you take. Ex: If your nickname is Madcap and you wanted to "wave" participants in the discussion, you would type the command /me waves. Your "wave" would appear on the screen like this: Ex: /Amy waves
/join channel	Joins the channel. All channel names begin with the "#" symbol. You must include that in the name. Ex: /join #WebTech
/part channel	Leaves the channel. Because you can be on many channels at once in IRC, you must always include the name of the channel you wish to leave. Ex: /part # WebTech
/nick new-nickname	Changes your nickname to a new one Ex: /nick new-technogeek
/quit	Quits IRC Ex: /quit

2.4.2.1 Internet Relay Chat Commands

A few IRC commands are listed in Table 2.3.

2.4.2.2 Few Architectural Issues of Internet Relay Chat

The IRC is vulnerable to issues pertaining to scalability, reliability, network congestion, and privacy. These issues are discussed in the following:

- *Scalability*: This protocol does not scale sufficiently well when used in a large arena because all the servers maintain information about all other servers and clients. Larger the network, the more difficult it is to propagate any updates.
- *Reliability*: As the only network configuration allowed for IRC servers is that of a spanning tree, each link between two servers is an obvious and quite serious point of failure.
- *Network congestion*: Due to the spanning tree architecture the IRC protocol is extremely vulnerable to network congestions. This problem is endemic (local), and should be solved for the next generation, i.e., if congestion and high traffic volume cause a link between two servers to fail, not only this failure generates more network traffic, but the reconnection (eventually elsewhere) of two servers also generates more traffic.
- *Privacy*: Besides not scaling well, the fact that servers need to know all information about other entities, the issue of privacy is also a concern.

FUN FACT: A single message is a string of characters with a maximum length of 512 characters.

2.5 Remote Login

Telnet, a standard TCP/IP protocol for virtual terminal service, proposed by ISO, enables the establishment of a connection to a remote system in such a way that the local terminal appears to be a terminal at the remote system. Telnet is an abbreviation for TErminaLNETwork. The Telnet protocol offers a user the possibility to connect and log on to any other host in the network from the user's own computer by offering a remote log-in capability. For the connections, Telnet uses the TCP protocol. The Telnet service is offered on the host machine at TCP port 23. The user at the terminal interacts with the local Telnet client. The Telnet client acts as a terminal accepting any keystrokes from the keyboard, interpreting them and displaying the output on the screen. The client on the computer makes the TCP connection to the host machine's port 23 where the Telnet server answers. The Telnet server interacts with applications in the host machine and assists in the terminal emulation (Figure 2.8).

As the connection is setup, both the ends of the Telnet connection are assumed to be originated and terminated at the network virtual terminal (NVT). The NVT is a network wide terminal which is host independent so that both the server and the client in the connection may not need to keep any information about each other's terminal's characteristics as both see each other as a NVT terminal. The Telnet has a set of options and these options can be negotiated through a simple protocol inside the Telnet. The negotiation protocol contains commands DO, WILL, WON'T, and DON'T.

Both Telnet and FTP are protocols that can be used to connect to servers on the Internet for two different purposes: Telnet is used to log on to an Internet server and look at information there. For example, you use telnet to log on to the library's server. You cannot download or upload files using telnet. To download or upload files, you use the File Transfer Protocol (FTP).

How do you find the files you want to transfer? One way is to use a client program called Archie. Telnet, FTP, and Archie are interrelated. The Archie database is made up of the file directories from hundreds of systems. When you search this database on the basis of a file's name, Archie can tell you which directory paths on which systems hold a copy of the file you want. To use Archie, you must Telnet to an Archie server. You can do that

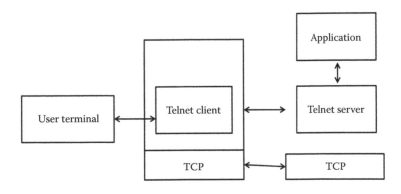

FIGURE 2.8
Telnet model.

by keying in a command such as **telnet://archie.internic.net** to get to the Archie server at that address and log on by keying in **archie** when prompted to do so. Once you do your Archie search, you must then go get the file using FTP, the Internet File Transfer Protocol. Thus, Telnet allows you to gain access to large electronic libraries of information and to access distant bulletin board systems without the expense of a long-distance telephone call. With Telnet, you access a remote computer, located somewhere else on the Internet. Often, the remote computer suggests a guest log-in name for you to type. If you reach the remote computer by clicking a link, the site with the link often tells you what to type when you see the words "Log In." Sometimes, though, all you see is a log-in prompt and no clues about what you should type. This usually means you must be a registered member or student with the institution providing the site. Only members receive log-in names and passwords, and the general public (you) can't access the site. Other times you'll see text explaining that you must pay for a log-in name and password before you can go farther. If you choose to do so, the transaction is between you and the organization providing the site, and it doesn't affect the Internet access fee you pay to your regular provider. Once you've logged in, you'll find each site has slightly different methods for navigation. When you Telnet, you are visiting a remote computer, and you have to learn and follow its rules. The screen often displays a menu of commands you can type to accomplish various tasks. Getting around usually is fairly easy, and most sites have online help systems. When you leave the site, you "return" to your computer and its methods and rules for accomplishing tasks.

FUN FACT: You can watch Star Wars Episode 4–in ASCII! Someone has recreated Star Wars in ASCII characters. $telnet towel.blinkenlights.nl

2.6 Usenet

Usenet is an acronym for USErNETwork. Like mailing lists, Usenet is also a way of sharing information. It was started by Tom Truscott and Jim Ellis in 1979. Initially it was limited to two sites but today there are thousands of Usenet sites involving millions of people. Usenet is a globally distributed discussion group where people can share views on topics of their interest. It is a collection of special interest groups, called newsgroups. Each newsgroup is devoted to a certain topic. Under each newsgroup, there are many messages called news articles. The article posted to a newsgroup becomes available to all readers of the newsgroup. The Network News Transport Protocol (NNTP) is used in transferring news articles between news clients and news servers, where news articles are stored. Thus, NNTP is the protocol that is used for posting/distributing/retrieving USENET news articles among news server. The step-by-step working is as follows:

- You use a news reader to read news, post news, follow-up on a piece of news, etc.
- Your news reader interacts with a news server.
- A news server negotiates with other servers to transfer certain newsgroups between each other. A news server holds the news articles for a certain pre-set period (controlled by the server's administrator) and eventually discards them at their expiration date.

The basic terminology used within the USENET is as follows:

- *News administrator*: A person who is in charge of running a news server.
- *News server*: A computer that saves, forwards, and manages news articles. Usually, a news server is running in one domain.
- *News reader*: A program that allows a user to read/post/subscribe/unsubscribe to a newsgroup.
- *Newsgroup*: An online forum that allows users from the Internet to join the discussion on a specific topic.
- *Usenet*: A collection of newsgroups.

2.6.1 Newsgroup Classification

The articles that users post to Usenet are organized into topical categories called newsgroups, which are logically organized into hierarchies of subjects. For instance, *sci.math* and *sci.physics* are within the *sci.** hierarchy, for science. There exist numerous newsgroups distributed all around the world. These are identified using a hierarchical naming system in which each newsgroup is assigned a unique name that consists of alphabetic strings separated by periods. The far-left portion of the name represents the top-level category of the newsgroup followed by the subtopic (as in the earlier example, *sci.** classifies the newsgroup as one that contains discussion of science related topics. The major set of worldwide newsgroups is contained within nine hierarchies, eight of which are operated under consensual guidelines that govern their administration and naming. The current *Big Eight* are:

- *comp.**: Computer-related discussions (*comp.software, comp.sys.amiga*)
- *humanities.**: Fine-arts, literature, and philosophy (*humanities.classics, humanities.design.misc*)
- *misc.**: Miscellaneous topics (*misc.education, misc.forsale, misc.kids*)
- *news.**: Discussions and announcements about news (Usenet, not current events) (*news.groups, news.admin*)
- *rec.**: Recreation and entertainment (*rec.music, rec.arts.movies*)
- *sci.**: Science related discussions (*sci.psychology, sci.research*)
- *soc.**: Social discussions (*soc.college.org, soc.culture.african*)
- *talk.**: Talk about various controversial topics (*talk.religion, talk.politics, talk.origins*)

2.7 World Wide Web

The services provided by the Internet can be classified into two categories: the communication services and the information services. The most important communication services on the Internet are electronic mail (and some derived services) and Usenet. Major information services are file transfer, telnet, and the World Wide Web (WWW or the Web). Unlike Telnet and FTP, the Web offers a view on one virtually unified but decentralized information space. The Web is the most sophisticated and most exciting new Internet service. It is essentially a huge client-server system with millions of servers distributed worldwide. Each server maintains a collection of documents; each document is stored as a file (although documents can also be generated on request). A server accepts requests for fetching a document and transfers it to the client. In addition, it can also accept requests for storing new documents. All communication on the Web between clients and servers is based on the Hypertext Transfer Protocol (HTTP). HTTP is a relatively simple client-server protocol; a client sends a request message to a server and waits for a response message.

Since 1994, Web development is primarily initiated and controlled by the World Wide Web Consortium. This consortium is responsible for standardizing protocols, improving interoperability, and further enhancing the capabilities of the Web. Its home page can be found at http://www.w3.org/.

As this book is primarily based on understanding the theoretical concepts, technologies, current practices, and future research of this latest information service of the Internet, the next parts of this book expound on the Web and examine each specification of these aspects explicitly and comprehensively.

FUN FACT: Gopher Protocol is one of the predecessors of Web. The Gopher Protocol was developed in the late 1980s to provide a mechanism for organizing documents for easy access by students and faculty at the University of Minnesota. Gopher is a protocol designed to search, retrieve, and display documents from remote sites on the Internet. It uses a server-client protocol to access and manage the files. The Gopher protocol is now obsolete, and it is not used anymore.

Review Questions

1. Answer the following:

    a. _____ communicate with one another using the protocol SMTP.

    b. When the MUA is a program installed on the user's system, it is called an _____.

    c. _____ and _____ are two primary mail access protocols.

    d. _____ is a protocol which encrypts the emails end-to-end and only the addressee is able to decrypt it, thus excluding any possibility of interception.

    e. _____ is a standard mechanism provided by TCP/IP for copying a file from one host to another.

    f. _____ FTP connection mode is used exclusively to transfer text and HTML.

    g. _____ protocol allows Internet telephony.

    h. Telnet is an acronym for_____.

    i. _____ protocol is used in transferring news articles between news clients and news server.

    j. _____ is responsible for standardizing protocols, improving interoperability, and further enhancing the capabilities of the Web.

2. Which set of Internet protocols enable the store-and-forward transfer of an email?

3. What meaning does the FTP server codes convey?

4. What are the basic components that enable Internet telephony? Give a few examples of VoIP.

5. What is the text-exchange process in a typical Internet Relay Chat (IRC)?

6. Describe the TCP/IP protocol for virtual terminal service that enables the establishment of a connection to a remote system in such a way that the local terminal appears to be a terminal at the remote system.

7. Web is a service provided by the Internet. Explain.

8. Differentiate between the following:

   a. Nuts-Bolts and Service Internet views

   b. Email Client and Webmail

   c. POP and IMAP

   d. Active and Passive FTP Transfer Modes

   e. Push and Pull Protocol

Section II

Web Theory

3

The World Wide Web

3.1 The Web

The World Wide Web (WWW or Web) is often confused with the Internet, but the concept of the Web was created when the Internet was already well established. Introduced by Sir Tim Berners-Lee in 1989 while working at CERN (The European Organization for Nuclear Research) in Geneva, Switzerland, the Web is a large transformable-information construct. It is a service, an application of the Internet. The Web is based on the Internet infrastructure and provides a hypertext-hypermedia interface to information resources on the Internet.

Technically, the Web is a set of technologies that allow information on the Internet to be linked together through the use of links, or connections, in documents. The language used to write these documents with links is HTML (Hypertext Markup Language). Let us first understand the notion of hypertext, a term that was first introduced by Ted Nelson. The standard way to read a book is in a linear fashion, starting from page one. The concept of hypertext allows a person to read or explore in a nonlinear fashion, as it contains "links" to other text. By following the links, the reader is not constrained to follow any particular order. Moreover, hypertext may contain links that do not necessarily lead to other text, but instead to audio or video files.

Sir Tim Berners-Lee was working at CERN, where there were scientists from many different countries so there were many different computer operating systems and document formats in use. It was difficult for a scientist working with one computer system to obtain information from a colleague using a different computer system. Berners-Lee realized that it would not be feasible to force the wide mix of researchers at CERN to reorganize their way of doing things to fit a new system. It was crucial that everyone could work with his or her own operating system, but still be able to easily share information. His solution was the alliance of hypertext and the Internet. This combination was the advent of the World Wide Web, which relied on three key components—Hypertext Transfer Protocol (HTTP), HTML, and the Uniform Resource Locator (URL)—all developed by Berners-Lee.

3.2 The Working Web

The first version of the Web was all about building a "web of nodes" storing "hypertext pages" viewed by "browsers" on a network. HTTP and HTML were the primary mechanisms used to make the Web work. HTTP is the simple way by which one computer (the client) asks another system (a server) for web pages. HTML is the way those pages are written so any computer can understand them and display the pages correctly with the help of a web browser. And the URL provides a uniform notation scheme for addressing accessible resources (web pages) over the network, as it provides the "address" of a web page. More formally:

- *HTTP (Hypertext Transfer Protocol)*: This is an application-layer protocol used to exchange information between a browser and a server. Detailed discussion on this is provided in Chapter 4.
- *HTML (Hypertext Markup Language)*: This is the language used by the browser to display the text and graphics on a web page. Chapter 8 discusses three client-side technologies for building web pages—HTML, CSS (Cascading Style Sheets), and JavaScript.
- *URL (Uniform Resource Locator)*: This is the "address" of a web page. When you click on a link in a web page, you are taken to a new location. The link contains the URL for your destination and follows a very specific syntax used in naming the destination. This is discussed in Chapter 1.

3.3 Web Terminology

The terminology related to the Web is diverse but not disjointed. We examine the terms web page, web site, web application (web app), and web service in this section.

3.3.1 Web Page

A web page is a document that can be displayed in a web browser. Web pages can be either static or dynamic. Static means the page is constant or unchanging, while dynamic means the page changes. Therefore, static web pages contain the same pre-built content each time the page is loaded, while the content of dynamic web pages can be generated on the fly. Standard HTML pages are static web pages. They contain HTML code, which defines the structure and content of the web page. Each time an HTML page is loaded, it looks the same. The only way the content of an HTML page will change is if a web developer edits and publishes an updated file. Figure 3.1 depicts the architectural flow for publishing a static web page.

Dynamic web pages, on the other hand, contain server-side code—such as PHP, ASP (Active Server Pages), or JSP (Java Server Pages)—that allows the server to generate unique content each time the page is loaded. For example, the server might display the current time and date on the web page. It might also output a unique response based on a web form the user completed. Many dynamic pages use server-side code to access database information, which enables the web page content to be generated from information stored in a database. The dynamic page request is addressed by a two-level response system that includes a web server and an application server. The web server's primary job is to display the site content while the application server is in charge of the logic, the interaction between the user and the displayed content. The terms web server and application server are often used interchangeably. However, web servers are well-suited for static content

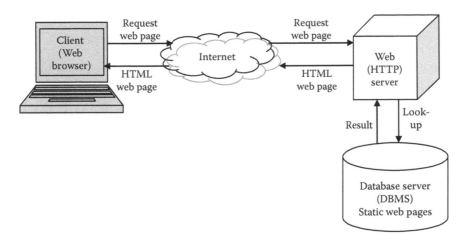

FIGURE 3.1
Publishing a static web page.

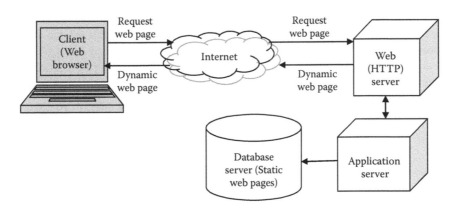

FIGURE 3.2
Publishing a dynamic web page.

and application servers for dynamic content. Figure 3.2 depicts the architectural flow for publishing a dynamic web page.

Section 3.4 gives a more detailed overview of the web architecture.

3.3.2 Web Page versus Web Site

A web site is a collection of web pages that are under one domain—for example, dtu.ac.in. This web site has several web pages like Home, Academics, Administrations, Academics, and Departments. A web page is an independent page of a web site. Typically, a web page can be accessed by one URL in a browser and that page can be copied and or sent to a friend for review—in other words, a web page is identified by a unique URL. Web pages can be created by user activity. For example, if you visit a web search engine and enter keywords on the topic of your choice, a page will be created containing the results of your search.

When we talk about a web site, we refer to a large amount of information spread over many pages; when we talk about a web page, we are referring to a screenshot, which is a small subset of the web site and can be used for a particular purpose. The difference between a web page and a web site can be summarized by these criteria:

- *Size*: Web sites can range from very simple, single page presences to huge web sites that contain thousands of web pages. One example of a huge web site is www.facebook.com, where each member has a web page on which he makes his profile and interacts with other members. A web site can run into several pages but can be a single web page too.
- *Content*: The content of the web site is varied, with different web pages containing different information. Big companies may have a "Contact Us" page, a "Sign Up" page, and so on. Content on a single web page contains specific information only.
- *Creation*: A web site is created in much the same way as a web page. After completing the web page, a navigational link is created to connect to the new page from other web pages on the web site (Figures 3.3 and 3.4).

Web sites can be further categorized as static and dynamic sites. A static web site is composed of web pages with content that remains constant. A static web site may consist of plain text or rich media. However, on visiting a static site, you will see the same content at all times regardless of the time of visit. On the other hand, a dynamic web site updates itself frequently depending on a set of parameters. In other words, a dynamic web site's content is renewed every time a user visits the site. A dynamic web page is created using a wide range of software and languages, such as JSP, ASP, PHP, Python, Perl, and so on.

FUN FACT: The first ever web site to go online is still online. It was built in 1991. You can access it at http://info.cern.ch/hypertext/WWW/TheProject.html.

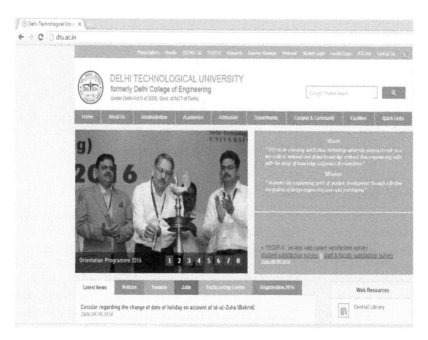

FIGURE 3.3
The web site of Delhi Technological University.

FIGURE 3.4
The Contact Us page from dtu.ac.in.

3.3.3 Web Site versus Web Application

Web sites are primarily informational. For example, http://cnn.com and http://php.net are web sites. Web applications (or web apps), however, allow the user to perform actions. A web app is a client-server software application for which the client (or user interface) runs in a web browser. They actually encompass all the applications that communicate with the user via HTTP. This includes light applications like Flash-based games, online calculators, and calendars, as well as more complex applications that use HTTP (Figure 3.5).

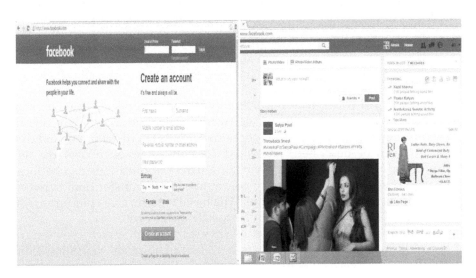

FIGURE 3.5
Facebook and a profile web page.

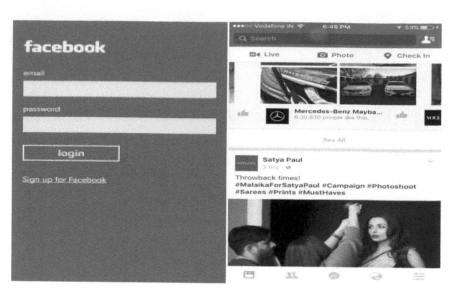

FIGURE 3.6
The Facebook app.

Web apps are task-centric. For example, you might use your smartphone or tablet to find an app that accomplishes a specific task, like making a call, checking your email, or finding a taxi nearby. Web sites and web apps differ in technicalities of development. Web apps have some defining attributes that distinguish them from web site development. Web apps

- Are self-contained.
- Require a rich/interactive user interface, possibly mimicking the native UI of the device.
- Use advanced device capabilities like geo-location, camera integration, or other technologies developed by the W3C Device APIs and Policy Working Group.
- Are action-oriented rather than information oriented (Figure 3.6).

3.3.4 Web App versus Web Service

As defined by the World Wide Web Consortium (W3C), web services provide a standard means of interoperating between different software applications running on a variety of platforms and frameworks. They are self-contained, modular, distributed, and dynamic applications that can be described, published, located, or invoked over the network to create products, processes, and supply chains. These applications can be local, distributed, or web-based, primarily used to communicate or transfer data between web applications running on different platforms. The basic web services platform is XML + HTTP (Extensible Markup Language + Hypertext Transfer Protocol).

A web application is an application that is accessed through a web browser running on client machine, whereas a web service is a system of software that allows different machines to interact with each other through a network. Web applications are intended for users and web services are intended for other applications. A web application is typically intended for human-to-computer interaction, whereas web services are typically intended for computer-to-computer interaction. A web service does not necessarily have a UI since it is typically used as a component in an application, while a web app is a complete application with a user interface. A web application can contain both a graphical user interface for human users, as well as a set of web services for computer "users" (clients). A web site might use a web service. A company, for example, might provide a web page with a web application and a web service—a payment service like PayPal, for instance, has both a GUI for human users and a set of web services through which back-end systems can access the PayPal services.

They are not entirely exclusive. A university web site might have web pages that provide information such as its address, tuition rates, and academic programs. In addition, it will likely have web applications that let users access university mail accounts, teachers manage course materials, and students register for courses. Meanwhile, a discussion forum is an example of a web service where an interface can be provided between a web page (for collecting data like user comments) and the backend system.

3.4 Web Architecture

The Web is a client-server system. Web browsers act as clients, making requests to web servers. Web servers respond to requests with requested information and/or computation generated by the client. Web applications are usually implemented with two-tier, three-tier, or multitier (N-tier) architectures. Each tier is a platform (client or server) with a unique responsibility.

In two-tier client-server architecture, Tier 1 is the client platform, hosting a web browser and Tier 2 is the server platform, hosting all the server software components. This architecture is inexpensive (single platform) but has limited scalability, no server redundancy, and highly interdependent components. It is suitable for 10–100 users and non-time-critical information processing, such as for a small company or organization like a law office (Figure 3.7). (Here, server redundancy means that if a primary server is unavailable due to a power outage, network connection loss, or other failure, a designated backup system takes over and enables the application to continue running.

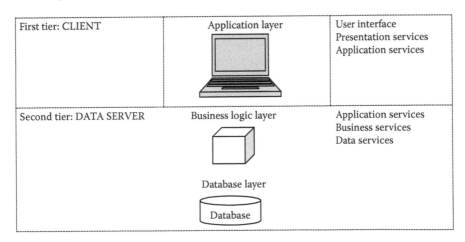

FIGURE 3.7
Two-tier client-server architecture.

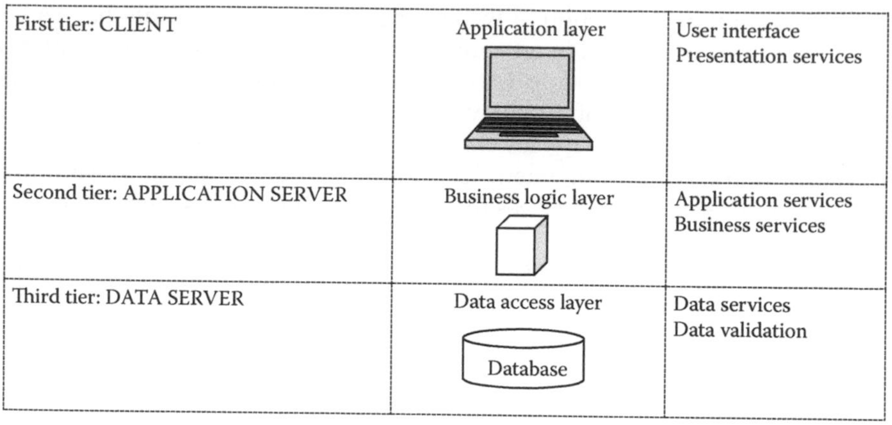

First tier: CLIENT	Application layer	User interface Presentation services
Second tier: APPLICATION SERVER	Business logic layer	Application services Business services
Third tier: DATA SERVER	Data access layer Database	Data services Data validation

FIGURE 3.8
Three-tier client-server architecture.

Backup servers behave as clients until their designated primary system fails. If the primary server fails, the first system designated as a backup server immediately takes over the primary server's role, enabling the application to continue running until the primary server is back online.)

In three-tier architecture, Tier 3 takes over part of the server function from Tier 2—typically data management (Figure 3.8). This architecture provides improved performance (from specialized hardware), has decreased coupling of software components, and offers improved scalability. But it, too, has no server redundancy. A typical application that involves a three-tier architecture might be a regional organization, such as a college. The three-tier structure can be extended to N-tier, containing several special application servers.

3.5 World Wide Web Challenges

With the increase in services provided by the Web, the challenges faced by web developers are also increasing. They are faced with providing new services in a timely manner and managing huge amounts of data. Some of the challenges encountered by stakeholders include:

- *Abundance*: With the phenomenal growth of the web, there is an ever increasing volume of data and information published in numerous web pages. According to worldwidewebsize.com, the indexed web contains at least 4.49 billion pages (as of May 2, 2017).

- *Web search results usually have low precision and recall*: For finding relevant information, the search service is generally a keyword-based, query-triggered process that results in problems of low precision and low recall. (Precision is the fraction of relevant documents retrieved to the total documents retrieved. Recall is the fraction of relevant documents retrieved from total existing relevant documents. These terms are further explained in Chapter 6.)

- *Limited query interface based on keyword-oriented search*: It is hard to extract useful knowledge out of information available because the search service used to find out specific information on the web is retrieval-oriented. Extracting potentially useful knowledge is a data-mining-oriented, data-triggered process.

- *Lack of personalization of information and limited customization to individual users*: Most knowledge on the web is presented as natural-language text with occasional pictures and graphics. This is convenient for human users to read and view but difficult for computers to understand. This also limits the state-of-the-art search engines, since they cannot infer contextual meaning. For example, does the word "Table" refer to a piece of furniture or to a mathematics-related table.

- *Heterogeneity*: Information and data on the web exists in almost all types (structured tables, texts, multimedia data, and so on).

- *Structure*: Much of the information on the web is semi-structured due to the nested structure of HTML code.

- *Hypertext*: Information on the web is typically linked to other information.

- *The web is noisy*: A web page typically contains a mixture of many kinds of information, such as content, navigational panels, copyright notices, and so on.

- *Dynamics*: Most anyone can publish information on the web at any time and from anywhere. Information on the web is constantly changing. It is a dynamic environment of information, whereas traditional systems are typically based on static document collections.

- *Duplication*: Several studies indicate that nearly 30% of the Web's content is duplicated, mainly due to mirroring.

Review Questions

1. Answer the following:
   a. The Web relies on three components: _____, _____, and _____.
   b. "Web of nodes" refers to the _____ generation of the Web.
   c. _____ is a document displayed in the web browser.
   d. _____ web pages are built on the fly.
   e. _____ is a client-server software application in which the client runs in a web browser allowing the user to perform actions.

2. How does the Web work?

3. Differentiate between the following:
   a. Web page and web site
   b. Web site and web app
   c. Web service and web app
   d. Two-tier and three-tier web architecture
4. How are web apps architecturally implemented?
5. What are the key challenges that the research community faces when dealing with the Web?

4

Hypertext Transfer Protocol (HTTP)

4.1 Hypertext Transfer Protocol

Web browsers interact with web servers with a simple application-level protocol called HTTP (Hypertext Transfer Protocol), which runs on top of TCP/IP network connections. HTTP is a client-server protocol that defines how messages are formatted and transmitted, and what action web servers and browsers should take in response to various commands. For example, when the user enters a URL in the browser, the browser sends a HTTP command to the web server directing it to fetch and transmit the requested web page. Some of the fundamental characteristics of the HTTP protocol are:

- The HTTP protocol uses the request/response paradigm, which is an HTTP client program sends an HTTP request message to an HTTP server that returns an HTTP response message. The structure of the request and response messages is similar to that of e-mail messages; they are a group of lines containing a message header, followed by a blank line, and then followed by a message body (Figure 4.1).

- HTTP is a *pull protocol*; the client *pulls* information from the server (instead of server *pushing* information down to the client).

- HTTP is a stateless protocol, that is, each request-response exchange is treated independently. Clients and servers are not required to retain a state. An HTTP transaction consists of a single request from a client to a server, followed by a single response from the server back to the client. The server does not maintain any information about the transaction. Some transactions require the state to be maintained, for example, in the case of a movie ticket booking web site will require the details of the user to be stored so that the next time the user visits the web site it will provide the user with movie suggestions based on their ticket purchasing history. To maintain the state, the web site uses proxies and cookies, which are discussed in detail in Section 4.6.

- HTTP is media independent: Any type of data can be sent by HTTP if both the client and the server know how to handle the data content. It is required for the client as well as the server to specify the content type using appropriate MIME-type.

More formally, the standard RFC-2616 defines HTTP as an application-level protocol for distributed, collaborative, hypermedia information systems. It is a generic, stateless, protocol that can be used for many tasks, beyond its primary use for hypertext, such as name servers and distributed object management systems. This is accomplished through the

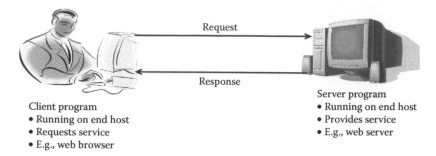

Client program
• Running on end host
• Requests service
• E.g., web browser

Server program
• Running on end host
• Provides service
• E.g., web server

FIGURE 4.1
A typical Web paradigm using the request/response HTTP.

extension of its request methods, error codes, and headers. In the next few sections, we elaborate these aspects of the HTTP protocol.

4.2 Hypertext Transfer Protocol Version

HTTP uses a <major>.<minor> numbering scheme to indicate versions of the protocol. The version of an HTTP message is indicated by an HTTP-Version field in the first line. Here is the general syntax of specifying HTTP version number:

```
HTTP-Version = "HTTP" "/" 1*DIGIT "." 1*DIGIT
```

The initial version of HTTP was referred to as HTTP/0.9, which was a simple protocol for raw data transfer across the Internet. HTTP/1.0, as defined by RFC (Request for Comments) 1945, improved the protocol. In 1997, HTTP/1.1 was formally defined, and is currently an Internet Draft Standard [RFC-2616]. Essentially all operational browsers and servers support HTTP/1.1. We therefore focus on HTTP/1.1 in this chapter.

FUN FACT: The latest version of HTTP, HTTP/2.0, was released in 2015. According to W3Techs, as of June 2016, 8.4% of the top 10 million websites are supported by HTTP/2 (originally named HTTP/2.0). At a high level, HTTP/2 is binary, instead of textual, fully multiplexed, instead of ordered and blocking, and can therefore use one connection for parallelism. It uses header compression to reduce overhead and allows servers to "push" responses proactively into client caches. The standard was prepared on an unrealistically short schedule and has some encryption issues. In lieu of this, it has faced a lot of criticism.

4.3 Hypertext Transfer Protocol Connections

How a client will communicate with the server depends on the type of connection established between the two machines. Thus, an HTTP connection can either be persistent or non-persistent. Non-persistent HTTP was used by HTTP/1.0. HTTP/1.1 uses the persistent type of connection, which is also known as a kept-alive type connection with multiple messages or objects being sent over a single TCP connection between client and server.

4.3.1 Non-Persistent Hypertext Transfer Protocol

HTTP/1.0 used a non-persistent connection in which only one object can be sent over a TCP connection. Thus, as shown in Figure 4.2, transmitting a file from one machine to other required two Round Trip Time (RTT)—the time taken to send a small packet to travel from client to server and back:

- One RTT to initiate TCP connection
- Second for HTTP request and first few bytes of HTTP response to return
- Rest of the time is taken in transmitting the file

While using non-persistent HTTP, the operating system has an extra overhead for maintaining each TCP connection, as a result many browsers often open parallel TCP connections to fetch referenced objects. The steps involved in setting up of a connection with non-persistent HTTP are:

1. Client (Browser) initiates a TCP connection to www.anyCollege.edu (Server): Handshake.
2. Server at host www.anyCollege.edu accepts connection and acknowledges.
3. Client sends HTTP request for file /someDir/file.html.
4. Server receives message, finds and sends file in HTTP response.
5. Client receives response. It terminates connection, parseObject.
6. Steps 1–5 are repeated for each embedded object.

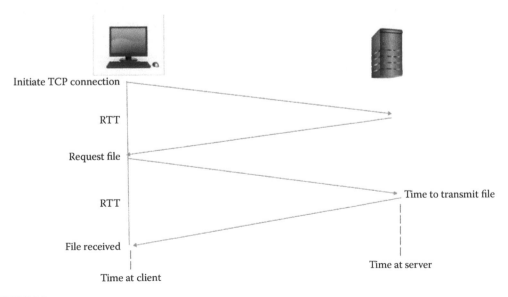

FIGURE 4.2
RTT in a non-persistent HTTP.

4.3.2 Persistent Hypertext Transfer Protocol

To overcome the issues of HTTP/1.0, HTTP/1.1 came with persistent connections through which multiple objects can be sent over a single TCP connection between the client and server. The server leaves the connection open after sending the response, so subsequent HTTP messages between same client/server are sent over the open connection. Persistent connection also overcomes the problem of slow start as in non-persistent each object transfer suffers from slow start, and overall number of RTTs required for persistent is much less than in non-persistent (Figure 4.3).

The steps involved in setting the connection of non-persistent HTTP are:

1. Client (Browser) initiates a TCP connection to www.anyCollege.edu (Server): Handshake.
2. Server at host www.anyCollege.edu accepts connection and acknowledges.
3. Client sends HTTP request for file /someDir/file.html.
4. Server receives request, finds and sends object in HTTP response.
5. Client receives response. It terminates connection, parseobject.
6. Steps 3–5 are repeated for each embedded object.

Thus, the overhead of HTTP/1.0 is 1 RTT for each start (each request/response), that is if there are 10 objects, then the Total Transmission Time is as follows:

```
TTT = [10 * 1 TCP/RTT] + [10 * 1 REQ/RESP RTT] = 20RTT
```

Whereas for HTTP/1.1, persistent connections[1] are very helpful with multi-object requests as the server keeps TCP connection open by default.

```
TTT = [1 * 1 TCP/RTT] + [10 * 1 REQ/RESP RTT] = 11 RTT
```

The visible advantages of a persistent connection include, saving of CPU time in routers and hosts, and the reduction in network congestion and latency on subsequent requests.

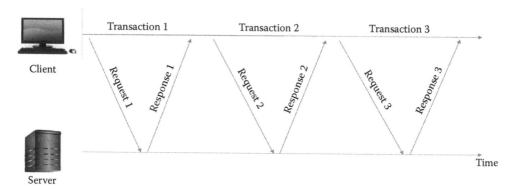

FIGURE 4.3
RTT in a persistent HTTP.

---

[1] Implies sequential request/response, a non-pipelined one where the next request is not sent until the response is received for the previous request [RTT: Round trip time (client to server and back to client)].

Persistent HTTP connections are used with or without pipelining. In persistent connections without pipelining, the client issues a new request only after the previous response has arrived. Whereas, in persistent connections with pipelining, the client sends the request as soon as it encounters a reference, i.e., multiple requests/responses.

HTTP/1.1 supports *pipelining*—it allows clients to send multiple requests at once, without waiting for a reply. Servers can also send multiple replies without closing their socket. This results in fewer round trips and faster load times. This is particularly useful for satellite Internet connections and other connections with high latency as separate requests need not be made for each file. Since it is possible to fit several HTTP requests in the same TCP packet, HTTP pipelining allows fewer TCP packets to be sent over the network, reducing network load. HTTP pipelining requires both the client and the server to support it.

4.4 Hypertext Transfer Protocol Communication

In its simplest form, the communication model of HTTP involves an HTTP client, usually a *web browser* on a client machine, and an HTTP server, more commonly known as a *web server*. The basic HTTP communication model has four steps:

- *Handshaking*: Opening a TCP connection to the web server.
- *Client request*: After a TCP connection is created, the HTTP client sends a request message formatted according to the rules of the HTTP standard—an *HTTP Request*. This message specifies the resource that the client wishes to retrieve or includes information to be provided to the server.
- *Server response*: The server reads and interprets the request. It takes action relevant to the request and creates an HTTP response message, which it sends back to the client. The response message indicates whether the request was successful, and it may also contain the content of the resource that the client requested, if appropriate.
- *Closing*: Closing the connection (optional).

4.4.1 Handshaking

For opening a TCP connection, the user on client-side inputs the URL containing the name of the web server in the web browser. Then, the web browser asks the DNS (Domain Name Server) for the IP address of the given URL. If the DNS fails to find the IP address of the URL, it shows an error (for example, "Netscape (Browser) is unable to locate error.") on the client's screen. If the DNS finds the IP address of the URL, then the client browser opens a TCP connection to port 80 (default port of HTTP, although one can specify another port number explicitly in the URL) of the machine whose IP address has been found.

4.4.2 Request Message

After handshaking in the first step, the client (browser) requests an object (file) from the server. This is done with a human-readable message. Every HTTP request message has the same basic structure as shown in Figure 4.4.

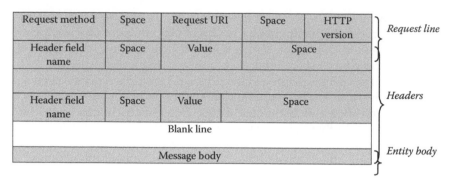

FIGURE 4.4
The HTTP request message format.

4.4.2.1 Start Line

Every start line consists of three parts: the request method, Request URI, and the HTTP version—with a single space used to separate these adjacent parts.

- *Request method*: It indicates the type of the request a client wants to send. They are also called methods. A method makes a message either a request or a command to the server. Request messages are used to retrieve data from the server whereas a command tells the server to do a specific task.

```
Method = GET | HEAD | POST | PUT| DELETE| TRACE | OPTIONS| CONNECT |
COPY| MOVE
```

The details of the types of HTTP request methods are discussed next:

- *GET*: Request server to return the resource specified by the Request-URI as the body of a response. It is the most frequently used method in the web. It is specified when a client wants to retrieve a resource from the server. The URL in the request line identifies the resource. If it is valid one, the server reads the content of the resource and sends the content back to the client, otherwise an error message is sent back to the client. The message body is empty for the GET method. This method may also be used to send information (possibly small) to the server for processing without using an HTML form. The information is sent by appending it to the URL using name-value pair.

- *HEAD*: Requests server to return the same HTTP header fields that would be returned if a GET method was used, but not return the message body that would be returned to a GET method (this provides information about a resource without the communication overhead of transmitting the body of the response, which may be quite large). It is useful to inspect the characteristics of the resource (possibly large) without actually downloading it. This effectively saves the bandwidth.

- *POST*: Request server to pass the body of this request message as data to be processed by the resource specified by the Request-URI. The actual information is included in the body part of the request message instead of appending it to the URL as done in the GET method. The most common form of the POST method is to submit an HTML form to the server. Since the information is included in the body, large chunks of data such as an entire file can be sent to the server. Consequently, the length of the request can be unlimited. It is more versatile but slower than using the GET method.

- *PUT*: Request server to store the body of this message on the server and assign the specified Request-URI to the data stored so that future GET request messages containing this Request-URI will receive this data in their response messages. It is used to upload a new resource or replace an existing document. The actual document is specified in the body part. It is vulnerable and is not permitted by most of the web servers. However, developers can customize their web servers to accept this method.

- *DELETE*: Request server to respond to future HTTP request messages that contain the specified Request-URI with a response indicating that there is no resource associated with this Request-URI.

- *TRACE*: Request server to return a copy of the complete HTTP request message, including start line, header fields, and body, received by the server. Used primarily for test purposes by instructing the web servers to echo the request back to the client.

- *OPTIONS*: Request server to return a list of HTTP methods that may be used to access the resource specified by the Request-URI. It is usually used to check whether a server is functioning properly before performing other tasks.

- *CONNECT*: It is used to convert a request connection into the transparent TCP/IP tunnel. It is usually done to facilitate secured socket layer (SSL) encrypted communication, such as HTTPS through an unencrypted HTTP proxy server.

- *COPY*: The HTTP protocol may be used to copy a file from one location to another. The method COPY is used for this purpose. The URL specified in the request line specifies the location of the source file. The location of the target file is specified in the entity header. This method is also vulnerable.

- *MOVE*: It is similar to the COPY method except that it deletes the source file.

- *Request-URI*: The second part of the start line is known as the Request-URI. It identifies the resource for which the request needs to be applied.

- *HTTP version*: HTTP/1.1 version is used as it is the latest available version.

4.4.2.2 Headers

HTTP headers are a form of message metadata. The enlightened use of headers makes it possible to construct sophisticated applications that establish and maintain sessions, set caching policies, control authentication, and implement business logic, as they collectively specify the characteristics of the resource requested and the data that is provided. For example, a client may want to accept the audio files only in some specified format.

The HTTP protocol specification makes a clear distinction between general headers, request headers, response headers, and entity headers. Both request and response messages have general headers but have no relation to the data eventually transmitted in the body. The headers are separated by an empty line from the request and response body. The format of a request header is shown in the following table:

General Header
Request Header
Entity Header

A header consists of a single line or multiple lines. Each line is a single header of the following form:

```
Header-name: Header-value
```

Each header line consists of a header name followed by a colon (:), one or more spaces, and the header value, as shown in the following:

Header Name	:		Header value

The header name is not case-sensitive; but the header value may be. If a header line starts with a space, then it is considered to be a part of the previous header line. This happens if a long header value is broken into multiple lines for easy reading. So, the following headers are equivalent.

```
Date: Mon, 12 Sept 2016 16:09:05 GMT
Date: Mon, 12 Sept 2016
16:09:05 GMT
```

4.4.2.2.1 General Headers

General headers do not describe the body of the message. They provide information about the messages instead of what content they carry. They are primarily used to specify the method for processing and handling messages. The earlier example of a header is actually an example of general header. Some of the general headers with their brief description are given in the following:

- *Date: Mon, 12 Sept 2016 16:09:05 GMT*

  This header specifies the time and date of the creation of the message.
- *Connection: Close*

  This header indicates whether the client or server, which generated the message, intends to keep the connection open.
- *Warning: Danger. This site may be hacked!*

  This header stores text for human consumption, something that would be useful when tracing a problem.
- *Cache-Control: no-cache*

  This header shows whether the caching should be used.

4.4.2.2.2 Request Header

It allows the client to pass additional information about themselves and about the request, such as the data format that the client expects. Some of the request headers with their brief description are given in the following:

- *User-Agent: Mozilla/4.75*

  Identifies the software (e.g., a web browser) responsible for making the request.
- *Host: www.netsurf.com*

  This header was introduced to support virtual hosting, a feature that allows a web server to service more than one domain.

- *Referer: http://wwwdtu.ac.in/~akshi/index.html*

  This header provides the server with context information about the request. If the request came about because a user clicked on a link found on a web page, this header contains the URL of that referring page.

- *Accept: text/plain*

  This header specifies the format of the media that the client can accept.

The response header corresponding to the response message will be explained later in Response format.

4.4.2.2.3 Entity Header

It contains the information about the message body or the target messages in case of the request messages have no body. Some of the entity headers with their brief description are:

- *Content-Type: mime-type/mime-subtype*

  This header specifies the MIME-type of the content of the message body.

- *Content-Length: 546*

  This optional header provides the length of the message body. Although it is optional, it is useful for clients such as web browsers that wish to impart information about the progress of a request. Where this header is omitted, the browser can only display the amount of data downloaded. But when the header is included, the browser can display the amount of data as a percentage of the total size of the message body.

- *Last-Modified: Sun, 11 Sept 2016 13:28:31 GMT*

  This header provides the last modification date of the content that is transmitted in the body of the message. It is critical for the proper functioning of caching mechanisms.

- *Allow: GET, HEAD, POST*

  This header specifies the list of the valid methods that can be applied on a URL.

4.4.2.3 Message Body

The message body part is optional for an HTTP message, but, if it is available, then it is used to carry the entity-body associated with the request. If the entity-body is associated, then usually Content-Type and Content-Length header lines specify the nature of the associated body. A message body is the one that carries the actual HTTP request data (including form data and uploaded, etc.). The example of HTTP request message with no message body is given in Figure 4.5.

4.4.3 Response Message

A server responds to the HTTP request of the client by providing the requested document (object, entity), then it transfers an HTML file. Before sending the real data, a status code is sent (e.g., 202, "Accepted"), as well as information about the document and the server. Similar to an HTTP request message, an HTTP response message consists of a status line, header fields, and the body of the response, in the following format (Figure 4.6).

GET/index.html HTTP/1.1	Request Line	
Date: Fri, 16 Sep 2016 22:08:32 GMT Connection: Close	General headers	
User-Agent: Mozilla/5.0 Host: www.drakshikumar.com Accept: text/html, text/plain Accept-Language: en-US Content- Length: 35	Request header	**HTTP Request**
BLANK LINE		
	Message Body	

FIGURE 4.5
A sample HTTP request message.

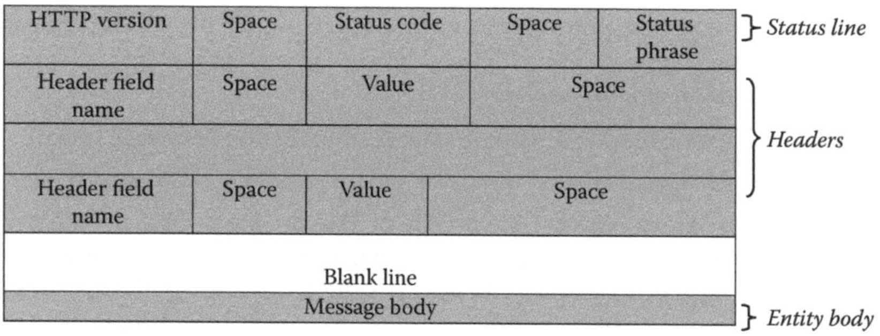

HTTP version	Space	Status code	Space	Status phrase	} *Status line*
Header field name	Space	Value	Space		
					} *Headers*
Header field name	Space	Value	Space		
Blank line					
Message body					} *Entity body*

FIGURE 4.6
The HTTP response message format.

4.4.3.1 Status Line

Status line consists of three parts: HTTP version, Status code, and Status phrase. Two consecutive parts are separated by a space.

HTTP version		Status Code		Status phrase

- *HTTP version*: This field specifies the version of the HTTP protocol being used by the server. The current version is HTTP/1.1.

- *Status code*: It is a three-digit code that indicates the status of the response. The status codes are classified with respect to their functionality into five groups as follows:

  - 1xx series (Informational)—This class of status codes represents provisional responses.

  - 2xx series (Success)—This class of status codes indicates that the client's request are received, understood, and accepted successfully.

  - 3xx series (Re-directional)—These status codes indicate that additional actions must be taken by the client to complete the request. The user agent may take further actions in order to fulfill the request automatically, provided that it uses either the HEAD or the GET method.

  - 4xx series (Client error)—These status codes are used to indicate that the client request had an error and therefore it cannot be fulfilled. Except when responding to a HEAD request, the body of the response message should contain the explanation that caused the error. The user agent should display the error message to inform the user.

- 5xx series (Server error)—This set of status codes indicates that the server encountered some problem and hence the request cannot be satisfied at this time. The reason of the failure is embedded in the message body. It is also indicated whether the failure is temporary or permanent. The user agent should accordingly display a message on the screen to make the user aware of the server failure.
- *Status phrase*: It is also known as Reason-phrase and is intended to give a short textual description of status code. Some of status phrases commonly encountered are given in Table 4.1. The respective status code, phrase and its description are provided in Table 4.1.

TABLE 4.1

HTTP Status Codes and Phrases

Status Code	Status Phrase	Description
100	Continue	The server has received the initial part of the request i.e., request headers, and the client may proceed further.
101	Switching	The server switches the protocol on receiving a request from the client to do the same.
102	Processing	The server has received the request which is currently under process and no response is available yet.
200	OK	Notifies that the request was valid.
201	Created	The request sent was successful and the desired resource has been created.
202	Accepted	The request is accepted for further processing.
300	Multiple Choices	The client may follow various available options for resources.
301	Moved Permanently	The resource request no longer exists. The client should redirect this and all the coming requests to the given URL.
302	Found	The request is not available currently. Clients (Server) should temporarily redirect requests to given URL.
400	Bad Request	The request cannot be fulfilled because of some syntax error in it.
401	Unauthorized	The request has failed to be authorized.
403	Forbidden	The request is valid but due to some reasons the server is refusing to respond to it.
404	Not Found	The requested resource could not be found but may be available in the future. Subsequent requests by the client are permissible.
408	Request Timeout	The server timed-out waiting for the request.
415	Unsupported Media Type	The request entity has a media type which the server or resource does not support. For example, the client uploads an image as image/svg+xml, but the server requires that images use a different format.
500	Internal Server Error	An error message including that a problem has occurred in the server.
501	Not Implemented	The server is unable to recognize the method specified and unable to fulfill the request.
502	Bad Gateway	The server is a gateway or proxy and has received an invalid response from the downstream server.
503	Service Unavailable	The server is currently unavailable (because it is overloaded or down for maintenance). Generally, this is a temporary state.
504	Gateway Timeout	The server was acting as a gateway or proxy and did not receive a timely response from the upstream server.
505	HTTP Version Not Supported	The server does not support the HTTP protocol version used in the request.
511	Network Authentication Required	The client needs to authenticate to gain network access. Intended for use by intercepting proxies used to control access to the network.

4.4.3.2 Headers

Headers in an HTTP response message are similar to the one in a request message except for one aspect, in place of request header in the headers it contains a response header. The general header and entity header has the same purpose and structure as the request message. The response header is discussed in the following:

General Header
Response Header
Entity Header

- **Response Header**

  Response headers help the server to pass additional information about the response that cannot be inferred from the status code alone, like the information about the server and the data being sent. Some response headers with their brief description are given in the following:

  - *Location: http://www.mywebsite.com/relocatedPage.html*

    This header specifies a URL towards which the client should redirect its original request.

    It always accompanies the "301" and "302" status codes that direct clients to try a new location.

  - *WWW-Authenticate: Basic*

    This header accompanies the "401" status code that indicates an authorization challenge. It specifies the authentication scheme which should be used to access the requested entity. In the case of web browsers, the combination of the "401" status code and the WWW-Authenticate header causes users to be prompted for ids and passwords.

  - *Server: Apache/1.2.5*

    This header is not tied to a particular status code. It is an optional header that identifies the server software.

  - *Age:22*

    This header specifies the age of the resource in the proxy cache in seconds.

4.4.3.3 Message Body

Similar to HTTP request messages, the message body in an HTTP response message is also optional. The message body carries the actual HTTP response data from the server (including files, images, and so on) to the client.

A sample response to the request message shown in Figure 4.5 is given in Figure 4.7.

HTTP/1.1 200 OK	Status Line	
Date: Fri, 16 Sep 2016 22:08:32 GMT Connection: Close	General headers	
Server: Apache/2.4.7 Accept-Ranges: bytes	Response header	
Content-Type: text/html Content- Length: 95 Last-Modified: Mon, 5 Sept 2016 10:14:24 GMT	Entity header	HTTP Response
BLANK LINE		
\<html> \<head> \<title> Welcome to my Homepage \</title> \</head> \<body> \<p> Coming Soon! \</p> \</body> \</html>	Message Body	

FIGURE 4.7
A sample HTTP response message.

4.5 Hypertext Transfer Protocol Secure

HTTPS is a protocol for secure communication over the Internet. It was developed by Netscape. It is not a protocol, but it is just the result of the combination of the HTTP and SSL/TLS (Secure Socket Layer/Transport Layer Security) protocol. It is also called secure HTTP, as it sends and receives everything in the encrypted form, adding the element of safety.

HTTPS is often used to protect highly confidential online transactions like online banking and online shopping order forms. The use of HTTPS protects against eavesdropping and man-in-the-middle attacks. While using HTTP, servers and clients still speak exactly the same HTTP to each other, but over a secure SSL connection that encrypts and decrypts their requests and responses. The SSL layer has two main purposes:

- Verifying that you are talking directly to the server that you think you are talking to.
- Ensuring that only the server can read what you send it, and only you can read what it sends back.

The really clever part is that anyone can intercept every single one of the messages you exchange with a server, including the ones where you are agreeing on the key and encryption strategy to use, and still not be able to read any of the actual data you send. This helps increase the trust that clients/customers have in a service or business. Let us understand the working process of HTTPS with an example: Suppose you visit a web site to view their online catalog. When you're ready to order, you will be given a web page order form with a Uniform Resource Locator (URL) that starts with https://.

When you click "Send," to send the page back to the catalog retailer, your browser's HTTPS layer will encrypt it. The acknowledgement you receive from the server will also travel in encrypted form, arrive with an https:// URL, and be decrypted for you by your browser's HTTPS sub-layer. The effectiveness of HTTPS can be limited by poor implementation of browser or server software or a lack of support for some algorithms. Furthermore, although HTTPS secures data as it travels between the server and the client, once the data is decrypted at its destination, it is only as secure as the host computer.

4.6 Hypertext Transfer Protocol State Retention: Cookies

HTTP is a stateless protocol. Cookies are an application-based solution to provide state retention over a stateless protocol. They are small pieces of information that are sent in response from the web server to the client. Cookies are the simplest technique used for storing client state. A cookie is also known as HTTP cookie, web cookie, or browser cookie. Cookies are not software; they cannot be programmed, cannot carry viruses, and cannot install malware on the host computer. However, they can be used by spyware to track a user's browsing activities. Cookies are stored on a client's computer. They have a lifespan and are destroyed by the client browser at the end of that lifespan.

A cookie is a combination of name and value, as in (name, value). A web application can generate multiple cookies, set their life spans in terms of how many milliseconds each of them should be alive, and send them back to a web browser as part of an HTTP response. If cookies are allowed, a web browser will save all cookies on its hosting computer, along with their originating URLs and life spans. When an HTTP request is sent from a web browser of the same type on the same computer to a web site, all live cookies originated from that web site will be sent to the web site as part of the HTTP request. Therefore, session data can be stored in cookies, thus, the state can be stored (Figure 4.8).

An HTTP cookie is a small file that is provided by the server as an HTTP response header, stored by the client and returned to the server as an HTTP request header. This is the simplest approach to maintain session data. Since the web server doesn't need to commit any resources for the session data, this is the most scalable approach to support session data of large number of users. But it is not secure or efficient for cookies to go between a web browser and a web site for every HTTP request, and hackers could eavesdrop for the session data along the Internet path.

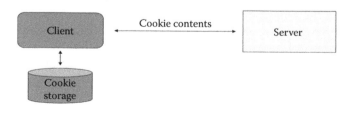

FIGURE 4.8
A HTTP cookie.

4.6.1 Creating Cookies

When receiving an HTTP request, a server can send a Set-Cookie header with the response. The cookie is usually stored by the browser and, afterwards, the cookie value is sent along with every request made to the same server as the content of a Cookie HTTP header. Additionally, an expiration delay can be specified as well as restrictions to a specific domain and path, limiting how long and to which site the cookies is sent to.

A simple cookie can be set like this:

```
Set-Cookie: <cookie-name>=<cookie-value>
```

There are various kinds of cookies that are used for different scenarios depending on the need. These different types of cookies are given with their brief description in Table 4.2.

A cookie may supply your name and e-mail to various websites resulting in various advertisements based on your recent web browsing history. A cookie may bring recommendations, shopping carts, authorization and user session state (web e-mail). Primary advantages include:

- *Persistence*: One of the most powerful aspects of cookies is their persistence. When a cookie is set on the client's browser, it can persist for days, months, or even years. This makes it easy to save user preferences and visit information and to keep this information available every time the user returns to a website. Moreover, as cookies are stored on the client's hard disk they are still available even if the server crashes.
- *Transparent*: Cookies work transparently without the user being aware that information needs to be stored.
- They lighten the load on the server's memory.

FUN FACT: Cookies are browser specific. Each browser stores the cookies in a different location. A cookie created in one browser (Google Chrome) will not be accessed by another browser (Internet Explorer or Firefox). Most of the browsers have restrictions on the length of the text stored in cookies. It is 4096(4kb), in general, but could vary from browser to browser. Some browsers limit the number of cookies stored by each domain (20 cookies). If the limit is exceeded, the new cookies will replace the old cookies.

TABLE 4.2

Types of Cookies

Cookies	Description
Session cookie	A session cookie only lasts for the duration of users using the website. The web browser normally deletes session cookies when it quits.
Persistent cookie/tracing cookie	A persistent cookie will outlast user sessions. If a persistent cookie has its max-age set to 1 year, then, within the year, the initial value set in that cookie would be sent back to the server every time the user visited the server.
Secure cookie	A secure cookie is used when a browser is visiting a server via HTTPS, ensuring that the cookie is always encrypted when transmitting from client to server.
Zombie cookie	A zombie cookie is any cookie that is automatically recreated after the user has deleted it.

4.7 Hypertext Transfer Protocol Cache

Fetching something over the network is both slow and expensive: large responses require many roundtrips between the client and server. As a result, the ability to cache and reuse previously fetched resources is a critical aspect of optimizing for performance. Caching is the term for storing reusable responses in order to make subsequent requests faster. The caching of web pages is an important technique to improve the Quality of Service (QoS) of the web servers. Caching can reduce network latency experienced by clients. For example, web pages can be loaded more quickly in the browser. Caching can also conserve bandwidth on the network, thus increasing the scalability of the network with the help of an HTTP proxy cache (also known as web cache). Caching also increases the availability of web pages. Web resources that are cached remain accessible even if the source of the resources or an intermediate network link goes down. Content can be cached at many different points throughout the delivery chain:

- *Browser cache*: Web browsers themselves maintain a small cache. Typically, the browser sets a policy that dictates the most important items to cache. This may be user-specific content or content deemed expensive to download and likely to be requested again.

- *Intermediary caching proxies (Web proxy)*: Any server in between the client and your infrastructure can cache certain content as desired. These caches may be maintained by ISPs or other independent parties.

- *Reverse cache*: Your server infrastructure can implement its own cache for backend services. This way, content can be served from the point-of-contact instead of hitting backend servers on each request.

A *Web proxy* is the most commonly used caching service. A proxy is an application program or a computer system that behaves like an intermediary between servers and clients looking for services from these servers. To access a resource, a client sends the request to proxy instead of the original web server. The proxy, in turn, searches for the resource in its cache. If the resource is found, it is delivered to the client. Otherwise, it contacts the specified server and gets the resource, puts that resource in its local cache, and finally returns the resource to the client. The subsequent requests for the same resource are served by the copy in its local cache thereby avoiding remote web server access. This way a proxy speeds up the access to the resource. Advantages of using a cache are:

- *Decreased network costs*: Content can be cached at various points in the network path between the content consumer and content origin. When the content is cached closer to the consumer, requests will not cause much additional network activity beyond the cache.

- *Improved responsiveness*: Caching enables content to be retrieved faster because an entire network round trip is not necessary. Caches maintained close to the user, like the browser cache, can make this retrieval nearly instantaneous.

- *Increased performance on the same hardware*: For the server where the content originated, more performance can be squeezed from the same hardware by allowing aggressive caching. The content owner can leverage the powerful servers along the delivery path to take the brunt of certain content loads.

- *Availability of content during network interruptions*: With certain policies, caching can be used to serve content to end users even when it may be unavailable for short periods of time from the origin servers.

FUN FACT: Certain content lends itself more readily to caching than others. Some very cache-friendly content include: Logos and brand images; Non-rotating images in general (navigation icons, for example); Style sheets; General JavaScript files; Downloadable Content; Media Files. These tend to change infrequently, so they can benefit from being cached for longer periods of time.

4.7.1 Cache Consistency

Cache consistency mechanisms ensure that cached copies of web pages are eventually updated to reflect changes in the original web pages. There are basically, two cache consistency mechanisms currently in use for HTTP proxies:

- *Pull method*: In this mechanism, each web page cached is assigned a time-to-serve field, which indicates the time of storing the web page in the cache. An expiration time of one or two days is also maintained, and it determines how long a web page should remain valid in the cache. If the time is expired, a fresh copy is obtained when user requests for the page.
- *Push method*: In this mechanism, the web server is assigned the responsibility of making all cached copies consistent with the server copy. Whenever a web page is modified, the web server sends an update request to every web proxy that cached this web page. The advantage of this is that the cached pages are modified only when the original copies are modified, but this also increases the load of the web server.

Review Questions

1. HTTP request and response messages are human readable (**True/False**).
2. What are the fundamental characteristics of HTTP?
3. Describe the HTTP Connection Types and their effects on the round-trip times for communication between the client-server machines.
4. A web page is downloaded, and it contains five images and an applet with two images embedded within the applet. How many RTTs does it take to download all objects in the web page using non-persistent HTTP, persistent HTTP without pipelining, and persistent HTTP with pipelining?

5. Explain the structure of HTTP Request message and list out the types of request methods.

6. Describe the HTTP response message. What is the meaning of HTTP response message status: 400?

7. What is the significance of Headers in HTTP request and response messages?

8. HTTP is a stateless protocol. What can be done to provide state retention over a stateless protocol?

9. Fetching something over the network is both slow and expensive. What can be done to improve the Quality of Service (QoS) of the web servers?

10. How is consistency in HTTP proxies maintained?

5

Evolution of Web

5.1 The Generations of Web

The first generation of the Web enabled the users to access a plethora of information, products, and services by serving as a simple medium—a place for businesses to broadcast their information to people. The early Web provided limited user interactions or content contributions, and only allowed users to search the information and read it. This generation of the Web was referred to as the Web of Documents, Web 1.0, the Web of Cognition, or the Read-only Web. An essential tool that enabled users to access the Web was the search engine, which ensured discovery of available information for the user. A vivid paradigm shift was observed in the early 2000s, when people became a prominent part of the Web evolution. The success of e-commerce, the abundant information discovery opportunities that the Web offered, and the emerging gamut of e-business models further amplified the involvement of users. Technological innovation enabled people to contribute content to the Web (e.g., with blogs) and engage in collectively organizing and structuring information (e.g., with wikis). At this step, the Web was characterized as a network where nodes were online resources or people; the edges in that network were contributions of resources by people, similarity among people or links between resources. Resources were not just static content (such as static HTML pages) on the server side, but also dynamic content that could be hosted on the client side. This second generation of the Web, which entailed collective intelligence applications, was referred to as the Web of people, the Web 2.0, the Web of Communication, or the Read-Write Web. Thus, the first generation *for the people* Web transformed into a *by the people, of the people, and for the people* Web. The following years progressed towards a more homogeneous, personalized, and a sustainable Web where the user-generated data was analyzed to develop advanced applications based on the collected data. It merged two main platforms—the available standardized semantic technologies and the social computing environment—to enable human-machine cooperation. This generation of the Web is referred to as the Web of Data, the Web 3.0, the Web of Cooperation, or the Read-Write-Execute Web. The added vision was a *Web for the people, of the people, by the people, to the people*; thus, building a Web that does not evolve around businesses but data analytics for new value models. The following sections expound the details of this colossal and pragmatic artifact, the Web.

5.2 Web 1.0

The first generation of the Web, Web 1.0, was introduced by Sir Tim Berners-Lee in late 1990s, as a technology-based solution for businesses to broadcast their information to people. It was defined as a system of interlinked, hypertext documents accessed via the Internet. It was static and somewhat mono-directional model with websites publishing the information for anyone at any time. This early Web was primarily informational in nature offering an online presence for resources, allowing the retrieving of relevant information, and reading it. It was one person or organization pushing content out to many people via websites and e-mail newsletters as a one-way communication. The core elements of Web 1.0 were HTTP, HTML, and URL. Eventually, it was imperative to have tools that facilitate quick and accurate access of available Web information. Web Search Engines have assumed a central role in the World Wide Web's infrastructure as tools that enable information retrieval from the largest available repository of data, the Web.

The Web 1.0, as an unlimited source of information with users from cross-section of society seeking to find information to satisfy their information needs, required an effective and efficient mechanism to access it. This read-only Web was accessible using an information retrieval system, popularly known as a web search engine, or simply search engine, which makes their existence imperative and a crucial part in the advent of Web. Information retrieval on the Web (Web IR) has been established as a distinguished field of study helping users complete the search tasks of finding a handful of relevant documents among thousands and thousands of pages of text with little structural organization. Search engines are the most popular implementation of Information Retrieval. We discuss the Web IR basics, the components, model categories, tools, tasks, and the performance measures extensively in the next chapter.

5.3 Web 2.0

The constant inflation of the World Wide Web and the familiarization of users with the Internet generated all the necessary preconditions for a wide adaptation of the basic Internet as a generic exchange platform, where any user becomes a content provider and, as a result, dramatically changed interactions with and usage of the Web. This came with the advent of Web 2.0, also known as the Read-Write Web. Web 2.0, first coined by Tim O'Reilly in 2004, helps the typical user to contribute content. "The user is the content" is its most popular slogan. The popularity of Web 2.0 grows within all its applications. This new collaborative Web (called Web 2.0) extends its reach through Web-based technologies like comments, blogs and wikis, and successful sites like Twitter or Facebook, which allow people to build social networks based on professional relationship, interests, and so on. The term "Web 2.0" is defined as the innovative use of the World Wide Web to expand social and business outreach and to exploit collective intelligence from the community. It advocates utilizing the architecture of the Web to promote users' participation and collaboration and to act as a basic platform for users to share, contribute, review, and enhance information resources. Although the term suggests a new version of the World Wide Web, it did not include any actual change in technical specifications. Rather it reflected the change in the way people use the Web.

Web 2.0 is a loose grouping of newer generation social technologies, whose users are actively involved in communicating and collaborating with each other as they build connections and communities across the Web. It allows for establishing friendly social communication among web users without obligating them to disclose their private identities. Hence, it significantly increases the participating interest of web users. Normal web readers (not necessarily being a standard web author simultaneously) then have a handy way of expressing their viewpoints without the need of disclosing who they are. The link between web readers and writers becomes generally connected, though many of the specific connections are still anonymous. The direct communication between web readers and writers is a fundamental distinction between Web 1.0 and Web 2.0. In short, Web 2.0 not only connects individual users to the Web, but it also connects these individual users to each other. It fixes the previous disconnection between web readers and writers by fostering a two-way communication in the online public commons. People can post comments and have a public conversation with an organization. It's one person or organization publishing content to many on social networking sites, which help to facilitate re-publishing the content to their friends, fans, followers, connections, and so on.

The use of the Web has shifted from passive consumption of content to more active collaboration. It focuses on user-created content, usability, and interoperability of data by the end-users. Web 1.0 websites functioned as a static outlet for information and products where content is posted by programmers to be viewed by users, while Web 2.0 websites function as applications, or programs, which can be updated from any computer, and users actively contribute to the content of the sites. Web 2.0 websites are designed in such a way that they allow for more user participation and encourage users to add value to the application as they use it. The characteristics of Web 2.0 include a rich experience, user participation, dynamic content, and scalability. Further characteristics such as openness, freedom, and collective intelligence by way of user participation make essential attributes of Web 2.0. Two of the main advantages of using Web 2.0 include, firstly, being able to pull information from a number of different places and having it personalized to meet the needs of a single user and, secondly, it makes the Internet a true democratic system where information flows freely and people can express their ideas without fear of repression. On the flip side, security is a bigger issue with Web 2.0, as many web services are offered free, and can be easily targeted by hackers hence compromising security and privacy of users.

5.3.1 Web 2.0 Technologies

Web 2.0 encourages a wider range of expression, facilitates more collaborative ways of working, enables community creation, fosters dialogue and knowledge sharing, and creates a setting for learners with various tools and technologies. A few of the most popular Web 2.0 tools are discussed next:

5.3.1.1 Blogging

Being a social creature, human beings have a natural tendency to express themselves; however, having audience for the same can be overwhelming for some people. The World Wide Web makes it possible for you to publish your thoughts (or whatever else you'd like) and distribute them to the entire world (of Internet-connected computer users). Nowadays, there are several good, reliable blogging tools available for free on the Web. You can set up your account and start blogging away within minutes. To understand this interactive tool of Web 2.0, one must be familiar with the basic terminology of blogging.

- *Weblog or Blog*: A Weblog, or "blog," is a personal journal or newsletter on the Web. Some blogs are highly influential and have enormous readership, while others are mainly intended for a close circle of family and friends. The power of Weblogs is that they allow millions of people to easily publish their ideas, and millions more to comment on them.

- *Blogger*: A blogger is someone who writes a blog.

- *Blogosphere*: Blogosphere is a word used to describe the online community of bloggers and their writings.

- *Permalink*: A permalink is the permanent identifier to a specific Weblog post or article. Bloggers love permalinks—they provide an easy way to capture specific references to posts or articles about which bloggers are writing.

- *Blog-roll*: A blog-roll is a list of blogs and bloggers that any particular blog-author finds influential or interesting. Blog-rolls indicate the online community that a blogger prefers or belongs to and where they are part of the conversations of the Blogosphere.

Some of the popular blogging resources are: Wordpress, Blogger, Technorati, Problogger (blogging for beginners), about.com, edublogs, and so on.

FUN FACT: More than 70 million blogs have been created since 2003. Blogosphere growth remains strong with over 120,000 blogs being created everyday.

5.3.1.2 Social Networking Sites

Social networking websites provide a "virtual community" for people interested in a particular subject or just a place to "hang out" together (Figure 5.1).

Social networking sites, with Facebook being the best-known, allow users to set up a personal profile page where they can post regular status updates, maintain links to contacts known as "friends" through a variety of interactive channels, and assemble and display their interests in the form of texts, photos, videos, group memberships, and so on. This might involve drawing in other Web 2.0 tools, such as RSS feeds, folksonomies, photos, and videos, from other social sharing sites. Social networking sites represent a fundamental shift from the content-oriented Web (where web pages were usually about topics) to the person-oriented Web (where web *pages* are about people). Basically, members create their own online profile page

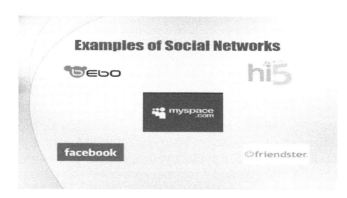

FIGURE 5.1
Social networking sites.

with biographical data, pictures, likes, dislikes, and any other information they choose to post. Users can communicate with each other via/through text, voice, chat, instant message, videoconference, and blogs. The services typically provide a way for members to contact friends of other members, thus enabling everyone's "network" to grow. YouTube is a special kind of social networking site, which is basically a video sharing tool of Web 2.0, with social networking features such as liking, sharing, and commenting on a particular video. YouTube videos are "streamed" to users on the YouTube site and can be easily "embedded" into other websites and blogs.

FUN FACT: The first ever YouTube video was "Me at the Zoo." It featured Jawed Karim—a founder of San Diego Zoo. The video was uploaded on April 23, 2005.

5.3.1.3 Podcasts

A Podcast is basically just an audio (or video) file. A podcast is different from other types of audio on the Internet because a podcast can be subscribed to by the listeners, so that when new podcasts are released, they are automatically delivered, or fed, to a subscriber's computer or mobile device.

- *Pod* refers to a mobile playback device such as iPod or any other mp3 player, and *casting* is derived from broadcasting, hence *podcasting* is the distribution of audio or video files over the Internet for playback on devices.
- If you are listening to a podcast on your computer, then it will be played on the video or audio player already installed on it. However, if you want to subscribe to podcast feeds, then you'll need to install "podcatcher" software on your computer. The most popular pod-catcher software is iTunes.
- The key difference between a podcast and a plain old audio file is the distribution model. Most podcasts are shared (syndicated) using the Real Simple Syndication (RSS) format. Through RSS, anyone can subscribe to and catch podcasts, which will be automatically downloaded and managed by a pod-catching program like iTunes.

5.3.1.4 Wikis

According to The Wiki Way, "Open editing has some profound and subtle effects on the wiki's usage. Allowing everyday users to create and edit any page in a Web site encourages democratic use of the Web and promotes content composition by nontechnical users" (Kajewski 2007). A Wiki is a website that allows its users to actively collaborate and modify its content and structure simply from a web browser. The collaborative encyclopedia "Wikipedia" is the most popular example of a wiki today.

- A single page in a wiki website is referred to as a wiki page.
- The entire collection of wiki pages, which are usually interconnected with hyperlinks, is "the wiki." A wiki is essentially a database for creating, browsing, and searching through information.
- A defining characteristic of wiki technology is the ease with which pages can be created and updated.
- Vandalism of wikis is a common problem. For example, due to its open nature anyone with an Internet connection and a computer can change wiki content to

FIGURE 5.2
Home page of Wikispace.

something offensive, adding nonsense or deliberately adding incorrect information can be a major problem.

- The following are the common platforms to create a wiki: wikispace, pbwiki, and
  wetpaint (Figure 5.2).

- Some popular wikis are Wikipedia, wikiwikiweb, memory alpha, wikivoyage,
  and susning.nu.

FUN FACT: The English Wikipedia has the largest user-base among wikis on the World
Wide Web, and it ranks in the top 10 among all Web sites in terms of traffic.

5.3.1.5 Micro-blogging

Micro-blogging is the practice of posting small pieces of digital content—which could be
text, pictures, links, short videos, or other media—on the Internet. Micro-blogging enables
users to write brief messages, usually limited to less than 200 characters, and publish
them via web browser-based services, email, or mobile phones. The most popular micro-
blogging service today is called Twitter. Micro-blogging is also known as "mobile social-
networking" or "themed Instant Messaging." It creates a sense of online community where
groups of friends and professional colleagues connect to each other, frequently update
content, and follow each other's posts.

- This is one of the best examples of subscription-based services where the subscribers must typically create accounts, which are linked with cell phones, e-mail
  accounts, instant messaging, web page, or any medium they will use to send
  updates in order to post a micro-blog or to read those posted by others.

- These posts might consist of short text snippets (maximum number of characters
  specified by the application), a photo, an audio clip, or a few seconds of video, any
  of which can be shared publicly or with a selected group of subscribers.

- The posting of micro-blogs has enjoyed a popular upsurge in the last few years with add-ons appearing regularly that enable more sophisticated updates and interaction with other applications.

Other micro-blogging sites are Friendfeed, Tumblr, Plurk, Yammer, and so on.

FUN FACT: Twitter co-founder Jack Dorsey sent the first tweet on March 21, 2006. The tweet he sent was "just setting up my twttr."

5.3.1.6 Social Bookmarking

Social bookmarking is a way to store, organize, search, manage, and share collections of websites. In a social bookmarking system, users save links to websites that they want to remember and/or share.

- These bookmarks are usually public, but can be saved privately, or shared only with specified people or groups. People can access these bookmarks chronologically, by category or tags, or via a search engine.
- Many social bookmarking services provide web feeds (RSS) for their lists of bookmarks and tagged categories. This allows subscribers to become aware of new bookmarks as they are saved, shared, and tagged by other users.
- As these services have matured and grown more popular, they have added extra features such as ratings and comments on bookmarks, the ability to import and export bookmarks from browsers, emailing of bookmarks, web annotation, and groups or other social network features.

Several Popular social bookmarking sites include: Del.icio.us, Digg, and Technorati.

5.3.1.7 E-portfolios

An E-portfolio is a digitized collection of artifacts including demonstration and accomplishments that represent an individual, group or institution.

- It is a collection of work developed across varied contexts over time.
- It may include input text, electronic files, images, multimedia, blog entries, and hyperlinks.

There are three main types of e-portfolios:

- *Developmental* (e.g., working): It shows the advancement of skill over a period of time.
- *Assessment*: It demonstrates skill and competence in a particular domain or area.
- *Showcase*: A showcase portfolio highlights stellar work in a specific area. It is typically shown to potential employers to gain employment. When it is used for a job application, it is sometimes called career portfolio.

Most e-portfolios are a mix of the three main types to create a hybrid portfolio. Today, electronic portfolios are gaining popularity in schools and higher education; job applications and continuing professional development; assessment and recognition of prior learning.

5.4 Web 3.0

Currently most of the Web content is suitable for human use. Today, typical uses of the Web include seeking information, publishing content, searching for people and products, shopping, reviewing catalogues, and so on. Dynamic pages are generated based on information from databases, but without original information structure found in databases. The problems with the current Web search results are high recall, low precision as the results are highly sensitive to vocabulary. Moreover, the results are single Web pages, and most of the published content is not structured to allow logical reasoning and query answering. The obvious shifts are from the era of "Web of Documents" to the "Web of People" to the "Web of Data." The Web of Data is an upgrade to the Web of Documents (also World Wide Web). The Web now has a huge amount of decentralized data, which can be accessed by various simple and standardized methods. Though this decentralized data is primarily machine accessible, it should also be made machine understandable in order to endorse Web as a powerful source for knowledge dissemination. Semantic Web, also known as Web 3.0, envisions the content to be machine-processable. According to the World Wide Web Consortium (W3C), "The Semantic Web provides a common framework that allows data to be shared and reused across application, enterprise, and community boundaries" (Berners-Lee et al. 2001). The term Semantic Web was coined by Tim Berners-Lee for a web of data that can be processed by machines. As per Berners-Lee et al. (2001), "The Semantic Web is an extension of the current web in which information is given well-defined meaning, better enabling computers and people to work in cooperation." The architecture of the Semantic Web is described by Semantic Web Stack. Figure 5.3 shows the Semantic Web Stack.

The core of Semantic Web Technologies includes four components, firstly *explicit metadata,* which is machine-processable, followed by *ontologies* that add meaning to make data machine-understandable. *Logic* modules are then employed for an inference mechanism, which is finally used by *software agents* to accomplish an intelligent task. These components are explained in detail as follows.

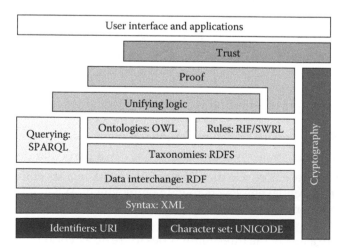

FIGURE 5.3
Semantic Web stack.

5.4.1 Explicit Metadata

Metadata captures part of the meaning of data. We annotate the natural language of web content explicitly with semantic metadata. This semantic metadata encodes the meaning (semantics) of the content, which can then be read and interpreted correctly by machines.

- *XML*: XML-based representations are more easily processable by machines since they are more structured. Meaning of XML-Documents is *intuitively* clear due to *"semantic"* Mark-Up primarily because tags are domain-terms. But, computers do not have intuition, and tag-names do not provide semantics for machines. Document Type Definitions (DTDs), or XML Schema, specify the structure of documents, *not* the meaning of the content in the document. Thus, XML lacks a semantic model as the representation makes no commitment on Domain specific ontological vocabulary (Which words shall we use to describe a given set of concepts?) and Ontological modeling primitives (How can we combine these concepts, for instance, "car is a-kind-of (subclass-of) vehicle"?). A pre-arranged agreement on vocabulary and primitives is hence required. Moreover, the metadata is restricted within documents, not across documents, and is prescriptive, not descriptive. As a solution, the next step is Resource Description Framework (RDF).

- *Resource Description Framework (RDF)*: A standard issued by W3C, RDF is an XML application defined by using a DTD, which explicates relationships between documents. RDF is made up of triples, which are like simple grammatical sentences with a subject, a verb, and an object (in that order). The subject and the verb will be an Uniform Resource Identifier (URI), the object may be an URI or may be a literal. A literal is a character string, or other primitive data-type, defined by XML. RDF is used to state facts and to exchange and represent knowledge. In principle, a *resource* can be everything that can be addressed or can be expressed. However, each resource must be uniquely identifiable and referenced. Resources are characterized by URIs and described by representing their properties and relationship among them. These relationships can be represented as graphs. This **framework** is based on a coalition of several web-based protocols such as URI, HTTP, and XML. The framework carries the semantics, which means the information expressed in RDF is machine understandable. Information expressed in RDF is represented as list of statements, and each statement follows a structure in the form of *<subject, predicate (property), object>*. This structure format is known as *triples* in RDF terminology. For example, consider a statement as follows:

```
"Akshi Kumar has phone number +9198XXX90XX9"
```

In the previous statement

Subject would be "Akshi Kumar",
Predicate would be "has phone number",
and **Object** would be "+9198XXX90XX9"

Thus, the RDF provides metadata about web resources in the form of Object -> Attribute-> Value triples using XML syntax. Chained triples form a graph referred to as a RDF Graph.

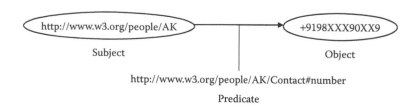

FIGURE 5.4
Sample RDF graph.

The constituents of a RDF graph covering the previous statements are shown in Figure 5.4.

In the earlier diagram, subject and predicate are the URI, whereas, Object is literal.

- *Resource Description Framework Schema (RDFS)*: RDFS is RDF vocabulary description language. RDFS allows for the definition of classes, properties, restrictions, and hierarchies for further structuring of RDF resources. Hierarchies include sub-classes and super-classes, as well as sub-properties and super-properties. RDFS vocabulary is as follows:

It has classes such as

- rdfs: Class

  Concept of a class, defines an abstract object and is applied (with rdf: type) to create instances

- rdf: Property

  It is a base class for properties

- rdfs: Literal

  Class for literals

- rdfs: Resource

  Every entity of an RDF model is the instance of this class

It has properties such as

- rdfs: subClassOf

  Transitive property to define inheritance hierarchies for classes

- rdfs: subPropertyOf

  Transitive property to define inheritance hierarchies for properties

- rdfs: domain

  Defines the domain of a property concerning a class

- rdfs: range

  Defines range of a property concerning a class

An example of RDFS is shown in Figure 5.5.

The earlier example shows a class in a university that runs two types of courses: a regular course and a part-time course. These two courses are also classes, but, they are sub-classes of the university class. The university is managed by (through isManagedBy property) classstaff, which again has two sub-classes of faculty and

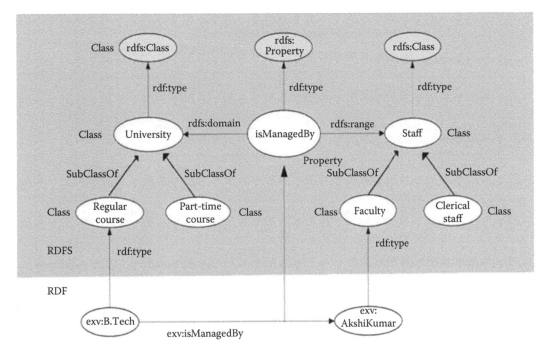

FIGURE 5.5
Example of RDFS.

clerical staff. The shaded region is the part of RDFS, whereas the unshaded area is the part of RDF. The RDF statement has resource as B.Tech course, predicate (property) as isManagedBy, and object as AkshiKumar.

- *SPARQL Protocol and RDF Query Language (or simply SPARQL)*: Pronounced as "Sparkle," it is a query language for RDF and RDFS databases that traverse the RDF graph to fetch the output. It is somehow inspired by the standard databases language know as SQL, which is used to query relational databases. It defines a protocol layer over HTTP known as SPARQL protocol layer. The output result of a SPARQL query is in XML format. Some of the features of SPARQL 1.0 are as follows:

  - It extracts the data in the form of URIs, blank nodes, typed and un-typed literals or can extract the entire RDF subgraph.
  - It can explore data for unknown relations.
  - Execution of complex, joint operations in a single query on heterogeneous data.
  - It can transform vocabulary of RDF data from one form to another.
  - It can result in the building of new RDF Graphs based on RDF Query Graphs.

To fetch data from a RDF database, the SPARQL must have a variable in query language. The variable must be prefixed with question mark (?) to fetch the particular information. For example

```
?student_name, ?book_price, ?employee_salary
```

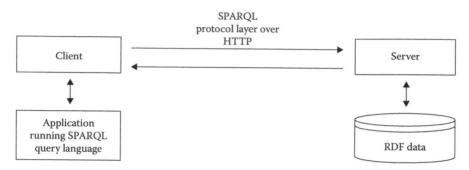

FIGURE 5.6
Client-Server communication via SPARQL.

It follows the same SELECT command to fetch information from RDF database that is used in the case of SQL. Therefore, select statement would be

```
SELECT ?roll_no, ?, ?name, ?phone_no, ?address from <https://
studentbiodata.com>
```

The previous query results in some way like this:

?roll_no	?name	?phone_no	?address
1	Alice	9XX4XX3XX1	New Delhi
5	Bob	7XX4XX2XX5	Mumbai
7	Garfield	04454XX7XX8	Chennai

Remember, the previous query is first executed in the client machine, then it is transferred to the server that holds the RDF database via the SPARQL protocol layer defined over HTTP. Figure 5.6 explains this phenomenon.

RDF enables a small ontological commitment to modeling primitives, and makes it possible to define vocabulary. However, it has no precisely defined meaning and no inference model. It cannot express other properties such as union, interaction, relationships, and so forth. Thus, with the need to develop richer language, Ontology languages were developed by the Semantic Web community for this purpose.

5.4.2 Ontologies

Ontologies are used to standardize concepts and the relationships between them. Ontology is an explicit, formal specification of shared conceptualization. The term is borrowed from philosophy, where Ontology is a systematic account of Existence. For artificial intelligence (AI) systems, what "exists" is that which can be represented. Here terminology such as *conceptualization, explicit, formal*, and *shared* has specific meaning. Conceptualization means formulation of an abstract model with a particular domain, identifying relevant concepts of domain and the relationship among them. Explicit means the meaning of all concepts must be clearly defined. Formal means the defined model should be machine understandable. Shared means that there should be some agreement about ontology on how to share it among different stakeholders. Web Ontology Language (OWL) is a language for expressing Ontologies. Components and models in Ontology are as follows:

- Classes: They represent overall concepts which are described via attributes. Attributes are Name Value pairs.
- Relations: They are special attributes whose values are objects of (other) classes.
- Instances: They describe individuals of an ontology.
- For Relations and Attributes Constraints (Rules) can be defined that determine allowed values.
- Classes, relations, and constraints can be put together to form statements/assertions.
- Special Case: Formal Axioms, which describe knowledge, cannot be expressed simply with the help of other existing components.

There are fundamentally four types of ontologies:

- Top level Ontologies (Upper Ontology or Foundational Ontology): They are general, cross domain ontologies. They are used to represent very general concepts.
- Domain Ontologies: They define concepts related to specific domain.
- Task Ontologies: They define concepts related to general activity or task.
- Application Ontologies: They are specialized ontologies focused on specialized task and domain.

Ontology editors are application tools that help in building and manipulating ontologies. A few popular tools are given in Table 5.1.

RDF is built on XML and OWL (Web Ontology Language) is built on RDF. We can express subclass relationships in RDF; additional relationships can be expressed in OWL. However, reasoning power is still limited in OWL. Therefore, the need for rules and subsequently a markup language for rules so that machines can understand.

5.4.3 Logic and Inference

This component of the Semantic Web defines unified language that expresses logical inferences made using rules and information, such as those specified by ontologies. Logic can

TABLE 5.1

Popular Ontology Editors

Tool	More Information
COE	http://cmap.ihmc.us/coe/
HOZO	http://www.ei.sanken.osaka-u.ac.jp/main/index-en.html
Onto- Track	http://www.informatik.uni-ulm.de/ki/ontotrack/
OWL Editor	http://www.modelfutures.com/owl
OWL-S Editor	http://owlseditor.semwebcentral.org/
Conzilla2	http://www.conzilla.org/wiki/Download/Main
SWOOP	http://www.mindswap.org/2004/SWOOP/
Protégé-2000	http://protege.stanford.edu/
WebOnto	http://www.aktors.org/technologies/webonto/
Adaptiva	http://www.aktors.org/technologies/adaptiva/

be used to specify facts as well as rules; New facts are derived from existing facts based on the inference rules; Descriptive Logic is the type of logic that has been developed for Semantic Web applications. The Semantic Web Rule Language (SWRL) is a proposed language for the Semantic Web that can be used to express rules as well as logic.

5.4.4 Software Agents

Software agents make use of all the above components, namely, explicit metadata, ontologies and logical inferences to help us perform a user-defined task. They are defined as a piece of software that runs without direct human control or constant supervision to accomplish goals provided by the user. Software Agents can

- Collect web content from diverse sources,
- Process that information and exchange the results with other programs (agents),
- Exchange proofs "proofs" written in Semantic Web's Unified Language.

Thus, we conclude that the World Wide Web is a huge, widely distributed, global source for information services, hyper-link information, access and usage information, and website content and organization. During the last decade, the World Wide Web has evolved as an information space. The following Table 5.2 provides the summary of the evolution of the Web.

TABLE 5.2

Summary of the Web Evolution

Evolution of the Web	Characteristics
Web 1.0 (1991–2003)	• It is a heteronym that refers to the state of the World Wide Web, and any website design style used before the advent of the Web 2.0 phenomenon. • Information-oriented Web. • It is Read-only Web. • Connects real people to the World Wide Web. • A Web of cognition. • Shopping carts and Static Web. • HTML/Portals.
Web 2.0 (2004–Till date)	• The term Web 2.0 is primarily linked with web apps that assist interactive information sharing, collaboration, user-centered design, and interoperability on the World Wide Web. • Social Web: connects real people who use the World Wide Web. • It is a Read-Write Web. • A Web 2.0 site gives its users the free choice to interact or collaborate with each other in the dynamic environment of social media in contrast to websites where users are limited to the passive viewing of content. • A Web of communication. • Blog, Social Media, and Video-streaming. • XML/RSS.
Web 3.0 (2006–Till date)	• It refers to the latest version of the Web. • Semantic Web; The Personal Portable Web. • The Read-Write-Execute Web. • There are two different perspectives for defining Web 3.0. It can either be viewed as the Semantic Web (or the meaning of data), or as Intelligent Web, where software agents will collate and integrate information to give "intelligent" responses to human operators. • A Web of co-operation. • RDF/RDFS/OWL.

5.5 Big Data: A Special Discussion

A term that has gained immense importance in the recent years by both researchers and practitioners is "Big Data." It is defined as *high-volume, high-velocity, and high-variety information assets that demand cost-effective, innovative forms of information processing for enhanced insight and decision making.* Big Data is used to refer to the collection of data sets that are too large and complex to manage and process by using traditional data processing applications. It usually includes data sets with sizes beyond the commonly used software tools' ability to capture, curate, manage, and process data within a tolerable elapsed time. The characteristics of Big Data are described in Table 5.3.

Big Data is a trending set of techniques that demand new ways of consolidation of the various methods to uncover hidden information from the massive and complex raw supply of data. User-generated content on the Web has been established as a type of Big Data, and, thus, a discussion about Big data is inevitable in any description of the evolution and growth of the Web. Following are the types of Big Data that have been identified across literature:

- *Social Networks (human-sourced information)*: Human-sourced information is now almost entirely digitized and stored everywhere from personal computers to social networks. Data are loosely structured and often ungoverned. Examples include: data from Facebook, Twitter, Blogs and comments, personal documents; pictures from Instagram, Flickr, Picasa; videos from YouTube; e-mails, Internet searches, and mobile data content, such as text messages amongst others.

TABLE 5.3

Big Data Characteristics

Volume Scale of data	It determines the amount of data that flows in, which can be stored and originated further. Depending on the amount of data that is stored, it is decided whether it can fall in the category of "big data" or not.
Variety Different forms of data	Different type and various sources of data are specified including both structured and unstructured data. For example, documents, emails, images, videos, audio etc.
Velocity Analysis of Streaming data	It is the aspect which deals with pace of the data in motion and its analysis where the content flow is assumed to be continuous and immense. Apart from the consideration of the speed of the input, it also contemplates the celerity of the generation of useful information from it.
Veracity Uncertainty of data	This characteristic of big data deals with the primary issue of reliability and whether the analysis of data is being accurately done, so that eventually there is a production of credible and quality solutions.
Variability Contextual meaning of data	It refers to the inconsistency of the information that is stored. In simpler words, it deals with rapidly changing and alternative meanings that are associated with the data.
Visualization Way to represent information/data	Visualization happens to make one of the crucial characteristics of big data because all the data that is being stored used as an input and generated as a result, needs to be sorted and viewed in a manner that is easy to read and comprehend.
Value Cost of using data	It deals with practice of retrieving the usefulness of the data. It is perceived that data in its original self won't be valuable at all. Under analysis, how data is turned into knowledge and information is what the "value" characteristic deals with.

- *Traditional Business systems (process-mediated data)*: These processes record and monitor business events of interest, such as registering a customer, manufacturing a product, and taking an order. Thus, the collected process-mediated data is highly structured and includes transactions, reference tables and relationships, as well as the metadata that establishes its context. Examples include: data from medical records data produced by public agencies and commercial transactions, such as banking/stock records, e-commerce and credit card purchases.

- *Internet of Things (machine-generated data)*: This type of Big Data is derived from the phenomenal growth in the number of sensors and machines used to measure and record the events and situations in the physical world. The output of these sensors is machine-generated data, and from simple sensor records to complex computer logs, it is well structured. Examples include: data from fixed sensors such as home automation, weather/pollution sensors, traffic sensors and webcams, and security/surveillance videos/images; data from mobile sensors (tracking) such as mobile phone locations, cars, and satellite images; and data from computer systems such as logs and web logs.

Review Questions

1. Which can be referred to as the Executing Web?
   a. Web 1.0
   b. Web 2.0
   c. Web 3.0
2. Social networking is:
   a. Related to Web 2.0
   b. Email related
   c. Share idea
   d. All of the above
3. Describe the journey of the Web from the Web of Documents to the intermittent Web of People to the current Web of Data.
4. What is micro-blogging? Give examples of popular micro-blogs.
5. What is an Ontology? Discuss its components and types.
6. What is Big Data? What are the seven V's describing Big Data?

6

Web IR: Information Retrieval on the Web

6.1 Web Information Retrieval

The field of information retrieval (IR) has long dealt with the problem of finding useful information. With the prevalence of the Web, this problem has compounded manifold.

The general task of information retrieval can be explained as "retrieving the amount of information a user needs in a specific situation for solving his/her current problem." The model of IR can be defined as a set of premises and an algorithm for ranking documents with regard to a user query. Web IR can be defined as the application of theories and methodologies from IR to the World Wide Web. It is concerned with addressing the technological challenges facing information retrieval in the setting of the Web. The characteristics of the Web make the task of retrieving information from it quite different than traditional (pre-web) information retrieval. Web IR is different from classical IR for two reasons: concepts and technologies. The Web is a seemingly unlimited source of information with users from a wide cross-section of society seeking to find information to satisfy their needs. The Web must be accessible through effective and efficient information retrieval systems that deliver information to fulfill needs through the retrieval of Web content.

While the task of "information seeking" on the Web is fairly similar to searching in classic information retrieval systems, there are notable differences. The considerable dissimilarity lies in the varied information resources and potential users with diverse goals and expectations found on the Web. Information resources on the Web are highly heterogeneous, semi-structured, and distributed. The information stored in traditional information systems, on the other hand, is typically well-organized and homogenous. The majority of the users of these traditional information systems have generally been experienced users, such as researchers and academicians with computer skills, subject knowledge, and search experience. In contrast, web users can be almost anybody, with extremely varied search behaviors, experience, goals, knowledge, and information needs.

6.2 Web Information Retrieval Tools

These are automated methods for retrieving information on the Web and can be broadly classified as search tools or search services (Figure 6.1).

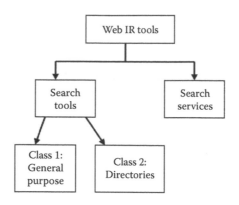

FIGURE 6.1
Categories of web IR tools.

6.2.1 Search Tools

A search tool provides a user interface (UI) where the user can specify queries and browse the results. Search tools employ "robots" that index web documents. At the heart of a search tool is the search engine, which is responsible for searching the index to retrieve documents relevant to a user query. Search tools can be divided into two categories based on the transparency of the index to the user. The two class categories are separated by the following criteria: the methods for web navigation, indexing techniques, query language (or specification scheme for expressing user queries), strategies for query-document matching, and methods for presenting the query output.

- *Class 1 search tools*: General purpose search tools completely hide the organization and content of the index from the user. Examples include AltaVista (www.altavista.com), Excite (www.excite.com), Google (www.google.com), Lycos (www.lycos.com), and HotBot (www.hotbot.com).
- *Class 2 search tools*: Subject directories feature a hierarchically organized subject catalog or directory of the Web, which is visible to users as they browse and search. Examples include Yahoo! (www.search.yahoo.com), WWW Virtual Library (vlib.org), and Galaxy (usegalaxy.org).

6.2.2 Search Services

Search services provide a layer of abstraction over several search tools and databases, aiming to simplify web search. Search services broadcast user queries to several search engines and various other information sources simultaneously. They then merge the results from these sources, check for duplicates, and present the results to the user as an HTML page with clickable URLs (uniform resource locators). Examples of these services include MetaCrawler (www.metacrawler.com) and (www.dogpile.com).

FUN FACT: Archie is often dubbed the first Internet search engine. It was actually designed for indexing FTP archives so that people could easily find specific types of files they were looking for.

6.3 Web Information Retrieval Architecture (Search Engine Architecture)

The ultimate challenge of web IR research is to provide improved systems that retrieve the most relevant information available on the Web to better satisfy the information needs of users. To address the challenges found in web IR, web search systems need very specialized architectures. In this section, we explore the components of a web IR system (popularly known as a search engine), primarily illustrating the architecture of a typical search engine. The architecture of a search engine is determined by two requirements: effectiveness (quality of results) and efficiency (response time and throughput). It has two primary parts: the indexing process and the query process.

6.3.1 The Indexing Process

The indexing process distills information contained within a body of documents into a format that is amenable to quick access by the query processor. Typically, this involves extracting document features by breaking down documents into their constituent terms, extracting statistics related to term presence within the documents, and calculating any query-independent evidence. Once the indexes are built, the system is ready to process queries. It consists of three steps, firstly *text acquisition*, which identifies and stores the documents for indexing, followed by *text transformation* where the documents are transformed into index terms or features, and finally the *index creation*, which takes index terms and creates data structures (*indexes*) to support fast searching. Figure 6.2 depicts the indexing process.

- *Text acquisition*: A search engine on the Web has a "crawler" (also known as a "spider" or a "bot"), which is typically programmed to visit web sites and read their pages and other information in order to create entries for a search engine index. A crawler is usually responsible for gathering the documents and storing them in a document repository. It identifies and acquires documents for the search engine. Web crawlers, which follow links to find documents, must efficiently find huge numbers of

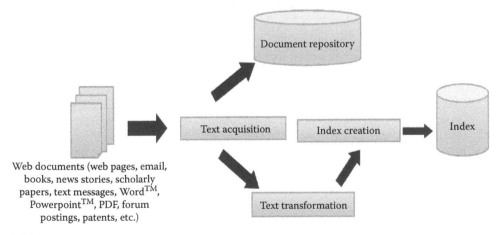

FIGURE 6.2
The indexing process.

web pages (coverage) and keep them up to date (freshness). Crawlers apparently gained this name because they crawl through a site a page at a time, following the links to other pages on the site until all pages have been read. They scan the Web, "reading" everything they find to see what words the pages contain and where those words are used. The web crawler is instructed to know that words contained in headings, metadata, and the first few sentences of the body are likely to be more important in the context of the page, and that keywords in prime locations suggest that the page is really "about" those keywords. Crawlers also take into account the real-time streams of documents, such as web feeds for news, blogs, video, radio, and television. Here, the Rich Site Summary (RSS) is the common standard. A variety of document types (HTML, XML, Word, or PDF) have to be converted into a consistent text plus metadata format. A Unicode standard like UTF-8 is used to convert text encoding for different languages. Similarly, ASCII (7 bits) or extended ASCII (8 bits) is used for English. Finally, information gathered is stored in the document repository. It stores text, metadata (document type, document structure, document length, etc.), and other related content for documents where metadata is information about the documents, such as type and creation date. Other content includes links and anchor text. The data store provides fast access to document contents for search engine components. It can also use a relational database system, but generally, a simpler, more efficient storage system is used due to the huge number of documents. Thus, text acquisition identifies and stores the documents for indexing by crawling the Web, then converts the gathered information into a consistent format, and finally stores the findings in a document repository.

- *Text transformation*: Once the text is acquired, the next step is to transform the captured documents into index terms or features. This is a kind of preprocessing step, which involves parsing, stop-word removal, stemming, link analysis, and information extraction as the sub-steps.

  - *Parser*: It is the processing of the sequence of text tokens in the document to recognize structural elements. For example, titles, links, headings, and so on. A tokenizer recognizes words in the text, considering issues like capitalization, hyphens, apostrophes, non-alpha characters, separators, and so on. Markup languages such as HTML and XML are often used to specify structure where tags are used to specify document elements and the document parser uses syntax of markup language (or other formatting) to identify structure.

  - *Stopping*: Commonly occurring words are unlikely to provide useful information and may be removed from the vocabulary to speed up processing. Stop word removal or stopping is a process that removes common words like "and," "or," "the," or "in." Stop word lists contain frequent words to be excluded. The top 20 stop words, according to their average frequency per 1000 words are: the, of, and, to, a, in, that, is, was, he, for, it, with, as, his, as, on, be, at, by. This can impact efficiency and effectiveness, and this can also be problematic for some queries.

  - *Stemming*: Stemming is the process of removing suffixes from words to get the common origin. It handles a group of words that are derived from a common stem. For instance, "engineer," "engineers," "engineering," "engineered." This process is usually effective, but not for all queries and that is why the benefits can vary for different languages.

- *Link analysis*: This makes use of links and anchor text in web pages and identifies popularity and community information—for example, PageRank™. Here, the anchor text can significantly enhance the representation of pages pointed to by the links and has a significant impact on web search, but has less importance in other applications.

- *Information extraction*: This process identifies the classes of index terms that are important for some applications. For example, named entity recognizers identify classes, such as people, locations, companies, and dates.

- *Classifier*: This identifies the class-related metadata for documents. It assigns labels to documents, such as topics, reading levels, sentiment, and genre. The use of classifier depends on the application.

- *Index creation*: Document statistics—such as counts of index term occurrences, positions in the documents where the index terms occurred, counts of occurrences over groups of documents, lengths of documents in terms of the number of tokens, and other features mostly used in ranking algorithms—are gathered. Actual data depends on the retrieval model and the associated ranking method. The index terms' weights are then computed (e.g., tf.idf weight, which is a combination of term frequency in document and inverse document frequency in the collection). Most indexes use variants of inverted files. An inverted file is a list of sorted words. Each word has pointers to the related pages. It is referred to as "inverted" because documents are associated with words, rather than words with documents. A logical view of the text is indexed. Each pointer associates a short description about the page that the pointer points to. This is the core of the indexing process, which tends to convert document-term information to term-document for indexing, but it is difficult to do that for very large numbers of documents. The format of inverted file is designed for fast query processing that must also handle updates.

  An inverted index allows quick lookup of document IDs with a particular word. The inverted index is built as follows, for each index term is associated with an *inverted list*:

  - Contains lists of documents or lists of word occurrences in documents and other information.
  - Each entry is called a *posting*.
  - The part of the posting that refers to a specific document or location is called a *pointer*.
  - Each document in the collection is given a unique number.
  - Lists are usually *document-ordered* (sorted by document number).

Let us consider a sample collection with three documents on Apple iPhone:

1. iPhone is a line of smartphone designed and marketed by Apple Inc.
2. The first generation iPhone was released on June 29, 2007.
3. Apple has released nine generations of iPhone models, each accompanied by one of the nine major releases of the iOS operating system.

TABLE 6.1

Sample Inverted Index

Term	#Document: Frequency
iPhone	I:1, II:3, III:1
line	I:1
Smartphone	I:1
designed	I:1
marketed	I:1
Apple	I:1, III:1
Inc.	I:1
First	II:1
Generation (generations)	II:1, III:1
Release (released, releases)	II:1, III:2
June	II:1
Most	II:1
Recent	II:1
Model (models)	II:1, III:1
Unveiled	II:1
Special	II:1
Event	II:1
September	II:1
Nine	III:1
Each	III:1
Accompanied	III:1
One	III:1
Major	III:1
iOS	III:1
operating	III:1
System	III:1

Stop words like "is," "a," and "the" have been removed and words like "released" and "releases" have been stemmed to the base word release. The inverted index with word counts is built as shown in Table 6.1.

FUN FACT: As updated on the Google page 'How Search Works' by May 2016, it had 130 trillion web pages indexed (Schwartz 2016).

6.3.2 The Query Process

The role of the indexing process is to build data structures that enable searching. The query process makes use of these data structures to produce a ranked list of documents for a user's query. Query processing takes the user's query and, depending on the application, the context, and other inputs, builds a better query and submits the enhanced query to the search engine on the user's behalf and displays the ranked results. Thus, a query process comprises a user interaction module and a ranking module (Figure 6.3). The user interaction module supports creation and refinement of a query and displays the results. The ranking module uses the query and indexes (generated during the indexing process) to generate a ranked list of documents.

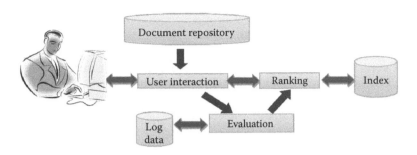

FIGURE 6.3
The query process.

The user interacts with the system through an interface where he inputs the query. Web queries are ad-hoc (often short and ill-defined). Users have different expectations and goals, such as informative, transactional and navigational as output to their query, and moreover impatiently look for the results mainly in the top 10 results. Query transformation is then employed to improve the initial query, both before and after the initial search. This can use a variety of techniques, such as spell checker, query suggestion (which provides alternatives to the original query), query expansion, and relevance feedback. The query expansion approach attempts to expand the original search query by adding further, new, or related terms. These additional terms are inserted into an existing query, either by the user (interactive query expansion or IQE) or by the retrieval system (automatic query expansion or AQE) and aim to increase the accuracy of the search. This new direction for search services basically incorporates context and corresponds to a novel field of research: the contextual information retrieval on the Web (C-Web IR). The details of C-WebIR will be discussed in Chapter 12 of this book.

The fundamental challenge of a search engine is to rank pages that match the input query and return an ordered list. Search engines rank individual web pages of a web site, not the entire site. There are many variations of ranking algorithms and retrieval models. Search engines use two different kinds of ranking factors: query-dependent factors and query-independent factors. Query-dependent are all ranking factors that are specific to a given query. These include measures such as word documents frequency, the position of the query terms within the document, and the inverted document frequency, which are all measures used in traditional IR. These are added to the classic IR measures, but they also focus on finding the most relevant documents to a given query mainly by comparing queries and documents. The tf-idf (term frequency-inverse document frequency) ranking is one the most basic query-dependent ranking algorithms. Query-independent factors are attached to documents, regardless of a given query, and consider measures such as an emphasis on anchor text, the language of the document in relation to the language of the query, and a measure of the "geographical distance between the user and the document." These are used to determine the quality of a given document, such that the search engines should provide the user with the highest possible quality and should omit low-quality documents. The most popular of these factors is PageRank™, which is a measure of link popularity used by the search engine Google. The output is displayed with ranked documents for a query and the snippets are generated to show how queries match the documents. The resultant output also highlights important words and passages and retrieves appropriate advertising in many applications. It might also provide clustering and other visualization tools. Thus, web search can be categorized into two phases: the offline phase, which includes crawling and indexing components, and the online phase, which includes the querying and ranking components of the Web IR system.

The results may be evaluated to monitor and measure retrieval effectiveness and efficiency. This is generally done offline and involves logging user queries and interaction, as this can be crucial for improving search effectiveness and efficiency. The query logs and click-through data are used for query suggestions, spell checking, query caching, ranking, advertising search, and other components. A ranking analysis can be done to measure and tune the ranking effectiveness, whereas a performance analysis is done to measure and tune system efficiency. We discuss the key Web IR performance measures in the next section.

6.4 Web Information Retrieval Performance Metrics

Like in the information retrieval community, system evaluation in Web IR (search engines) also revolves around the notion of relevant and not relevant documents. This implies that with respect to a given query, a document is given a binary classification as either relevant or not relevant. An information retrieval system can be thought of as a two-class classifier which attempts to label documents as such. It retrieves the subset of documents which it believes to be relevant. To measure information retrieval effectiveness, we need:

- A test collection of documents
- A benchmark suite of queries
- A binary assessment of either relevant or not relevant for each query-document pair (Figure 6.4)

In a binary decision problem, a classifier labels examples as either positive or negative. The decision made by the classifier can be represented in a structure known as a confusion matrix or contingency table. The confusion matrix has four categories: True positives (TP) are examples correctly labeled as positives. False positives (FP) refer to negative examples incorrectly labeled as positive—they form Type-I errors. True negatives (TN) correspond to negatives correctly labeled as negative. And false negatives (FN) refer to positive examples incorrectly labeled as negative—they form Type-II errors (Figure 6.5).

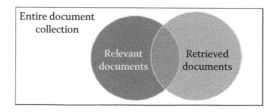

FIGURE 6.4
The web IR information space.

	Not Retrieved (Predicted NO)	Retrieved (Predicted YES)
Irrelevant (**Actual NO**)	True Negatives (TN) (irrelevant and not retrieved)	False Positives (FP) (irrelevant and retrieved)
Relevant (**Actual YES**)	False Negatives (FN) (relevant and not retrieved)	True Positives (TP) (relevant and retrieved)

FIGURE 6.5
Confusion matrix.

In an information retrieval scenario, the most common evaluation is retrieval effectiveness. The effect of indexing exhaustivity and term specificity on retrieval effectiveness can be explained by two widely accepted measures: precision and recall.

- *Precision*: This is defined as the number of relevant documents retrieved by a search divided by the total number of documents retrieved by that search:

$$P = \frac{\text{Total number of relevant retrieved documents}}{\text{Total number of relevant documents}} \times 100$$

That is, $P = \dfrac{TP}{(TP + FP)}$

This provides the proportion of retrieved and relevant documents to all the documents retrieved. A perfect Precision score of 1.0 means that every result retrieved by a search was relevant—but it says nothing about whether all relevant documents were retrieved.

- *Recall*: This is also known as true positive rate or sensitivity or hit rate. It is defined as the number of relevant documents retrieved by a search divided by the total number of existing relevant documents (that should have been retrieved). This represents the proportion of relevant documents that are retrieved out of all relevant documents available:

$$R = \frac{\text{Total number of relevant retrieved documents}}{\text{Total number of relevant documents}} \times 100$$

That is, $R = \dfrac{TP}{(TP + FN)}$

A perfect Recall score of 1.0 means that all relevant documents were retrieved by the search, but says nothing about how many irrelevant documents were also retrieved.

Precision and recall are inversely related. You can always get a recall of 1 (but very low precision) by retrieving all documents for all queries. Recall is a non-decreasing function of the number of documents retrieved. On the other hand, precision usually decreases as the number of documents retrieved is increased. Nevertheless, the two quantities clearly trade off against one another; the following graph depicts this tradeoff (Figure 6.6).

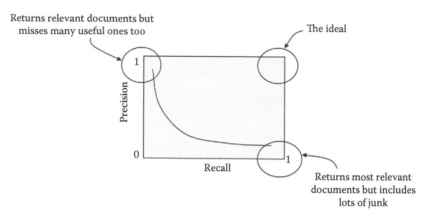

FIGURE 6.6
The recall-precision tradeoff graph.

Some other measures that evaluate the performance are as follows:

- *Accuracy*: This is the proportion of the total number of predictions that were correct.

$$AC = \frac{TP + TN}{n}$$

- *Misclassification Rate* or *Error-rate*:

$$Error = \frac{(FP + FN)}{n}$$

or

$$Error = 1 - AC$$

- *False Positive Rate (False Alarm Rate or Fallout)*: This is defined as the probability to find an irrelevant document among the retrieved documents. It measures how quickly precision drops as recall is increased:

$$Fallout = \frac{FP}{(TN + FP)}$$

- *Specificity*: This is a statistical measure of how well a binary classification test correctly identifies the negative cases:

$$Specificity = \frac{TN}{(TN + FP)} = 1 - Fallout$$

- *F-measure (in information retrieval)*: This can be used as a single measure of performance. The F-measure is the harmonic mean of precision and recall. It is a weighted average of the true positive rate (recall) and precision:

$$F\text{-measure} = \frac{2 * Precision * Recall}{Precision + Recall}$$

Let us understand the computation of these performance measures with the help of an example. We are trying to evaluate the performance of a predictive search engine whose entries in the confusion matrix are as follows:

n=165	Predicted: NO	Predicted: YES	
Actual: NO	TN=50	FP=10	60
Actual: YES	FN=5	TP=100	105
	55	110	

The performance measures are thus computed from the confusion matrix for a binary classifier as follows:

- *Accuracy*: Overall, how often is the classifier correct?
  (TP + TN)/total = (100 + 50)/165 = 0.91 implies 91% accuracy
- *Misclassification rate or the error rate*: Overall, how often is it wrong?
  (FP + FN)/total = (10 + 5)/165 = 0.09 implies 9% error rate (equivalent to 1 minus Accuracy)
- *Recall or true positive rate or sensitivity*: When it's actually yes, how often does it predict yes?
  TP/actual yes = 100/105 = 0.95 implies 95% recall
- *False positive rate or fall-out*: When it's actually no, how often does it predict yes?
  FP/actual no = 10/60 = 0.17
- *Specificity*: When it's actually no, how often does it predict no?
  TN/actual no = 50/60 = 0.83 (equivalent to 1 minus false positive rate)
- *Precision*: When it predicts yes, how often is it correct?
  TP/predicted yes = 100/110 = 0.91 implies 91% precision
- *F-measure*: 2 * precision * recall/precision + recall
  2 * 0.91 * 0.95/0.91 + 0.95 = 1.729/1.86 = 0.92956989 ~ 0.93

6.5 Web Information Retrieval Models

Retrieval models form the theoretical basis for computing the answer to a query. A retrieval model is a formal representation of the process of matching a query and a document. The model of Web IR can be defined as a set of premises and an algorithm for ranking documents with regard to a user query. More formally, a Web IR model is a quadruple [D, Q, F, R(q_i, d_j)] where D is a set of logical views of documents, Q is a set of user queries, F is a framework for modeling documents and queries, and R(q_i, d_j) is a ranking function that associates a numeric ranking to the query q_i and the document d_j. The model is characterized by four parameters:

- Representations for documents and queries, which define the model
- Matching strategies for assessing the relevance of documents to a user query, which involves learning parameters from query

- Methods for ranking query output
- Mechanisms for acquiring user-relevance feedback

In general, retrieval models can be categorized into "exact match" or "best match" models. An exact match model is where the query specifies precise retrieval criteria and every document either matches or fails to match the query. The result is an unordered set of documents with pure exact matches. These models work well when we know exactly (or roughly) what the collection contains and what we're looking for—that is, basically, we are looking for precise documents using structured queries. Employing exact match models has many advantages, such as they can be very efficiently implemented and are predictable and easy to explain. But at the same time, a notable disadvantage of using an exact match model is scalability where the difficulty to match increases with collection size. Moreover, structured query formulation is difficult for most. Thus, these models show acceptable precision scores, which generally imply an unacceptable recall. In the other variant, that is, the "best match" or "rank-based" models, the query describes "good" or "best" matching documents and every document matches the query to some degree. The result is a ranked list of documents. These are significantly more effective than the exact match model and support textual queries but suffer from problems related to natural language understanding. The efficiency is also less as compared to the exact match models owing to their incapability to reject documents early.

The primary types of IR models that are extended to the Web are the standard Boolean model, the algebraic model (which includes the vector space and extended Boolean model), the probabilistic retrieval models (basic probabilistic model, Bayesian inference networks, and language models), and the citation analysis models (such as Hubs-Authority and PageRank). The Boolean model is the only model that fits into the "exact match" type, whereas the others fall under the "best match" category. The detailed classification of Web IR models that have been found across literature is presented in the following. The focus of this book is to confer broader concepts relating to the Web that describe it as a technology in research and practice and so we cover limited discussion on the Web IR models.

- *Standard Boolean model*: The standard Boolean model is based on Boolean logic and classical set theory where both the documents to be searched and the user's query are conceived as sets of terms. Retrieval is based on whether the documents contain the query terms. A query is represented as a Boolean expression of terms in which terms are combined with the logical operators AND, OR, and NOT (Unconstrained NOT is expensive, so often not included). It specifies precise relevance criteria and documents are retrieved if and only if (iff) they satisfy a Boolean expression. The documents are returned in no particular order and thus are an unranked Boolean model where all terms are equally weighted. The Boolean model is depicted as follows:

  Model:
    - Retrieve documents iff they satisfy a Boolean expression.
    - Query specifies precise relevance criteria.
    - Documents are returned in no particular order (unranked Boolean).

  Operators:
    - Logical operators: AND, OR, and NOT (Unconstrained NOT not included).
    - Distance operators: Proximity.

- String matching operators: Wildcard (The wildcard operator "search*" matches "search," "searching," "searched," and so on. This was common before stemming algorithms were introduced).
- Field operators: Date, Author, Title.

A Boolean retrieval model always uses Boolean queries. However, Boolean queries can also be used with other retrieval models (e.g., probabilistic).

- *Algebraic model*: Documents are represented as vectors, matrices, or tuples. Using algebraic operations, these are transformed to a one-dimensional similarity measure. Implementations include the vector space model and the generalized vector space model, (enhanced) topic-based vector space model, and latent semantic indexing (a.k.a. latent semantic analysis). The strength of this model lies in its simplicity. Relevance feedback can be easily incorporated into it. However, the rich expressiveness of query specification inherent in the Boolean model is sacrificed. In algebraic models, the similarity of the query vector and document vector is represented as a scalar value.

  - *Vector space model (VSM)*: The VSM is an algebraic model used for information retrieval where the documents are represented through the words that they contain. It represents natural language documents in a formal manner by the use of vectors in a multi-dimensional space. Any text object (documents, queries, sentences) can be represented by a term vector and similarity is determined by distance in a vector space—for example, the cosine of the angle between the vectors.

    Model:
    - Each document is broken down into a word frequency table. The tables are called vectors and can be stored as arrays.
    - A vocabulary is built from all the words in all the documents in the system.
    - Each document and user query is represented as a vector based against the vocabulary.
    - Calculating similarity measure.
    - Ranking the documents for relevance.

    Vector space modeling is based on the assumption that the meaning of a document can be understood from the document's constituent terms. Documents are represented as "vectors of terms $d = (t1, t2, ..., tn)$ where ti $(1 <= i <= t)$ is a non-negative value denoting the single or multiple occurrences of term i in document d." Each unique term in the document represents a dimension in the space. "Similarly, a query is represented as a vector $Q = (t1, t2, ..., tn)$ where term ti $(1 <= i <= n)$ is a non-negative value denoting the number of occurrences of ti (or, merely a 1 to signify the occurrence of term) in the query." Once both the documents and query have their respective vectors calculated, it is possible to calculate the distance between the objects in the space and the query, allowing objects with similar semantic content to the query should be retrieved. Vector space models that don't calculate the distance between the objects within the space treat each term independently. Using various similarity measures, it is possible to compare queries to terms and documents in order to emphasize or de-emphasize properties of the document collection. A well-known example of this, "the dot product (or, inner product) similarity measure finds the Euclidean distance between the query and a term or document in the space."

Consider the following two documents:

Document A: A student and a teacher

Document B: A school

a. *Building the vector space model*:

Step-1: Each document is broken down into a word frequency table. The tables are called vectors and can be stored as arrays.

Document A: A student and a teacher

A	Student	And	Teacher
2	1	1	1

Document B: A school

A	School
1	1

Step-2: A vocabulary is built from all the words in all the documents in the system. The vocabulary contains all the words used—a, student, and, teacher, baby.

Step-3: The vocabulary needs to be sorted—a, and, student, teacher, school.

Step-4: Each document is represented as a vector based against the vocabulary.

Vector for Document A: A student and a teacher

A	Student	And	Teacher	School
2	1	1	1	0

Vector: (2,1,1,1,0)

Vector for Document B: A school

A	Student	And	Teacher	School
1	0	0	0	1

Vector: (1,0,0,0,1)

The queries are also represented as vectors in the same way as documents. For example, Teacher = (0,0,0,1,0)

b. *Similarity measures/coefficient*: Using a similarity measure, a set of documents can be compared to a query and the most similar documents are returned. The similarity in VSM is determined by using associative coefficients based on the inner product of the document vector and query vector, where word overlap indicates similarity. There are many different ways to measure how similar two vectors are, like Inner Product, Cosine Measure, Dice Coefficient, or Jaccard Coefficient.

The most popular similarity measure is the cosine coefficient, which measures the angle between a document vector and query vector. The cosine measure calculates the angle between the vectors in a high-dimensional virtual space. For two vectors d and d' the cosine similarity between d and d' is given by:

$$\frac{(D * D')}{|D| * |D'|}$$

Here, d X d' is the vector product of d and d', calculated by multiplying corresponding frequencies together.

Step-5: Calculate the similarity measure of query with every document in the collection.

For Document A, d = (2,1,1,1,0) and d' = (0,0,0,1,0)

$$dXd' = 2X0 + 1X0 + 1X0 + 1X1 + 0X0 = 1$$
$$|d| = sqrt\ (2^2 + 1^2 + 1^2 + 1^2 + 0^2) = sqrt(7) = 2.646$$
$$|d'| = sqrt(0^2 + 0^2 + 0^2 + 1^2 + 0^2) = sqrt(1) = 1$$
$$Similarity = 1/(1\ X\ 2.646) = 0.378$$

For Document B, d = (1,0,0,0,1) and d' = (0,0,0,1,0)

$$dXd' = 1X0 + 0X0 + 0X0 + 0X1 + 1X0 = 0$$
$$|d| = sqrt(1^2 + 0^2 + 0^2 + 0^2 + 1^2) = sqrt(2) = 1.414$$
$$|d'| = sqrt(0^2 + 0^2 + 0^2 + 1^2 + 0^2) = sqrt(1) = 1$$
$$Similarity = 0/(1\ X\ 1.414) = 0$$

c. *Ranking documents*: A user enters a query and the query is compared to all documents using a similarity measure. The user is shown the documents in decreasing order of similarity to the query term.

Step-6: Rank in descending order and display to user.

Document A	0.378
Document B	0

Stop word removal and stemming can further improve the result precision of VSM.

- *Extended Boolean model*: Several methods have been developed to extend the Boolean model to address the following issues: Firstly, the Boolean operators are too strict and ways need to be found to soften them. Secondly, the standard Boolean approach has no provision for ranking. The smart/extended Boolean approach and methods provide users with relevance ranking. The goal of the extended Boolean model is to overcome the drawbacks of the Boolean model as it doesn't consider term weights in queries and the result set of a Boolean query is often either too small or too big. The idea of the extended model is to make use of partial matching and term weights as in the vector space model. It combines the characteristics of the vector space model with the properties of Boolean algebra and ranks the similarity between queries and documents. This way a document might be somewhat relevant if it matches some of the queried terms and will be returned as a result, whereas in the standard Boolean model, this document wasn't returned. Documents are returned by ranking them on the basis of frequency of query terms (ranked Boolean).

The concept of term weights was introduced to reflect the (estimated) importance of each term. There are many variations on how term weight is calculated. The prominent ones are:

- *Term frequency (tf)*: One technique is to pick the most frequently occurring terms (words with high term frequency or *tf*). However, the most frequent word is a less useful metric since some words like "*this*" or "*a*" occur very frequently across all documents. Hence, we also want a measure of how unique a word is, such as how infrequently the word occurs across all documents (inverse document frequency or *idf*).

- *Term frequency * inverse document frequency (tfidf)*: The product of tf *idf of a word gives a product of how frequent this word is in the document multiplied by how unique the word is across the entire corpus of documents. Words in the document with a high tfidf score occur frequently in the document and provide the most information about that specific document. Consider a document containing 100 words wherein the word "*world*" appears 3 times. The term frequency (i.e., tf) for "*world*" is then (3/100) = 0.03. Now, assume we have 10 million documents and the word "*world*" appears in one thousand of these. Then, the inverse document frequency (i.e., idf) is calculated as (10,000,000/1,000) = 4. Thus, the tf-idf weight is the product of these quantities: 0.03 * 4 = 0.12.

Consider another generalized example, given a document containing terms with given frequencies A(3), B(2), and C(1). Assume the collection contains 10,000 documents and document frequencies of these terms are: A(50), B(1300), and C(250).

$$\text{Then: A: tf} = \frac{3}{3}; \text{idf} = \log\left(\frac{10000}{50}\right) = 5.3; \text{tf-idf} = 5.3$$

$$\text{B: tf} = \frac{2}{3}; \text{idf} = \log\left(\frac{10000}{1300}\right) = 2.0; \text{tf-idf} = 1.3$$

$$\text{C: tf} = \frac{1}{3}; \text{idf} = \log\left(\frac{10000}{250}\right) = 3.7; \text{tf-idf} = 1.2$$

Fuzzy logic approaches may be used to extend the Boolean model.

- *Probabilistic models*: Information retrieval deals with uncertain information. Probability theory seems to be the most natural way to quantify uncertainty. A document's relevance is interpreted as a probability. Document and query similarities are computed as probabilities for a given query. The probabilistic model takes these term dependencies and relationships into account and, in fact, specifies major parameters, such as the weights of the query terms and the form of the query-document similarity. Common models are the basic probabilistic model, Bayesian inference networks, and language models. Prominent probabilistic approaches to IR include probability ranking principle, information retrieval as probabilistic inference, probabilistic indexing, and Bayesian nets in IR. It is beyond the scope of this book to discuss all probabilistic research models in detail, but we do list out a few.

Probabilistic theorems like the Bayes theorem are often used in these models as follows:

Let a and b be two events.

Bayesian formulas are as follows:

$$p(a|b)p(b) = p(a \cap b) = p(b|a)p(a)$$

$$p(a|b) = \frac{p(b|a)p(a)}{p(a)}$$

$$p(\bar{a}|b)p(b) = p(b|\bar{a})p(\bar{a})$$

- *Probability ranking principle*

  Let x be a document in the collection. Let R represent relevance of a document w.r.t. given (fixed) query and let NR represent non-relevance.

  To find $p(R|x)$, probability that a retrieved document x is relevant.

$$p(R|x) = \frac{p(x|R)p(R)}{p(x)}$$

$$p(NR|x) = \frac{p(x|NR)p(NR)}{p(x)}$$

  where:

  $p(R)$, $p(NR)$ is the prior probability of retrieving a (non) relevant document.

  $p(x|R)$, $p(x|NR)$ is the probability that if a relevant (non-relevant) document is retrieved, it is x.

  Ranking Principle (Bayes' Decision Rule):

  If $p(R|x) > p(NR|x)$ then x is relevant, otherwise x is not relevant.

- The state-of-the-art system developed by Turtle and Croft (1991) uses Bayesian inference networks to rank documents by using multiple sources of evidence to compute the conditional probability P (Info need | document) such that an information need is satisfied by a given document. An inference network consists of a directed acyclic dependency graph, where edges represent conditional dependency or causal relations between propositions represented by the nodes. The inference network consists of a document network, a concept representation network that represents indexing vocabulary, and a query network representing the information need. The concept representation network is the interface between documents and queries. To compute the rank of a document, the inference network is instantiated and the resulting probabilities are propagated through the network to derive a probability associated with the node representing the information need. These probabilities are used to rank documents.

  - *Citation analysis models*: Using citations as links, standard corpora can be viewed as a graph. The structure of this graph, independent of content, can provide interesting information about the similarity of documents and the structure of information.

Hubs   Authority

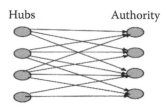

FIGURE 6.7
The HITS Bipartite graph.

- *Hyperlink-induced topic search (HITS)*: This is an algorithm developed by Kleinberg in 1998. It defines *authorities* as pages that are recognized as providing significant, trustworthy, and useful information on a topic. *In-degree* (number of pointers to a page) is one simple measure of authority. However, in-degree treats all links as equal. *Hubs* are index pages that provide lots of useful links to relevant content pages (topic authorities). It attempts to computationally determine hubs and authorities on a particular topic through analysis of a relevant sub-graph of the Web. This is based on mutually recursive facts that hubs point to lots of authorities and authorities are pointed to by lots of hubs. Together, they tend to form a bipartite graph (Figure 6.7).

  Algorithm:
  - Computes hubs and authorities for a particular topic specified by a normal query.
  - First determines a set of relevant pages for the query called the *base* set *S*.
  - Analyze the link structure of the web sub-graph defined by *S* to find authority and hub pages in this set.

- *PageRank™ (Google)*: An alternative link-analysis method is used by Google, known as the PageRank given by Brin and Page in 1998. It does not attempt to capture the distinction between hubs and authorities. It ranks pages just by authority and is applied to the entire web rather than a local neighborhood of pages surrounding the results of a query. The PageRank is discussed in detail in the following section.

6.6 Google PageRank

Google is a search engine with the mission statement to "organize the world's information and make it universally accessible and useful." The largest search engine on the Web, Google receives more than 200 million queries each day through its various services.

The Google search engine uses multiple machines for crawling. Its crawler works as follows. The crawler consists of five functional components, which run in different processes. A URL server process reads URLs out of a file and forwards them to multiple crawler processes. Each crawler process runs on a different machine, which is single threaded. It uses asynchronous I/O to fetch data from up to 300 web servers in parallel. The crawlers transmit downloaded pages to a single store server process, which compresses the pages and stores them on a disk. Then the indexer process reads pages from disk. It extracts links from the pages and saves them to a different disk file. A URL resolver process reads the link file, analyzes the URLs contained therein, and saves the absolute URLs to the disk file that is read by the URL server.

The ranking algorithm of Google, PageRank is a numeric value that represents the importance of a page present on the Web. It was proposed by Sergey Brin and Larry Page stating that a web page is important if it is pointed to by other important web pages. The general idea is that when one page links to another page, it is effectively casting a vote for the other page. More votes imply more importance of a web page in context to other web pages. In short, PageRank is a "vote" by all the other pages on the Web, about how important a page is. A link to a page counts as a vote of support. If there's no link, there's no support (but this is an abstention from voting rather than a vote against the page). Importance of the page that is casting the vote determines the importance of the vote. Therefore, the rank of the page casting the vote plays a key role itself and thereby creates a chain of values to be computed. A web page is important if it is pointed to by other important web pages. Google calculates a page's importance from the votes cast for it. The importance of each vote is taken into account when a page's PageRank is calculated. PageRank is Google's way of deciding a page's importance. It matters because it is one of the factors that determine a page's ranking in the search results. A PageRank value is represented as *PR*.

- *Nomenclature*: The Web's hyperlink structure forms a massive directed graph. The nodes in the graph represent web pages and the directed arcs or links represent the hyperlinks. Hyperlinks coming to a page are called in-links and point into nodes and out-links point out from nodes. The types of links are categorized as follows:
  - *Inbound links or in-links*: Inbound links are links into the site from the outside. In-links are one way to increase a site's total PageRank. Sites are not penalized for in-links.
  - *Outbound links or out-links*: Outbound links are links from a page to other pages on a site or other sites.
  - *Dangling links*: Dangling links are simply links that point to any page with no outgoing links.
- *General concept*: A link from your page to page A is an endorsement of page A. The more in-links a page has, the more important that page is. However, some links are more valuable than others. A link to page A from a very important page is more valuable. The more important a page is, the more it should contribute to the importance of the pages to which it links. A link to page A from a page with a large number of out-links is not so valuable. The more out-links a page has, the less valuable is the recommendation provided by each of its individual out-links.

6.6.1 Algorithm

The original PageRank algorithm, which was described by Larry Page and Sergey Brin, assumes that a page A has pages T1...Tn which point to it (i.e., are citations). The PageRank of a page A is given as follows:

$$PR(A) = (1-d) + d \left(\frac{PR(T1)}{C(T1)} + ... + \frac{PR(Tn)}{C(Tn)} \right)$$

where:
- PR(A): PageRank of page A.
- PR(Tn): PageRank of pages Tn, which link to page A. Each page has a notion of its own self-importance. That's PR(T1) for the first page in the Web all the way up to PR(Tn) for the last page.
- C(Tn): Number of outbound links on page Ti. Each page spreads its vote out evenly among all of its outgoing links. The count, or number, of outgoing links for page 1 is C(T1), C(Tn) for page n, and so on for all pages.
- C(Tn) is the PR(Tn)/C(Tn): If page A has a back link from page n, the share of the vote page A will get is PR(Tn)/C(Tn).
- d: All these fractions of votes are added together, but to stop the other pages having too much influence, this total vote is "damped down" by multiplying it by 0.85 (the factor "d").
- (1 – d): The PageRanks form a probability distribution over web pages so the sum of PageRanks of all web pages will be one. The (1 – d) bit at the beginning is a bit of probability math magic so the sum of all web pages' PageRanks will be one, it adds in the bit lost by the d. It also means that if a page has no links to it (no back links) even then it will still get a small PR of 0.15 (i.e., 1 –0.85).

PageRank or PR(A) can be calculated using a simple iterative algorithm. It corresponds to the principal eigenvector of the normalized link matrix of the Web. As the PageRanks form a probability distribution over web pages, the sum of all web pages' PageRanks will be one. The probability for the random surfer not stopping to click on links is given by the damping factor d, which depends on, probability and therefore, is set between 0 and 1. The higher d is, the more likely it is that the random surfer will keep clicking links. Since the surfer jumps to another page at random after he stopped clicking links, the probability therefore is implemented as a constant (1 – d) into the algorithm. Regardless of inbound links, the probability for the random surfer jumping to a page is always (1 – d), so a page always has a minimum PageRank.

A simple way of representing the formula is:

(d = 0.85) *Page Rank (PR) = 0.15 + 0.85 * (a share of the PageRank of every page that links to it)*

The amount of PageRank that a page has to vote will be its own value * 0.85. This value is shared equally among all the pages that it links to. The calculations do not work if they are performed just once. Accurate values are obtained through many iterations. Suppose we have two pages, A and B, which link to each other and neither have any other links of any kind. The PageRank of page A depends on the PageRank value of page B and the PageRank of B depends on the PageRank value of A. We can't work out A's PageRank until we know B's PageRank, and we can't work out B's PageRank until we know A's PageRank. But performing more iteration can bring the values to such a stage where the PageRank values do not change and, hence, necessitates iterations while calculating PageRanks.

Consider a simple example with two pages, each pointing to the other:

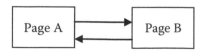

Each page has one outgoing link (the outgoing count is 1, i.e., $C(A) = 1$ and $C(B) = 1$).

Guess 1

We do not know what their PR should be to begin with, so let's take a guess at 1.0 and do some calculations:

$$d = 0.85$$
$$PR(A) = (1 - d) + d(PR(B)/1)$$
$$PR(B) = (1 - d) + d(PR(A)/1)$$

i.e.

$$PR(A) = 0.15 + 0.85 * 1 = 1$$
$$PR(B) = 0.15 + 0.85 * 1 = 1$$

The numbers aren't changing at all. So it looks like we started out with a lucky guess.

Guess 2

Let's start the guess at 0 instead and re-calculate:

$$PR(A) = 0.15 + 0.85 * 0 = 0.15$$
$$PR(B) = 0.15 + 0.85 * 0.15 = 0.2775$$

NB. we've already calculated a "next best guess" at PR(A) so we use it here

And again:

$$PR(A) = 0.15 + 0.85 * 0.2775 = 0.385875$$
$$PR(B) = 0.15 + 0.85 * 0.385875 = 0.47799375$$

And again

$$PR(A) = 0.15 + 0.85 * 0.47799375 = 0.5562946875$$
$$PR(B) = 0.15 + 0.85 * 0.5562946875 = 0.622850484375$$

And so on. The numbers just keep going up. But will the numbers stop increasing when they get to 1.0? What if a calculation over-shoots and goes above 1.0?

Guess 3

Well, let's see. Let's start the guess at 40 each and do a few cycles:

$$PR(A) = 40$$
$$PR(B) = 40$$

First calculation

$$PR(A) = 0.15 + 0.85 * 40 = 34.25$$
$$PR(B) = 0.15 + 0.85 * 0.385875 = 29.1775$$

And again:

$$PR(A) = 0.15 + 0.85 * 29.1775 = 24.950875$$
$$PR(B) = 0.15 + 0.85 * 24.950875 = 21.35824375$$

These numbers are heading down and it surely looks like the numbers will get to 1.0 and stop.

Principle: It doesn't matter where you start your guess, once the PageRank calculations have settled down, the *"normalized probability distribution"* (the average PageRank for all pages) will be 1.0. We get a good approximation of the real PageRank values after only a few iterations. According to publications of Lawrence Page and Sergey Brin, about 100 iterations are necessary to get a good approximation of the PageRank values of the whole Web.

Review Questions

1. Differentiate between the following:
   a. Classical IR and web IR
   b. Precision and recall
   c. Boolean model and algebraic model
   d. Term frequency (tf) and inverse document frequency (idf)

2. What are the categories in which web IR tools can be divided?

3. How is an index created in a typical web IR system? Represent diagrammatically and elaborate the steps involved in the process.

4. Evaluate the performance of a predictive engine whose entries in the confusion matrix are:

n=200	Predicted: NO	Predicted: YES
Actual: NO	TN=60	FP=10
Actual: YES	FN=5	TP=125

5. Calculate the precision, recall, accuracy, error, fall-out, and f-measure for a dataset having 10 records with expected and predicted set of outcomes generated as follows:

Expected	Predicted
Man	Woman
Man	Man
Woman	Woman
Man	Man
Woman	Man
Woman	Woman
Woman	Woman
Man	Man
Man	Woman
Woman	Woman

6. Consider a small web consisting of three pages A, B, and C, with the following in-link, out-link structure as shown in the following. Calculate Google's PageRank for 5 iterations.

Section III

Web Development

7

Web Development Basics

The current generation of web technology is built around dynamic content. We expect the Web to be interactive, user-driven, and constantly changing. The architecture of a typical Web application is depicted in Figure 7.1.

The web browsers on the client side provide the graphic user interface for users to interact with web applications. The web apps can run on most operating systems with limited hardware or software requirements. A web server is the server on which the web site is hosted. The web server receives document requests and data submissions from web browsers through the HTTP protocol on top of the Internet's TCP/IP layer. The main function of the web server is to feed HTML files to the web browsers. This server will have installed web server software such as IIS, Apache, or Nginx.

The application server provides access to business logic for use by client application programs. It is responsible for computing the business logics of the web application, like carrying out a bank account fund transfer or computing the shortest route to drive from one city to another. If the business logic is simple or the web application is only used by a small group of clients, the architecture might not include an application server, with the web server handling business logic. Likewise, most application servers include web server as an integral component, which means an app server can do whatever a web server is capable of doing. The data server (database management system) hosts one or more databases, such as Oracle, SQL Server, or MySQL to provide data persistency.

FUN FACT: Although many web site addresses start with "www," there is no requirement that they begin this way. It was just an early convention to help people recognize that someone was running a web server.

7.1 Elements of Web Development

Although the user experience of a web site is fascinating, dynamic, and interactive, Web development itself is complex, as it involves much more in terms of concepts, tools, and technologies. Though the set of tools and technologies is constantly expanding, there are essential tools and technologies that every web developer should be acquainted with:

- *Browsers*: As the interpreters of the Web, browsers request information and on receiving a response, display the web page in a human-readable format. Examples of popular web browsers include:
  - *Google Chrome* (currently, the most popular browser)
  - *Safari* (Apple's web browser)

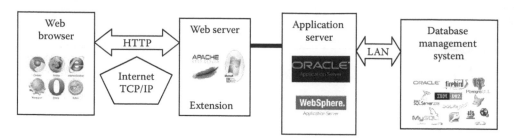

FIGURE 7.1
Web app client-server architecture.

- *Firefox* (an open-source browser supported by the Mozilla Foundation)
- *Internet Explorer* (Microsoft's browser)
- *HTML*: The Hypertext Markup Language provides structure to web pages and web sites so the web browser knows what to display.
- *CSS*: Cascading Style Sheets enable web designers to control colors, fonts, animations, and transitions on the web. CSS makes the web look good.
- *Programming languages*: Programming languages allow you to communicate with computers and tell them what to do. Among the many available, there is no concept of one being better than the other. It's the programmer's capabilities and application requirements that typically drive this choice. The prominent ones are:
  - JavaScript: Supported by all web browsers.
  - *Python*: Used by the Django framework.
  - *Ruby*: Used by the Ruby on Rails framework.
  - *PHP*: Used by WordPress, Joomla Content Management Systems.
  - *Objective-C*: Led by Apple, this is the programming language behind iOS.
  - *Swift*: Apple's newest programming language.
  - *Java*: Used by Android (Google) and many desktop applications.
- *Frameworks*: Frameworks are built to make building and working with programming languages easier. Frameworks typically take all the difficult, repetitive tasks in setting up a new web application and either do them for you or make them easier to complete. Examples include:
  - *Meteor*: A full-stack (front- and back-end) JavaScript framework.
  - *Node.js*: A server-side JavaScript framework.
  - *Ruby on rails*: A full-stack framework built using ruby.
  - *Django*: A full-stack framework built using python.
  - *Ionic*: A mobile framework.
  - *Bootstrap*: A UI (user interface) framework for building with HTML, CSS, and JavaScript.

- *Content management systems (CMS)*: WordPress, Joomla, and Drupal are popular solutions that support the creation and modification of digital content.
- *NET*: A full-stack framework built by Microsoft.
- *Angular.js*: A front-end JavaScript framework.
- *Libraries*: Libraries are groups of code snippets that enable a large amount of functionality without your having to write it all. Libraries typically ensure code is efficient and works well across browsers and devices (though this is not always the case). Examples include jQuery and Underscore.
- *Databases*: Databases are where you store data. A database is like a bunch of filing cabinets, with folders filled with files. They come mainly in two flavors: SQL and NoSQL. SQL provides more structure, which helps with making sure all the data is correct and validated. NoSQL provides a lot of flexibility for building and maintaining applications. Examples include:
  - *MongoDB*: This open-source NoSQL database is currently the only database supported by Meteor.
  - *Redis*: The most popular key-value store, this database is lighting fast for retrieving data but does not allow for much depth in the data storage.
  - *PostgreSQL*: A popular open-source SQL database.
  - *MySQL*: Another popular open-source SQL database, MySQL is used in WordPress sites.
  - *Oracle*: An enterprise SQL database.
  - *SQL Server*: A SQL server manager created by Microsoft.
  - Neo4j: A graph-based NoSQL variant.
- *Client (or client-side)*: A client is one user of an application. For accessing www.facebook.com on a client (computer, tablet, or mobile device), there are typically multiple clients interacting with the same application stored on a server.
- *Server (or server-side)*: The server is where the web application code is typically stored. Requests are made to the server from clients, and the server gathers the appropriate information and responds to those requests. Some of the common servers include: web server, application server, FTP server, chat server, online game server, IRC server, and mail server. Examples of popular web servers include Apache and IIS.
- *Front-end*: The front-end is comprised of HTML, CSS, and JavaScript. This is how and where the web site is displayed to users.
- *Back-end*: The back-end is comprised of your servers and databases. This is where functions, methods, and data manipulation happen that you don't want the client to see.
- *Protocols*: Protocols are standardized instructions for how to pass information back and forth between computers and devices.
  - *HTTP*: Hypertext Transfer Protocol is how the data from a web site gets to your browser. Whenever you type a web site address (such as http://www.google.com), this protocol requests the web site from Google's server and then receives a response with the HTML, CSS, and JavaScript of the web site.

- *DDP*: Distributed data protocol is a new protocol created in connection with Meteor. The DDP protocol uses web sockets to create a consistent connection between the client and the server. This constant connection lets web sites and data on those sites update in real-time without having to refresh the browser.

- *REST*: Representational state transfer is a protocol mainly used for APIs. It has standard methods like GET, POST, and PUT that let information be exchanged between applications.

- *API*: An application programming interface is created by the developer of an application to allow other developers to use some of the application's functionality without sharing code. Developers expose "end points," which are like inputs and outputs for the application. API access can be controlled with API keys. Examples of good APIs are those created by Facebook, Twitter, and Google for their web services.

- *Data formats*: Data formats are the structure of how data is stored. Common examples include:

  - *JSON*: JavaScript Object Notation is quickly becoming the most popular data format.

  - *XML*: The main data format in the earlier days of the Web, eXtensible Markup Language was predominantly used by Microsoft systems.

  - *CSV*: Comma-Separated Values is data formatted by commas. Excel data is typically formatted this way.

- *GitHub*: Referred to as a developer's collaborative platform, GitHub is now the largest online storage space of collaborative works that exist in the world. One of the main misconceptions about GitHub is that it is a development tool. In reality, GitHub itself is simply a social network like Facebook or Instagram where you build a profile, upload projects to share, and connect with other users by following their accounts. Git is the version control software that runs at the heart of GitHub. GitHub is a graphical interface, which manages changes to a project without overwriting any part of that project. Thus, GitHub makes Git easier to use in two ways. First, if you download the GitHub software to your computer, it provides a visual interface to help you manage your version-controlled projects locally. Secondly, creating an account on GitHub.com brings your version-controlled projects to the Web and ties in social network features for good measure.

- *Web hosting*: Hosting your own web site doesn't have to cost a monthly fee or require a lot of technical knowledge to setup. If you just need to host a small web site that only has few visitors, you can turn your Windows PC into a WAMP (Windows, Apache, MySQL, and PHP) server—a local development server. Downloading WAMP simply downloads a program that installs three different things: Apache, MySQL, and PHP. WAMPs are convenient because they allow you to download and install all of the packages needed for hosting dynamic web content. (If you're running Linux instead of Windows, you can install a LAMP.) It's also possible to host a web site on Windows using IIS so you don't have to install any third-party software.

7.2 Client-Side and Server-Side Scripting

Let us first understand the concepts of markup, scripting, and programming languages:

- *Markup language*: Markup languages are the building blocks of the Web and were initially a set of text and some formatting instructions when web sites were just static pages. Originating from typesetting processes used in early printing presses, these languages have long been used to annotate the text of a site, dictating both the architecture of a site and the display of text. Markup languages were designed for the processing, definition, and presentation of text. The language specifies code for formatting both the layout and style within a text file. The code used to specify the formatting is referred to as tags. HTML is an example of a widely known and used markup language. With an elaborate history, markup languages have evolved and are in no way obsolete. They are very much a part of the current generation of dynamic web and are still used to control the presentation of data.

- *Programming Language*: A programming language is a notation for writing programs, which are specifications of a computation or algorithm. They are used to transform the data or we can say are used to instruct the computer to perform logic. These are compiled, that is, they take text files, run them through a compiler, and the compiler creates binary instruction files (binaries). Examples include C, C++, Java, Objective-C, and Swift.

- *Scripting language*: Scripting languages are programming languages, but they fit into a category called interpreted languages (i.e., Python, Ruby, PHP). They use an interpreter or some running application to take programming commands and turn them into instructions to be executed. Basically, scripting languages are programming languages. The theoretical difference between the two is that scripting languages do not require the compilation step and instead are interpreted. This is a historical distinction that is almost obsolete and in the today's environment, they are used interchangeably.

For a web app to work, two programs run at the same time:

- The code that lives on the server and responds to HTTP requests, referred to as the server-side code.
- The code that lives in the browser and responds to user input, referred to as the client-side code.

Table 7.1 elaborates on the difference between the two.

Web development ranges from creating plain text pages to complex web-based applications, social networks, and business apps, which is accomplished by choosing among the gamut of available technology options. It is not in the scope of this book to cover all languages, technologies, tools, and frameworks of web development. But we do present a few prominent ones in the following chapters.

TABLE 7.1

Client-Side Scripting versus Server-Side Scripting

	Client-Side Scripting	Server-Side Scripting
Definition	Client-side scripting is used when the user's browser already has all the code and the page is altered on the basis of the user's input.	Server-side scripting is used to create dynamic pages based on a number of conditions when the user's browser makes a request to the server.
Execution	The web browser executes the client-side scripting on the user's computer.	The web server executes the server-side scripting that produces the page to be sent to the browser.
Access	Client-side scripting cannot be used to connect to the databases and cannot access the file systems on the web server.	Server-side scripting is used to connect to the databases and access the file systems that reside on the web server.
Blocking	It is possible for a client-side script to be blocked by the user.	Server-side scripting cannot be seen or blocked by the user.
Response Time	Response from a client-side script is faster as compared to a server-side script because the scripts are processed on the local computer.	Response from a server-side script is slower as compared to a client-side script because the scripts are processed on the remote computer.
Use	• Interactive web pages • Make pages work dynamically • Interact with temporary storage • Provide an interface between user and server • Send requests to the server • Retrieve data from server • Interact with local storage • Provide remote access for client server program	• Processing user input • Displays requested pages • Structure web applications • Interaction with servers and storage • Interact with databases • Query databases • Encoding data into HTML • Operations over databases such as delete and update
Advantages	• Allow for more interactivity by immediately responding to user actions • Execute quickly because they do not require a trip to the server • May improve the usability of web sites • Can be substituted with alternatives (for example, HTML) if a user's browser does not support scripts • Reusable and obtainable from many free resources	• User can create one template for the entire web site • The site can use a content management system, which makes editing simpler • Generally quicker to load than client-side scripting • User is able to include external files to save coding • Scripts are hidden from view, making it more secure (users only see the HTML output) • User does not need to download plug-ins like Java or Flash
Disadvantages	• Not all browsers support scripts, therefore, users might experience errors if no alternatives have been provided. • Different browsers and browser versions support scripts differently, thus more quality assurance testing is required. • More development time and effort might be required (if the scripts are not already available through other resources).	• Page postback can introduce processing overhead that can decrease performance and force the user to wait for the page to be processed and recreated. (Once the page is posted back to the server, the client must wait for the server to process the request and send the page back to the client.) • Many scripts and content management systems tools require databases in order to store dynamic data. • Requires scripting software to be installed on the server. • The nature of dynamic scripts creates new security concerns, in some cases making it easier for hackers to gain access to servers by exploiting code flaws.

(Continued)

TABLE 7.1 (*Continued*)

Client-Side Scripting versus Server-Side Scripting

	Client-Side Scripting	Server-Side Scripting
Examples	• JavaScript • VBScript • HTML (Structure) • CSS (Design) • AJAX • jQuery	• PHP • ASP.NET • JavaScript (Node.js) • Java and JSP • Python (Django) • Ruby (Rails)

7.3 Model-View-Controller Architecture for Web Application Development

Model-View-Controller (or MVC, as it is popularly called) is a software design pattern for developing web-based, desktop, and mobile applications. It has been a widely adopted web development framework written to split up the business logic, database access, and presentation layers, thus separating the input, processing, and output of an application. The framework has three interconnected components: the model, the view, and the controller. The idea is to isolate the application logic from the user interface layer and support separation of concerns. The controller receives all requests for the application and then works with the model to prepare any data needed by the view. The view then uses the data prepared by the controller to generate a final presentable response (Figure 7.2).

Thus, each component plays a distinct role:

- *Model*: The lowest level of the pattern, which is responsible for maintaining data. It concerns the data structure/database schema used. It responds to the request from the view and also responds to instructions from the controller to update itself.
- *View*: This is about "what a user sees." It is responsible for displaying all or a portion of the data to the user. It presents the data in a particular format triggered by a controller's decision.

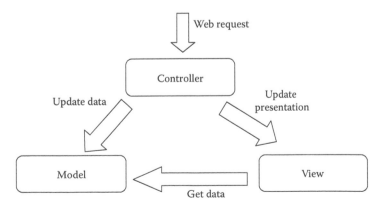

FIGURE 7.2
MVC architecture.

- *Controller*: The code that controls the interactions between the model and the view. The controller is responsible for responding to user input and performs interactions on the data model objects. The controller receives the input, it validates the input, and then it performs the business operation that modify the state of the data model.

MVC has been adopted and established as a great architecture for application development no matter what language you are using for development. Essentially, it allows for the programmer to isolate these very separate pieces of code into their own domain, which makes code maintenance and debugging much simpler than if all these items were chunked into one massive piece. MVC supports rapid and parallel development with proven cost and time benefits. The advantages and disadvantages of using MVC framework are as follows.

- *Advantages*:
    - *Simultaneous development*: Multiple developers can work simultaneously on model, controller, and views.
    - *High cohesion*: MVC enables logical grouping of related actions on a controller. The views for a specific model are also grouped together.
    - *Low coupling*: The very nature of the MVC framework is such that there is low coupling among models, views, or controllers.
    - *Ease of modification*: Because of the separation of responsibilities, future development or modification is easier.
    - *Multiple views for a model*: Models can have multiple views.
- *Disadvantages*:
    - *Code navigability*: The framework navigation can be complex because it introduces new layers of abstraction and requires users to adapt to the decomposition criteria of MVC.
    - *Multi-artifact consistency*: Decomposing a feature into three artifacts causes scattering. Thus, requiring developers to maintain the consistency of multiple representations at once.
    - *Pronounced learning curve*: Knowledge on multiple technologies becomes the norm. Developers using MVC need to be skilled in multiple technologies.

Review Questions

1. A Web browser is:
    a. A program to view HTML documents
    b. A program to display a web page
    c. A program to enable users to access resources on the Web
    d. All of the above

2. What does a dynamic Web page do?
   a. Content remains same every time it is viewed
   b. Generates on demand of a program
   c. Generates on request from browser
   d. Both b and c
3. What is a web development framework? Give a few examples.
4. What do you understand by API? Why are they used?
5. What is the role of databases in web development?
6. Differentiate between the following:
   a. Programming language, scripting language, and markup language
   b. Client-side scripting and server-side scripting
7. Explain the Model-View-Controller architecture for web application development.

8

Client-Side Technologies

8.1 HTML: Hypertext Markup Language

Hypertext Markup Language (HTML) is a simple text formatting language for annotating a document in a way that is syntactically distinguishable from the text, thus creating hypertext documents. A hypertext document is viewed in a web Browser, such as Internet Explorer or Netscape Navigator. The browser is a program that understands the document written in HTML and displays it by interpreting the document contents. A unique feature of this versatile language is that it allows the creation of links, also known as hyperlinks. These links are references to data that the user follows by clicking or hovering. A hyperlink may point to a whole document or to a specific element within a document. Thus, "hypertext" means machine readable text, "markup" means to structure it in a specific format, and "hyperlinks" are links from a hypertext document to another location, activated by clicking on highlighted text, an icon, or a graphic image.

8.1.1 Creating an Hypertext Markup Language Document

Before we create an HTML document, let's consider the following facts:

- Every HTML document corresponds to a single page.
- An HTML document consists of HTML elements.
- HTML is a tag-oriented language (most HTML elements consist of a Start Tag and an End Tag).
- HTML is not case sensitive (HeAD and hEAd mean the same thing).
- A file containing HTML elements can only be saved with the file extension as .HTM or .HTML.

Now, to create an HTML document, open the Notepad application by accessing the Start Menu on the Taskbar:

Start->Programs->Accessories->Notepad

Add the HTML code in Notepad and save the file, naming it MyFirstHtmlPage.htm (Figure 8.1).

To view the HTML page in your browser, open the My Documents folder on your computer and double-click on the file MyFirstHtmlPage.htm which will automatically open in the default browser program and display the result as shown in Figure 8.2.

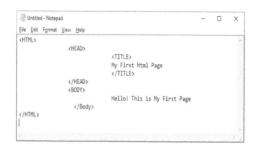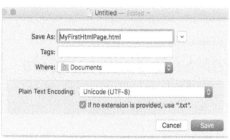

FIGURE 8.1
Writing first HTML page.

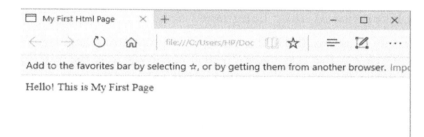

FIGURE 8.2
Viewing the HTML page.

8.1.2 Tags

Tags are control text used to denote various elements in an HTML document. A tag in HTML comprises a left angular bracket (<), followed by a tag name, and closed by a right angular bracket (>). For example: <html>, <body>, and <title>. The tags described here are examples of start tags. Every start tag must have an end tag, which is similar to the start tag but with a forward slash sign before the tag name: </html>, </body>, and </title>.

```
<TAG> tag content </TAG>
```

8.1.2.1 Hypertext Markup Language Element

HTML elements are fundamental blocks of a web page. Here is an overview of HTML elements:

```
<HTML>----------------</HTML> is an HTML element
<BODY>---------------</BODY> is a Body element
```

- *Container elements:* All container elements are paired (i.e., they have start and end tags). The start tag consists of the tag name enclosed in left and right angular brackets (for instance, <body>). The end tag is identical to the start tag except for a slash (/) that preceeds the text within angular brackets of the end tag (e.g., </body>). Container elements contain parameters and parameters of an element are given between the start tag and the end tag.

    Elements in HTML also contain attributes that can be given along with the tag name in the angular brackets of the start tag.

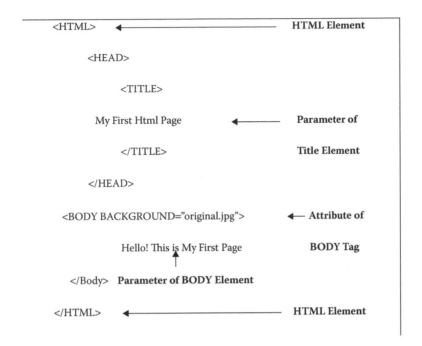

FIGURE 8.3
Basic structure of an HTML page.

- *Empty elements:* Empty elements have only a start tag and no end tag. Hence, an empty element has no parameters, but can take attributes, which are given within the angular brackets of the start tag.
- *HTML attributes:* Attributes are used to define the characteristics of an HTML element and they are placed inside the element's opening tag. All attributes are made up of two parts: a name (the property that you want to set) and a value (the value of the named property). The value is always put in quotes. Attribute names and values are not case sensitive, but lowercase is recommended. For example, in Figure 8.3, the <body> tag has an attribute named *background* whose value has been set to an image named "original.jpg."

8.1.2.2 *Parts of a Hypertext Markup Language Document*

The basic structure of an HTML document is given by the following elements, known as document structure elements.

```
<HTML>
    <HEAD>
        ------------------------------
    </HEAD>
    <BODY>
        ------------------------------
    </BODY>
</HTML>
```

The most frequently used HTML tags are described in Table 8.1.

TABLE 8.1

HTML Tags

Tag	Description
<html>	Identifies the document as an HTML document. The <html> element does not affect the appearance of the document but gives a hint to the browser that the document is an HTML document.
<head>	Defines the HTML document header and does not contribute in the appearance of the document. The header contains information about the document.
<title>	This element specifies and displays the title of the HTML document in the browser window. The browser does not display any information in the header, except for the text contained in the <title> tag.
<body>	Contains the main contents of the document as parameter. The <body> element has BACKGROUND, BGCOLOR, TEXT, LINK, ALINK, and VLINK as important attributes.
 	Wraps the text to start from next line without adding extra space. The BR element is used to give line breaks, as in HTML white spaces are ignored.
<p>	Used to specify text in paragraph form and inserts a line break with extra space in the beginning of the first line.
<hn>	Can be used to give section headings. The heading element is written as <hn>.....</hn>, where n is the level of the heading and can have values from 1 to 6.
<b>	This tag displays the text in bold form.
<i>	This tag displays the text in italic.
<tt>	This tag displays text in typewriter font.
<u>	Underlines the text it encloses. Gaps between words in the enclosed text are also underlined.
<center>	Centers the content mentioned in the start and end tag. It also lets us center elements, such as images, and arbitrary content that could not otherwise be centered. You can place the <center> tag anywhere, such as in the middle of a paragraph.
<hr>	Draws a horizontal line across the document frame or window. You can use a horizontal line to visually divide information or sections.
<sub>	Displays text as subscript. Subscript appears slightly below the baseline (bottom edge) and in a smaller font.
<sup>	Displays text as superscript. Superscript appears slightly above the top of the preceding text and in a smaller font.
<li>	Whenever it is required to make a list of certain items, we use the <li> (list item) element. This tag is used inside list elements, such as <ol> to produce an ordered list and <ul> to produce an unordered list.
<ol>	Displays the list that is preceded by a number or a letter. This tag is used when the items are to be placed in a specific order.
<ul>	Displays a bulleted list. This tag is used when the items are not to be placed in a specific order.
<dl>	This tag (definition list) is used when you need to form a list of terms along with their definitions. You can write terms under the <dt> tag and their definition under the <dd> tag.
<dt>	Specifies the term in the definition list.
<dd>	Displays a definition description in a defined list.
<img>	Specifies an image to be displayed in an HTML document. Syntax: <img src="location">
<strike>	Displays text with a line through it.
<nobr>	Ensures that a line does not wrap to the next line. This tag is useful for words or phrases that must be kept together in one line.

(Continued)

TABLE 8.1 (*Continued*)

HTML Tags

Tag	Description
<span>	Delimits an arbitrary piece of text. You can apply colors to different spans of text.
<table>	This is the basic element for creating a table. The table element is a container element. Syntax: <table align="left/right/center"> ..... </table>
<tr>	Used to define table rows. This is a container element used inside the <table> element. The number of rows in a table corresponds to the number of instances of the <tr> element within the table element.
<td>	Specifies the text in a cell of a table. It is a container element used inside the <tr> tag. The number of columns in a table depends on the number of <td> elements within the <tr> element.
<th>	Used to create header values. This tag specifies a table cell whose contents are usually displayed in a bolder font than those of regular table cells. The intent of the <th> tag is that you use it for column or row headings.
<a>	An anchor defines a place in a document. It is a container element. Syntax: <a href="location">............ </a>
<form>	This tag can contain interface elements (such as text, buttons, checkboxes, radio buttons, and selection lists) that allow the user to enter text and make choices. Each interface element in the form must be defined between the <form> and </form> tags.
<input>	This tag is required when the user has to give input data. This tag is always used within the <form> tag. Thus, the <input> tag defines a form element that can receive user input. The type attribute determines the specific sort of form element to be created. The value of the type attribute can be text, email, radio, password, and so on. Syntax: <input type="text" name="name">
<select>	Defines a selection list on an HTML form. A selection list displays a list of options from which the user can select an item. From a selection list, any one item can be selected at a time, or more than one. Syntax: <select name="selectname" multiplesize="list length">.................</select>
<textarea>	Defines a multiline input field on an HTML form. A <textarea> field lets the user enter words, phrases, or numbers. Scrollbars appear in the text area if the text in the text area element exceeds the number of specified columns or rows.
<frame>	Creates a frame, which is an independently scrollable region of a web browser's client window. Syntax: <framebordercolor="color">
<frameset>	Defines a set of frames that appear in a web browser window. The frameset tag contains one or more <frame> tags, each describing a frame. A frameset can describe that its frames are laid out in rows or columns. Syntax: <framesetcols="columnwidthlist" rows="rowwidthlist">.......................</frameset>

- Attributes of the <body> element include the following.
  - *Background*: Used to specify the URL (uniform resource locator) of an image that will be used as a background for the document and the image tiles on the entire background. For example, <body background="original.jpg">---------</body>.

    The image to be copied should have an extension of either .JPG or .GIF. To display a .BMP file, it must first be converted into .JPG or .GIF format.

- *Bgcolor*: This sets the color of the background. There are three major colors RED, BLUE, and GREEN. If combination is required then the value for *bgcolor* can be given as #RRGGBB.
- *Text*: Sets the color of the normal text in the document. Color values can be given in the same way as that of *bgcolor* attribute.
- *Link*: Sets the default color of the unvisited links in the document. An unvisited link is a link that has not been clicked on (or followed).
- *Vlink*: Specifies the text color of visited (or followed) links in a document.
- *Alink*: Specifies the color to which links briefly change when clicked. After flashing the *alink* color, visited links change to the *vlink* color if it has been specified; otherwise they change to the browser's default visited link color.
- *Leftmargin, Rightmargin*: These are used to specify the margin from the left and right sides of the document, respectively. For example, <body leftmargin="100", rightmargin="100">-------</body>
- *Topmargin, Bottommargin*: These are used to specify the margin from the top and bottom of the document, respectively. For example, <body topmargin="100", bottommargin="100">--------</body>

Figure 8.4 shows the HTML code for different attributes of the <body> tag with output.

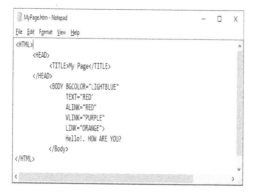
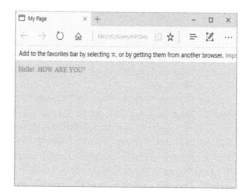

FIGURE 8.4
Sample use of various <body> tag attributes.

- *Special Characters in HTML*

Several characters in HTML have special meanings with a specialized purpose. For example, the less than symbol < in HTML signifies the beginning of a tag to be interpreted by the browser. Therefore, the < character cannot be used in normal text within the HTML document. Similarly, special characters, such as copyright symbols, the registered trademark symbol, angle brackets, and the ampersand symbol (&), require special treatment. To use these symbols, a replacement code has to be used instead. These characters are referred to as "entities" and are referenced using a particular code that is rendered by the browser for the correct character. The code always begins with an ampersand '&' and ends with a semicolon ';'. For example, the entity for the ampersand is '&'. Table 8.2 lists the special characters and their codes.

TABLE 8.2

Escape Sequence in HTML

Symbol	Code	Description
"	"	Quotation Mark
&	&	Ampersand
>	>	Greater than
<	<	Less than
c	©	Copyright
r	®	Registered trademark
		Nonbreaking space
¼	¼	Fraction of one fourth
½	½	Fraction of one half

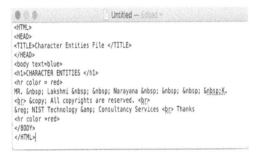 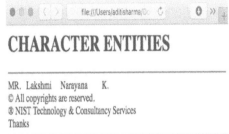

FIGURE 8.5
Sample use of various escape sequences.

Note: Unlike the rest of HTML, the escape sequences are case-sensitive (Figure 8.5).

Sample use of HTML is provided in Appendix A of this book. Web page development in HTML is simple with a mild learning curve. This is primarily due to the keyword-based formatting instructions dedicated to style certain words, sentences, and paragraphs. It is suitable when the page has less content and few formatting requirements. Scaling this for a larger, more complex web page would involve multiple keywords in each section repeated multiple times in a single page, making the code unnecessarily lengthy. Moreover, separating the content of the document from the presentation style of the document would make site maintenance easier. Cascading Style Sheets (CSS) offer a solution as a core technology, simplifying styling with apparent benefits as the size of the page grows. Web page creation and troubleshooting are both much easier when using CSS. The following section discusses CSS in detail.

8.2 CSS: Cascading Style Sheets

CSS is the style language that defines layout of HTML documents to control the look and feel of the content. HTML is used to structure content, whereas CSS is used to format this structured content.

The word "Cascading" means that styles can fall (or cascade) from one style sheet to another, enabling multiple style sheets to be used on one HTML document. The simplest HTML document may have three or more style sheets associated with it:

- *The browser's style sheet*: The default style sheet applied to all web documents.
- *The user's style sheet*: A user is anyone who looks at your web site, and so this style sheet allows users to set their own style sheets within their browser.
- *The author's style sheet*: The author is the person who created the web site.

Thus, CSS provides a powerful and flexible way to control the details of web documents. It is just a set of style rules in a specific format. They are stored in plain text files with the CSS filename extension. Style sheets contain multiple style definitions. CSS is a language that defines the format for incorporating style information in a style sheet. While HTML is more concerned about the content, CSS is used to impose a particular style on the document. It separates the appearance from the content written in HTML.

Advantages of using CSS:
- *Efficiency in design:* You can create rules and apply them to many elements throughout the web site.
- *Consistency:* The main benefit of CSS is that styles are applied consistently across multiple web pages. One change can control several areas at one time, which is quite advantageous if there are changes that need to be made.
- *Greater control over layout and appearance:* Fonts, sizes, color, line spacing, margins, indentation, and so on.
- *Faster page downloads:* The rules are only downloaded once by the browser, then cached and used for each page load. This leads to lighter page loads and improved performance.
- *Low maintenance:* Easier site maintenance as the structure is separate from visual appearance.

Disadvantages of using CSS:
- *Fragmentation*: CSS renders different dimensions with each browser. Programmers are required to consider and test all code across multiple browsers for compatibility before taking any web site or mobile application live.
- *Come in different levels:* There is CSS, CSS1 up to CSS3, which has resulted in confusion among developers and web browsers.
- *Lack of security:* Because it is an open text-based system, CSS doesn't have the built-in security that will protect it from being overridden. Anyone who has read/write access to a web site can change the CSS file, alter the links, or disrupt the formatting, whether by accident or design.

8.2.1 Basics of Style Sheets

CSS is not a replacement to HTML and relies on an underlying markup structure, such as HTML. Although CSS is used in HTML pages, its use is not limited to HTML alone—it can be used on other languages, such as XML. Without binding to an element, a style really does not do anything. The purpose of a style sheet is to create a presentation for an element or set of elements. Binding an element to a style specification is very simple. It consists of an element, followed by its associated style defined within curly braces: Element {Style Specification}.

For example, for binding a style rule to the element such that a 28 point impact font is used every time, the following rule would display the desired result:

```
h1 {font-family:  Impact;   font-size:  28pt;  color:  "red"}
```

In general, a style can be specified in a document using four methods: inline, internal (embedded), external, and imported. A single style sheet can be utilized for multiple documents. The following sections discuss these briefly.

8.2.2 Cascading Style Sheets Page Layout

A CSS file consists of one or more style rules. Every rule specifies the appearance of content of HTML documents. A style rule further is divided into two body parts—the selector and the declaration. For example:

```
body {background-color : gray;}
```

Here, body is the selector whereas the declaration is included in curly braces. Selector specifies which body part will be affected by this style rule.

- *Inline style sheets*: This is the simplest way to attach a style tag–simply include a style attribute with the tag along with a list of properties and their values. The browser uses those style properties and values to render the contents of just this instance of the tag. For example:

```
<h1   style = "color: blue;   font-style:  italic">
I' m Mr. K.  L.   Narayana
<h1>
```

This type of style definition is called inline because it occurs with the tag as it appears in the document. The scope of the style covers that tag only. It is the least flexible method.

- *Internal style sheets*: These are also known as document-level style sheets and embedded style sheets. The real power of style sheets becomes more evident when you place a list of presentation rules within the head of a document. Enclosed within their own <style> and </style> tags, these "document-level" style sheets affect all the same tags within that document except for tags that consists an overriding inline style attribute. The <style> tag must appear within the <head> of a document. Everything between the <style> and </style> tags is considered part of the style rules to be applied to the document. To be perfectly correct, the contents of the <style> tag and HTML or XHTML are not bound by the normal rules for mark-up content.

Syntax: Selector {Property: Value}

For example, H1 {color: red}

P {font-size: 12 pt; font-face: Verdana sans-sarif;}

Note that several property-value pairs can be used but they must be separated by semi-colons. Values are dependent on the properties. Some properties can have numeric values while some take a value from a predetermined set valid values (Figure 8.6).

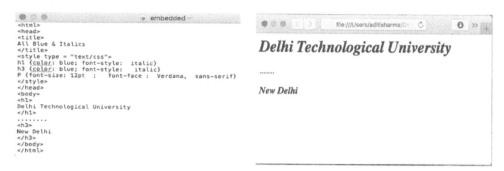

FIGURE 8.6
Sample use of an internal style sheet.

- *External style sheets*: Style rules can be kept in a separate file with a .CSS extension and then linked up with one or more HTML documents. This linking can be done by using the <link> tag within the <head>, as shown in the following example (Figure 8.7).

```
<head>
<link REL="STYLESHEET"  HREF="/path /stylesheet.css" TYPE ="text/css">
</head>
```

FIGURE 8.7
Sample use of an external style sheet.

- *Imported style sheets*: Importing a style into a document is another way to use a document window style. The idea is similar to linking. An external style sheet is transferred, but in this case, reference is similar to macro expansion inline. The syntax for importing the style definitions is @import followed by the URL of the style sheet to include. This rule must be included in the <style> element; it has no meaning outside the element (Figure 8.8).

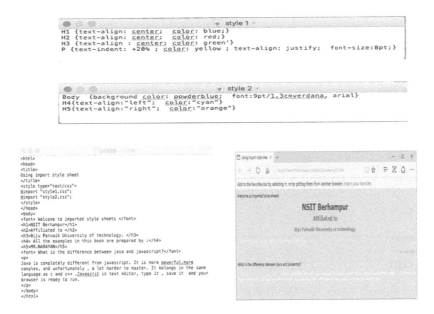

FIGURE 8.8
Sample use of an imported style sheet.

Imported style sheets are also known as multi-special suits. This approach has an advantage over linking. Multiple style sheets can be linked to the same document, which is otherwise not possible using a standard <link> tag.

8.2.3 Properties of Style Sheets

CSS defines more than 50 different properties and values, and browser vendors are busy devising new ones all the time. Some of them are shown in Table 8.3.

HTML and CSS are technologies that create static web pages as you can't do anything dynamic just by using its tags. They are actually not technically programming languages—they are just page structure and style information. For an interactive web page that is clickable, hoverable, and generally dynamic, you need to manipulate its HTML and CSS. JavaScript is one programming language that lets web developers design interactive sites. It is a web-adapted version of actual programming code, intended to write applets (small, web-based applications) for use on web sites. Thus, HTML provides the basic structure of sites, which is enhanced and modified by other technologies like CSS and JavaScript. CSS is used for styling to control presentation, formatting, and layout. while JavaScript adds functionality by controlling the behavior of different elements. The next section elaborates JavaScript.

TABLE 8.3

CSS Properties

Property	Possible Values
Font-family	family name, generic family name
Font-style	normal, italic, oblique
Font-variant	normal, small-caps
Font-weight	normal, bold, bolder, lifter, 100- 900 (normal is 400)
Font-size	absolute size, relative size, length, percentage
Absolute sizes	xx-small, x-small, small, medium, large, x-large, x-length
Relative sizes	smaller, larger, color, color value
Line-height	normal, number, length, percentage
Word-spacing	normal, spacing
Letter-spacing	normal, length
Text Transformation	none, capitalize, lowercase, uppercase
Text-align	center, justify, left, right

8.3 JavaScript

JavaScript is a lightweight, interpreted programming language (all scripting languages are programming languages) designed for creating network-centric applications. And it allows building interactivity into otherwise static HTML pages.

- *JavaScript is not just Java simplified*

  One of the most common misconceptions about JavaScript is that it is a simplified version of Java, the programming language from Sun Microsystems. Other than an incomplete syntactic resemblance and the fact that both Java and JavaScript can deliver executable content over networks, the two languages are entirely unrelated. The similarity of names is purely a marketing ploy.

- *Features of JavaScript*
  - An interpreted language.
  - Embedded within HTML.
  - Minimal syntax, easy to learn.
  - Supports quick development and better performance.
  - Designed for programming user events.
  - Platform independent.

- *JavaScript capabilities*
  - *Rich interface*: Improves the user interface of a web site.
  - *Increased interactivity*: Makes your site easier to navigate and creates popup windows.

- *Less server interaction*: Validates user input before sending the page off to the server. This reduces server traffic, which means reduced load on the server.
- *Form validation*
- *What JavaScript can't do*
  - JavaScript doesn't have any graphics capabilities except for the ability to format and display HTML.
  - For security reasons, client-side JavaScript doesn't allow the reading or writing of files.
  - JavaScript doesn't support networking of any kind.
  - Used in limited context.
  - It doesn't have any multithreading capabilities.
- *Client-side JavaScript*

  When a JavaScript interpreter is embedded in a web browser, the result is client-side JavaScript. Client-side JavaScript encompasses the core language plus the predefined objects only relevant to running JavaScript in a browser. A client-side JavaScript is embedded directly in HTML pages and interpreted by the browser completely at run time.
- *Server-side JavaScript*

  Netscape calls its server-side JavaScript product LiveWire or LiveScript. An obvious capability of server-side JavaScript is to dynamically generate HTML to be displayed by the client. Its most powerful features come from the server-side objects it has access to. For example, the database object allows a script to perform SQL database queries and updates.

8.3.1 Basic Syntax

A script is a small program code that is written within the <head> tag of the HTML document to perform a task. The <script> tag is used to write a script as follows:

```
<Script LANGUAGE ="JavaScript">
. . . . . . . . . . . . . . .
</SCRIPT>
```

The <script> tag indicates to the browser that the text written within the script tags is part of a script. This tag can be used one or multiple times in the <head> as well as in the <body> element. But it is typically recommended that you keep the <script> tag within the <head> tags. The *language* attribute specifies that the language used for writing the script/program is JavaScript. Netscape navigator uses JavaScript as the default scripting language, but Microsoft Internet Explorer uses JScript. Both languages are syntactically similar. The following two script statements are equivalent:

<script language="JavaScript">

<script> (Note that no language attribute is specified.)

The <script> tag takes three attributes as follows:

- *Language*: Specifies the language used for the script.
- *SRC*: Indicates the URL of a file that contains an external script load.
- *Type*: Indicates the MIME type of script to be run.

JavaScript statements are composed of values (fixed values called literals and variable values called variables), operators, expressions, reserve words (keywords), and comments. Syntactical, features of JavaScript are:

- *Whitespace and line breaks*: JavaScript ignores spaces, tabs, and newlines that appear between tokens in programs except those that are part of string constants.
- *Optional semicolons*: Simple Statements in JavaScript are generally followed by a semicolon. In JavaScript, however, you are allowed to omit the semicolon if your statements are each placed on a separate line. For example: A=3 or B=4.
- *Comments*: JavaScript supports both C and C++ style comments.
  - *Single line comments*: //HI, I am Rachel.
  - *Multi-line comments*: /*Hi, I am Rachel*/
- *Literals*: A literal in JavaScript is a data value that appears directly in a program. These are numbers, strings, Boolean values, and special value NULL. Types include:
  - *Integer literals*: Base 10 integers may be simply represented as an optional minus sign followed by a sequence of digits that doesn't begin with 0. For example: 3, -12, or 10,000,000.
  - *Octal and hexadecimal literals*: You can specify integers as octal (base 8) and hexadecimal (base 16) values. An octal value begins with an optional minus sign, followed by the digit, followed by a sequence of digits between 0 and 7. A hexadecimal literal begins with an optional minus sign, followed by "0x" or "0X," followed by a sequence of digits from 0-9 or letters A-F. For example: -0123, -0xCAFE911.
  - *Floating point literals*: These can have a decimal point. For example: 1.413 or 6.02e+23.
  - *String literals*: Strings are any sequence of 0 or more characters enclosed within single or double quotes. Single quote characters may be contained within strings delimited by double quotes, and double quote characters may be contained within strings delimited by single quotes. For example: "learn" or "3.14" or 'name = "mypage"'.

    Escape sequences in string literals: The backslash character (/) has a special purpose in JavaScript strings. Combining this with the character that follows it, it represents a character that is not otherwise represented within the strings, just like in C++. For example: \b is for backspace and \n is for newline.
- *Variables*: JavaScript uses the *var* keyword to declare variables. An equal sign is used to assign values to variables. For example, the following defines x as a variable and then assigns x the value 14:

Var x;
x = 14;

- *Operators*: JavaScript supports arithmetic operators, comparison operators, logical (or relational) operators, assignment operators, and conditional (or ternary) operators.
- *Expression*: An expression is a combination of values, variables, and operators, which computes to a value. The computation is called an evaluation. For example: 14 * 10, which evaluates to 140.
- *Reserve words*: These are keywords allowed in JavaScript. For example: int, char, if, while, var, and public.

8.3.2 JavaScript Display Possibilities

JavaScript can "display" data in different ways:

- Writing into an HTML element using *innerHTML*: To access an HTML element, JavaScript can use the *document.getElementById(id)* method. The *id* attribute defines the HTML element. The *innerHTML* property defines the HTML content (Figure 8.9).

```
<!DOCTYPE html>
<html>
<head>
 <title> FIRST JAVASCRIPT PROGRAM </title>
<body>
<h2>My JavaScript Web Page</h2>
<p>My First Attempt!</p>
<p id="demo"></p>
<script>
document.getElementById("demo").innerHTML = 24 + 14;
</script>
</body>
</html>
```

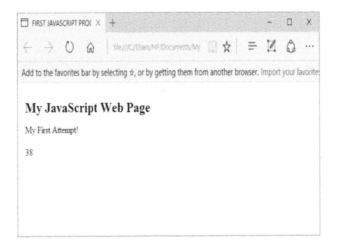

FIGURE 8.9
Sample use of the document.getElementById() method.

- Writing into the HTML output using *document.write()*: Here, the "document" is the object that contains information used by the script, and "write ()" is the method (or function) associated with the object, which provides service to the script. Thus, the document object allows the text to be displayed in the document and the write () method is used to write a line of text within that document (Figure 8.10).

```
<html>
<head>
<title> FIRST JAVASCRIPT PROGRAM </title>
<script language="JavaScript">
document.write("<i> It's the first Script</i>");
document.write("<h2> The program is very interesting</h2>");
</script>
</head>
<body>
<h1> Welcome to the Web Page </h1>
</body>
</html>
```

FIGURE 8.10
Sample use of the document.write() command.

- Writing into an alert box, using *window.alert()*: This command is used to produce an alert message in a separate window. Here, the object is "window" and "alert()" is the method. This command creates a dialog box that can be used to display important messages to the user or interact with the user browsing the web page. The dialog box automatically includes OK button, which allows the user to hide the dialog/message by pressing the button. So, as the dialog box appears and OK is clicked, the text written within the <body> tag is displayed in the browser window (Figure 8.11).

```
<html>
<head>
<title> FIRST JAVASCRIPT PROGRAM </title>
<script language="JavaScript">
window.alert("Hi ! and Welcome ");
</script>
<body>
<b><i>Press F5 or click refresh button to run the program again</i></b>
</body>
</html>
```

FIGURE 8.11
Sample use of the window.alert() command.

After the OK button is clicked, the following output appears as shown in Figure 8.12:

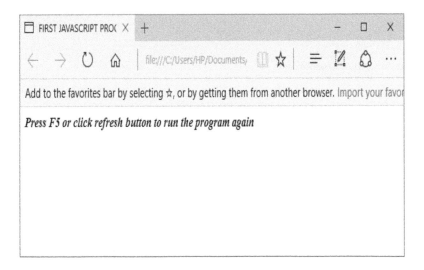

FIGURE 8.12
Output of OK in the window.alert() command.

- A *window.prompt()* command produces a dialog box in which the user can enter some value that can either be a number or characters. Thus, the command allows the user to input a value that can be used in the script at any point of time. Let us look at the program written in the following (Figure 8.13):

```
<html>
<head>
<title> FIRST JAVASCRIPT PROGRAM </title>
<script language="JavaScript">
window.prompt("Enter some value");
</script>
<body>
<b><i>Press F5 or click refresh button to run the program again</i></b>
</body>
</html>
```

FIGURE 8.13
Sample use of window.prompt() command.

- Writing into the browser console, using *console.log()*.

```
<!DOCTYPE html>
<html>
<body>
<script>
console.log(14+24);
</script>
</body>
</html>
```

8.3.3 Sample Programs in JavaScript

Example 8.1: Program to Display the Name and Age of a Friend Entered by User (Figure 8.14)

```html
<html>
<head>
<title> LEARNING JAVASCRIPT </title>
<script language="JavaScript">
var first, second;
first = window.prompt("Enter your name", "NAME");
second = window.prompt("Enter your age", "AGE");
document.write("<h1>Hi my friend : "+ first +"</h1>");
document.write("<h2>Even my age is : "+ second +"</h2>");
</script>
<body>
<b><i>Press F5 or click refresh button to run the program again</i></b>
</body>
</html>
```

FIGURE 8.14
Output of program in JavaScript to display name and age.

Example 8.2: Program to Display the Sum of Two Numbers Entered by User (Figure 8.15)

By default, values stored in variables are stored as character strings not as numbers. Thus, to perform the calculation in a proper way, the program makes use of the parseInt function, meaning it parses the string and returns an integer.

```html
<html>
<head>
<title>LEARNING JAVASCRIPT </title>
<script language="JavaScript">
var number1, number2, sum;
number1 = window.prompt("Enter first number", "0");
number2 = window.prompt("Enter second number", "0");
sum = parseInt(number1) + parseInt(number2);
document.writeln("<h1>The sum is : "+ sum +"</h1>");
</script>
<body>
<b><i>Press F5 or click refresh button to run the program again</i></b>
</body>
</html>
```

FIGURE 8.15
Output of program in JavaScript to display the sum of two numbers entered by user.

8.3.4 AJAX

AJAX is an acronym for asynchronous JavaScript and XML. It is not a programming language. It is simply a combination of

- A browser built-in XMLHttpRequest object (to request data from a web server).
- JavaScript and HTML DOM (to display or use the data).

AJAX allows you to send and receive data asynchronously without reloading the web page. It only sends the important information to the server and not the entire page. So, only valuable data from the client-side is routed to the server-side, making the web application interactive and fast. Many popular web applications like Gmail, Facebook, Twitter, Google maps, and YouTube use AJAX technology. A few advantages and disadvantages of using AJAX are listed in the following:

- *Advantages*
  - *Reduced server interactivity:* Reduces server traffic in both side requests. Also reduces the time consumed on both side responses.
  - *Better interaction and easier navigation:* AJAX is responsive, with a small amount of data transferred at a time.
- *Disadvantages*
  - View source is allowed and anyone can view the code source written for AJAX. Security is less in AJAX applications, as all files are downloaded at client side.
  - AJAX is not well integrated with any browser. In addition, JavaScript-disabled browsers cannot use AJAX applications.
  - Data of all requests is URL-encoded, which increases the size of the request.

8.4 Bootstrap Framework

Bootstrap is the most popular open source front-end (HTML, CSS, and JavaScript) framework for developing responsive, mobile-first projects on the Web. It includes HTML- and CSS-based design templates for typography, forms, buttons, tables, navigation, modals, image carousels, and more, as well as optional JavaScript plug-ins. Bootstrap was developed by Jacob Thornton and Mark Otto at Twitter and was released as an open source product in August 2011 on GitHub (Figure 8.16).

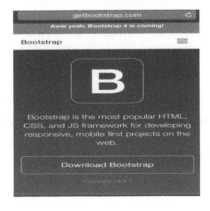

FIGURE 8.16
Bootstrap framework.

Bootstrap has three main files:

- *bootstrap.css*: A CSS framework
- *bootstrap.js*: A JavaScript/jQuery framework
- *glyphicons*: A font (an icon font set)

Additionally, Bootstrap requires jQuery to function. jQuery is an extremely popular and widely used JavaScript library, which simplifies and adds cross-browser compatibility to JavaScript. Thus, the Bootstrap package includes:

- *Scaffolding*: A basic structure with Grid System, link styles, and background
- *CSS*: Global CSS settings, fundamental HTML elements styled and enhanced with extensible classes, and an advanced grid system
- *Components*: Over a dozen reusable components built to provide iconography, dropdowns, navigation, alerts, pop-overs, and much more
- *JavaScript plug-ins*: More than a dozen custom jQuery plug-ins. One can easily include all of them at once or one at a time
- *Customization*: The ability to customize Bootstrap's components, LESS variables, and jQuery plug-ins to get your very own version

The biggest advantage of using Bootstrap is that it consists of tools for creating flexible and responsive web layouts, as well as common interface components. Responsive web design is about creating web sites that automatically adjust themselves to look good on all devices, from small phones to large desktops. Bootstrap uses a variety of techniques, such as grid systems and flexible images, to adjust to desktops, tablets, and mobile phones. This ensures that a user's experience with a web site is not diminished.

Some of the key features and capabilities that make Bootstrap a powerful and popular option are:

- *Easy to use:* Bootstrap is very easy to use. A lot of time and effort can be saved when using the Bootstrap predefined design templates and classes.
- *Responsive features:* Bootstrap gives you the ability to easily create responsive designs. The responsive features make your web pages appear correctly on different devices and screen resolutions without any change in markup.
- *Consistent design:* All Bootstrap components share the same design templates and styles through a central library so the designs and layouts of your web pages are consistent.
- *Compatible with browsers:* Bootstrap is created with modern browsers in mind and it is compatible with all modern browsers, such as Mozilla Firefox, Google Chrome, Safari, Internet Explorer, and Opera.
- *Open source:* It is completely free to download and use.

8.5 AngularJS Framework

AngularJS is an open source JavaScript-based development framework for building well structured, easily testable, and maintainable front-end applications. It provides developers with options for writing client-side applications using JavaScript following the MVC (Model-View-Controller) architecture (some coding specialists prefer to follow MVW [whatever] architecture for AngularJS).

AngularJS changes static HTML to dynamic HTML and extends the ability of HTML by adding built-in attributes and components. It also provides an ability to create custom attributes using simple JavaScript. Applications written in AngularJS are cross-browser compliant, i.e., AngularJS automatically handles JavaScript code suitable for each browser.

8.5.1 The Model-View-Controller Architecture of AngularJS

AngularJS is based on an MVC framework that defines how to organize the web application. The application is defined with modular components that can depend on each other.

- *Model*: A model in AngularJS is a primitive data type, such as number, string, Boolean, object, etc. It is a simple JavaScript object without any getter or setter methods.
- *View*: In AngularJS, Document Object Model (DOM) is what users see. In order to display the data from controller, Angular expressions can be added to the view which will coordinate model and view about any modification.
- *Controller*: Controller is a collection of JavaScript classes where application logic is defined. Model resides inside controller. The controller encapsulates the behavior of application.

8.5.2 Key Features of AngularJS

AngularJS is a new, powerful, client-side technology that provides a way of accomplishing powerful things in a way that embraces and extends HTML, CSS, and JavaScript. Figure 8.17 illustrates the key concepts that define AngularJS.

AngularJS, which has been developed and maintained by Google, is a popular structural framework for creating dynamic web sites. It is the tool of choice for building single page and multipage applications and web sites, as it's easy to maintain and test web and mobile apps using AngularJS. It has the following key advantages and disadvantages:

- *Advantages of AngularJS*
  - *Easy to use*: AngularJS provides the capability to create single page applications in a very clean and maintainable way.
  - *Two-way data binding*: Two-way data binding implies that when you update any properties in your model, the UI will update and similarly that when

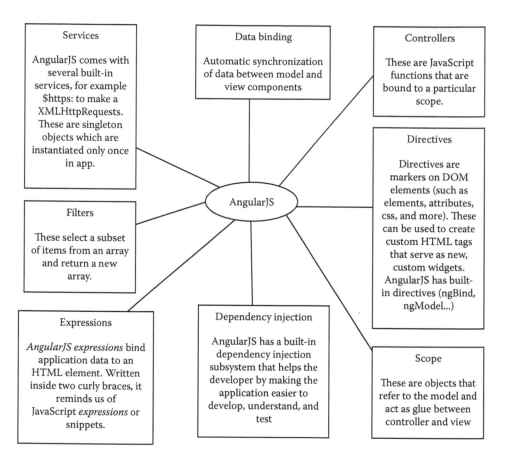

FIGURE 8.17
Key features of AngularJS.

UI elements are updated, the changes will be reflected to model properties. AngularJS provides this two-way data binding capability to HTML, enabling view and model to coordinate with the changes in one another, delivering a rich and responsive experience.

- *Testable code:* AngularJS is designed with testability in mind so that testing of your AngularJS applications is as easy as possible. It allows you to write basic flow end-to-end testing, unit testing, and UI mocks.

- *Dependency injection:* AngularJS uses dependency injection and makes use of separation of concerns.

- *Reusable components:* AngularJS provides reusable components, allowing developers to write less code and get more functionality.

- *Browser support:* On top of everything, AngularJS applications can run on all major browsers and smart phones including Android and iOS phones and tablets.

- *Disadvantages of AngularJS*

Though AngularJS provides many advantages, at the same time it suffers from a few disadvantages:

- *Not secure:* As it is a JavaScript-only framework, applications written in AngularJS are not safe. Server-side authentication and authorization is a must to keep an application secure.
- *Not degradable:* If an application user disables JavaScript, the user will just see the basic page and nothing more.

8.5.3 Creating an Application in AngularJS

AngularJS is a JavaScript framework. It can be added to an HTML page with a <script> tag.

```
<script src="https://ajax.googleapis.com/ajax/libs/angularjs/1.4.8/
angular.min.js"></script>
```

It extends HTML attributes (control features) by attaching directives to web pages and binds data to HTML with expressions. AngularJS extends HTML with *ng-directives*.

- The *ng-app* directive defines and links an AngularJS application to HTML.
- The *ng-model* directive binds the values of AngularJS application data to HTML controls (input, select, textarea).
- The *ng-bind* directive binds the AngularJS application data to the HTML tags.

Creating an application in AngularJS can be defined as a four step process. The first step is to load the framework using the <script> tag. In the second step, we define the application using the ng-app directive. In the third step, we define a model name using the ng-model directive. And finally, in the fourth step, we bind the value of the earlier defined model using the ng-bind directive. Let us create an application page "My first attempt with AngularJS" following these steps.

AngularJS applications are a combination of HTML and JavaScript, so the first thing you need is an HTML page and then you need to include the AngularJS file in the HTML page in order to use all the attributes of AngularJS. Thus, we load the framework using the <script> tag as follows:

```
<!DOCTYPE html>
<html>
  <head>
    <title>My first attempt with AngularJS</title>
    <script src="https://ajax.googleapis.com/ajax/libs/angularjs/1.4.8/
    angular.js">
    </script>
  </head>
  <body>
  </body>
</html>
```

In the next step, you need to specify the AngularJS section in your HTML page. To do this, you need to add the ng-app attribute to the root element of the section where you want to add AngularJS. Typically, the root element can be the HTML, BODY or a DIV element of page. The following example shows the ng-app attribute added in the <html> tag for defining the application.

```
<!DOCTYPE html>
<html ng-app>
  <head>
      <title>My first attempt with AngularJS</title>
      <script src="https://ajax.googleapis.com/ajax/libs/angularjs/1.4.8/
      angular.js">
      </script>
  </head>
  <body>
  </body>
</html>
```

In the third step, we need to define a model name using the ng-model directive. So we add an HTML input text element that contains the ng-model attribute. Finally, we bind the value of the previous model defined using the ng-bind directive (Figure 8.18).

```
<!DOCTYPE html>
<html ng-app>
  <head>
    <title>My first AngularJS code</title>
    <Script SRC="https://ajax.googleapis.com/ajax/libs/angularjs/1.2.13/
    angular.js">
    </Script>
  </head>
  <body>
    <h1> Say Hello in AngularJS </h1>
    <p>Enter your first name:</p>
    <input ng-model="myName" type="text"  placeholder="Your name">
    <p>Hello <span ng-bind = "myName"></span></p>
  </body>
</html>
```

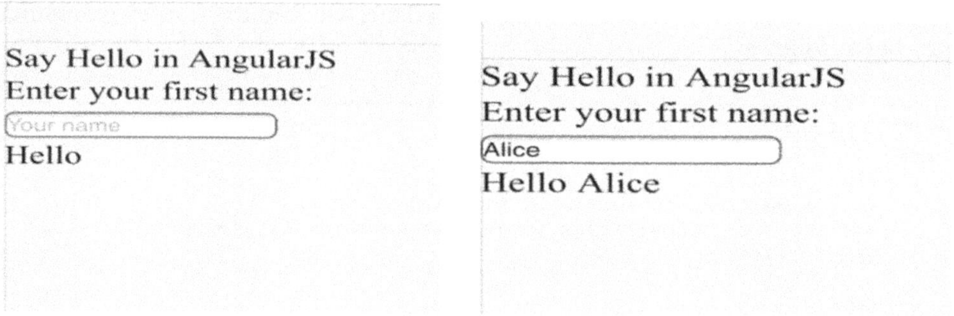

Say Hello in AngularJS
Enter your first name:
[Your name]
Hello

Say Hello in AngularJS
Enter your first name:
[Alice]
Hello Alice

FIGURE 8.18
Sample output in AngularJS.

Thus, AngularJS extends HTML by providing directives that add functionality to your markup, allowing you to create powerful dynamic templates. You can also create your own directives, crafting reusable components that fill your needs and abstracting away all the DOM manipulation logic. It also implements two-way data binding, seamlessly connecting your HTML (views) to your JavaScript objects (models). In simple terms, this means that any update on your model will be immediately reflected in your view without the need for any DOM manipulation or event handling (e.g., with jQuery).

Review Questions

1. Create a webpage with HTML describing your department. Use paragraph and list tags.
2. Insert an image and create a link such that clicking on the image takes the user to another page. Change the background color of the page. At the bottom, create a link to take the user to the top of the page using HTML.
3. Using HTML, design a page that has five equal columns. The table should look the same in all screen resolutions.
4. What is the significance of "Cascading" in CSS?
5. What are the key features and capabilities of JavaScript?
6. Create a simple form to submit user input, such as his name, age, address, and favorite subject. Using JavaScript, put validation checks on values entered by the user (such as the age should be a value between 1 and 150).
7. Write a JavaScript program to:
   a. Display an information box as soon as the page loads.
   b. Implement an odd/even number check.
   c. Find when January 1st is a Sunday between 2014 and 2050.
8. What components are included in a Bootstrap package?
9. Describe the MVC architecture of AngularJS.
10. List the advantages and disadvantages of:
    a. CSS
    b. AJAX
    c. Bootstrap
    d. AngularJS

9

Server-Side Technologies

9.1 Server-Side Scripting

Server-side scripting refers to the dynamic generation of web pages served up by the web server, as opposed to static web pages in the server storage that are served up to the web browser. In other words, some part of the content sent in response to an HTTP request is determined on the fly by a program that executes on the server after the HTTP request has been received and generates content as a result of the execution. For example, insertion of continuously changing content into a web page, such as news, weather, or stock quotes, and retrieval of data in response to query string parameters and insertion into a web page are perhaps the most common uses of server-side scripting. All server-side technologies share a common set of features:

- Read data submitted by the user.
- Generate HTML dynamically based on user input.
- Determine information about the client browser.
- Access database systems.
- Exploit the HTTP protocol.

The marketplace for server-side web development solutions is a crowded one, with several available options, such as CGI (Common Gateway Interface), Perl, ASP (Active Server Pages), PHP (Hypertext Preprocessor), JSP (Java Server Pages), Cold Fusion, and Node.js.

CGI, an open-source software, represents one of the earliest, practical methods for generating web content and is the most common way to cater these needs as it allows browsers to request the execution of server-resident software CGI as a part of the approach often called LAMP (Linux, Apache, MySQL, Px—where the Px is Perl, PHP, or Python). CGI is primarily written in the Perl programming language. Though Perl is a mature, cross-platform language, it can be hard to understand. PHP is a cross-platform, open-source alternative with lots of built-in features. PHP has been dubbed "Perl killer" as it can do almost everything that Perl can, and it is usually quicker and easier. Unlike Perl, which usually runs as a CGI program invoked by the web server to handle each page request, PHP integrates with the web server to operate much more efficiently. This scripting language, released in 1995, has been considered a leading back-end development language for over 20 years for making scalable, dynamic web applications, such as e-commerce applications. More recently, Node.js, a platform built on Chrome's V8 JavaScript, has emerged as a key player in server-side development for easily building fast, scalable, network applications like chat apps. Released in 2009, it is considered a popular platform that is defining the web's future. The following sections are a primer to these two server-side competitors: PHP and Node.js.

9.2 Personal Home Pages

PHP was originally an acronym for personal home pages, but is now a recursive acronym for PHP: Hypertext Preprocessor. It is a server-side scripting language used to make HTML pages dynamic. Considering the Model-View-Controller (MVC) for web application development framework, the database forms the bottom most layer (the model), PHP runs as the middle layer (the controller), and HTML forms the topmost layer (the view).

As PHP is a server-side technology, a server is needed to run it and there are several options for doing so. You can choose a host server that supports PHP, you can install PHP on your computer, or you can even use XAMPP (a program that lets you run the PHP directly on your computer without having to install PHP). Once the server is up and running, we can create the sample page.

9.2.1 Sample Page in Personal Home Pages

Basically, a PHP file is a text file with the .php extension. It consists of:

- Text
- HTML tags
- PHP Scripts

PHP is about writing commands to a server. It was designed to work with HTML, basically embedding into the HTML code. Though, you can create PHP files without any HTML tags, it is referred to as a pure PHP file.

```
<HTML> <PHP CODE> </HTML>
```

First, we need to inform the server when the PHP begins and ends. Thus, you mark the beginning and end with the special markup tags <*?php* and *?>* that are recognized by the PHP parser, delineating PHP code that the server must execute. Now we add the following simple code snippet to your HTML code (Figure 9.1):

```
<html>
  <head>
    <title>My first PHP page</title>
  </head>
  <body>
    <?php
    echo "<h1>Hello World!</h1>";
    ?>
  </body>
</html>
```

FIGURE 9.1
My first PHP page.

We asked the server to write "Hello World!" The string function echo is used to write a specified string to the client where the semicolon ends the command. The PHP echo statement is often used to output data to the browser. When you look at the HTML code in the browser, you'll see that the PHP code is gone—only the server sees the PHP code, whereas the client only sees the result. This is what appears by selecting view source in the browser (Figure 9.2).

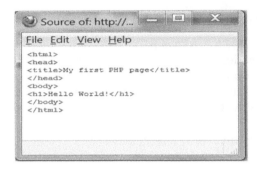

FIGURE 9.2
View source in browser.

Let's now make the server write the current date and time (Figure 9.3).

```html
<html>
  <head>
    <title>My first PHP page</title>
  </head>
  <body>
    <?php
        echo date("r");
    ?>
  </body>
</html>
```

FIGURE 9.3
Displaying current date and time.

The corresponding HTML code is shown in Figure 9.4.

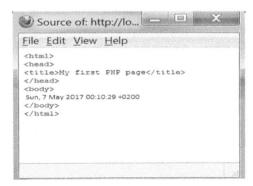

FIGURE 9.4
Corresponding code for displaying current date and time.

We make the server write the date and time when the PHP page is displayed. The HTML code contains only the date—not the PHP code. Therefore, the example is not affected by which browser is used. In fact, all functionalities that are made with server-side technologies always work in all browsers. Whenever you refresh the page in the browser, a new time is written. The server writes the current date and time each time the page is sent to the client.

9.2.2 Personal Home Pages Syntax

PHP is similar to C/C++ when it comes to basic syntax, though it has its own variations. The PHP interpreter provides the functionality to "preprocess hypertext," which means executing PHP commands and producing the desired HTML. It supports many databases like MySQL, PostgreSQL, and Oracle. In fact, it supports any database that supports the Open Database Connectivity (ODBC) standard. Key syntactical rules that PHP follows are:

- Each statement is terminated by a semicolon.
- Space insensitive.
- Keywords (if, else, while, echo, and so on), classes, functions, and user-defined functions are not case sensitive. For example, all the following echo statements are legal (and equal).

```
ECHO "Hello
World!<br>";
echo "Hello World!<br>";
EcHo "Hello World!<br>".
```

- All variable names are case sensitive.
- Comments in PHP can be given as:

  // for a single-line comment.

  # is also for a single-line comment.

  /* begins a multi-line comment block that spans over multiple lines.

  */ appears at the end of a multi-line comment block.
- Blocks are defined using braces {}.

9.2.2.1 Personal Home Pages Variables and Constants

9.2.2.1.1 Variables in PHP

Variables are containers for storing information. In PHP, a variable starts with the $ sign, followed by the name of the variable. A variable name must start with a letter or the underscore character. It cannot start with a number and can only contain alpha-numeric characters and underscores (A–z, 0–9, and _). Variable names are case sensitive ($color and $COLOR are two different variables) and cannot contain spaces. PHP has no command for declaring a variable. A variable is created the moment you first assign a value to it. In PHP, a variable does not need to be declared before adding a value to it. It automatically converts the variable to the correct data type, depending on its value. After declaring a variable, the variable can be reused throughout the code. The assignment operator = is used to assign value to a variable.

Thus, a PHP variable can be defined as:

```
$var_name = value;
```

Consider the following example where we create two variables. The first one is assigned a string value and the second is assigned a number. We display the variable values in the browser using the echo statement (Figure 9.5).

```php
<?php
// Declaring variables
$txt = "Hello World!";
$number = 2414;

// Displaying variables value
echo $txt;   // Output: Hello World!
echo $number; // Output: 2414
?>
```

FIGURE 9.5
Variables in PHP.

9.2.2.1.2 *Constants in PHP*

A constant is a name or an identifier for a fixed value. Constants are defined using PHP's *define()* function, which accepts two arguments: the name of the constant and its value. Once defined, the constant value can be accessed at any time just by referring to its name. The naming convention for constants is similar to that of variables, except that the $ prefix is not required for constant names (Figure 9.6).

```html
<!DOCTYPE html>
<html lang="en">
<head>
<title>PHP Constants</title>
</head>
<body>
 <?php
 // Defining constant
  define("SITE_URL", "http://www.dtu.ac.in/");
 // Using constant
 echo 'Thanks for visiting homepage -' . SITE_URL;
 ?>
</body>
</html>
```

The output of the previous code will be:

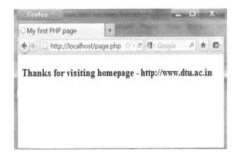

FIGURE 9.6
Constants in PHP.

9.2.2.2 Personal Home Pages Data Types

Although PHP has automatic data type recognition and does a lot of type casting internally, in some cases it does explicit casting and checks the data types to make sure that a variable is assigned to a certain data type. Table 9.1 describes the data-types in PHP.

TABLE 9.1

Data Types in PHP

Data Type	Description
Int, integer	Numeric values with no commas
Double, real	Floating-point number
String	A sequence of characters
Array	A pool of values
Object	An artificial, user-defined data type

9.2.2.3 Personal Home Pages Strings

A string is a sequence of letters, numbers, special characters, and arithmetic values or a combination of all of these. The simplest way to create a string is to enclose the string literal (i.e., string characters) in single quotation marks ('), as follows:

```
$my_string = 'Hi World';
```

You can also use double quotation marks ("). However, single and double quotes work in different ways. Strings enclosed in single quotes are treated almost literally, whereas the strings delimited by double quotes replace variables with the string representations of their values as well as interpret certain escape sequences. These replacements are shown in Table 9.2.

TABLE 9.2

Escape Sequence in PHP

Escape Sequence	Replacement
\n	Newline character
\r	Carriage return character
\t	Tab character
\$	Dollar sign itself ($)
\"	Single double quote (")
\\	Single backslash (\)

Figure 9.7 illustrates the difference between the single and double quote strings.

```
<?php
$my_str = 'World';
echo "Hi, $my_str!<br>";  //
Displays: Hi World!
echo 'Hi, $my_str!<br>';  // Displays: Hi,
$my_str!

echo '<pre>Hi\tWorld!</pre>'; // Displays:
Hi\tWorld!
echo "<pre>Hi\tWorld!</pre>"; // Displays:
Hi    World!
echo 'I\'m loving it';   // Displays: I'm
loving it
?>
```

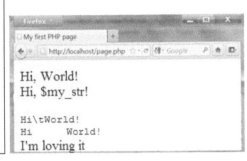

FIGURE 9.7
Strings in PHP.

String manipulations are possible in PHP similar as to in C. Some examples of basic string functions are shown in Table 9.3.

TABLE 9.3

String Functions in PHP

Syntax	Description	Example

strlen(string);	Displays the length of any string	`<?php`
		`echo strlen("Welcome to my Homepage"); //will`
		`  return the length of given string`
		`?>`

str_word_ count (string);	Displays the number of words in any specific string	`<?php`
		`echo str_word_count("Welcome to my Homepage");`
		`  //will return the number of words in the string`
		`?>`

strev(string)	Reverses a string	`<?php`
		`echo strev("Welcome to my Homepage"); // will`
		`  return the string in reverse. The result here will be:`
		`  egapemoH ym ot emocleW`
		`?>`

9.2.2.4 Personal Home Pages Arrays

Arrays are complex variables that allow us to store more than one value or a group of values under a single variable name. There are three types of arrays that you can create in PHP. These are:

- *Indexed array*: An array with a numeric key. Here the indices of the data elements are numbers that start with 0 (zero indexed) and grow incrementally.

```
$numeric_array = array('value_1', 'value_2',   'value_3');
```

Here the indexes of the 3 elements or values are 0, 1, and 2, respectively. For example:

```php
<?php
// Define an indexed array
$colors= array("Red", "Green", "Blue");
?>
```

This is equivalent to the following example, in which indexes are assigned manually:

```php
<?php
$colors[0] = "Red";
$colors[1] = "Green";
$colors[2] = "Blue";
?>
```

- *Associative array*: An array where each key has its own specific value. That is, in an associative array, the keys assigned to values can be arbitrary and user defined strings. In the following example, the array uses keys instead of index numbers:

```php
<?php
// Define an associative array
$rollnos = array("Alice"=>14, "Bob"=>24, "Garfield"=>28);
?>
```

- *Multidimensional array*: An array containing one or more arrays within it. In a multidimensional array, each element can also be an array and each element in the sub-array can be an array or further contain an array within itself and so on. An example of a multidimensional array will look something like this Figure 9.8.

```
<?php
// Define a multidimensional array
$friends = array(
  array(
    "name" => "Rachel Green",
    "email" => "rachelgreen@mail.com",
  ),
  array(
    "name" => "Ross Geller",
    "email" => "rossgeller@mail.com",
  ),
  array(
    "name" => "Monica Geller",
    "email" => "monicageller@mail.com",
  )
array(
    "name" => "Phoebe Buffay",
    "email" => "phoebebuffay@mail.com",
  )
);
// Access nested value
echo "Rachel Green's Email-id is: " . $friends[0]["email"];
?>
```

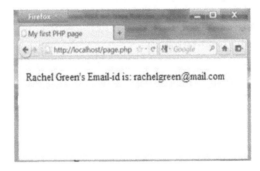

FIGURE 9.8
Multidimensional arrays in PHP.

9.2.2.5 Personal Home Pages Functions

A function is a self-contained block of code that performs a specific task. They are used to enhance reusability of code, by segregating logically connected code segments. These code segments or parts can then be used by making a call to the function.

Argument passing and returning of values from functions are similar to that of C programming. PHP has a huge collection of internal or built-in functions that you can call directly within your PHP scripts to perform specific tasks, including gettype(), print_r(), and var_dump. In addition to the built-in functions, PHP also allows you to define your own functions. The basic syntax for creating a custom function can be given with:

```
function functionName(){
    // Code to be executed
}
```

A function name must start with a letter or underscore character (not with a number), and can contain more letters, numbers, and underscore characters. Function names are not case sensitive. The declaration of a user-defined function starts with the word function, followed by the name of the function you want to create, followed by parentheses, and then your function's code placed between curly brackets. You can also specify parameters while defining the function to accept input values at run time:

```
function myFunc($firstParameter, $secondParameter){
    // Code to be executed
}
```

A simple example of a user-defined function, getSum(), which outputs the sum of two numbers is depicted in the following:

```
<?php
// Defining function
function getSum($num1, $num2){
 $sum = $num1 + $num2;
 echo "Sum of the two numbers $num1 and $num2 is : $sum";
}
// Calling function
getSum(10, 20);
?>
```

The output of the earlier code will be the sum of the two numbers (10 and 20): 30.

9.2.2.6 Personal Home Pages Control Structures

In PHP, there are two primary types of control structures: conditional statements and control loops. The basic control structures (if, switch, while, for) behave as they do in C, including supporting break and continue. The foreach loop in PHP is a variation of the for loop, but it only works with arrays. One notable difference is that switch in PHP can accept strings as case identifiers.

9.2.2.7 Personal Home Pages Operators

The assignment operators (=, +=, *=, and so on), the Boolean operators (&&, ||, !), the comparison operators (<,>, <=, >=, ==, !=), and the basic arithmetic operators (+, -, *, /, %) all behave in PHP as they do in C.

Coding in PHP is expansive and is also used for manipulation of databases. We have tried to cover only the basics of PHP for beginners in this section of this book. PHP is recommended for making high-level web applications because:

- It has a huge community and extensive guidance because of its long development era.
- PHP has an enormous base on Web as majority of the websites are coded using it. Most content management systems (like WordPress, Drupal, Joomla, Magento) popular for building websites are written in PHP.
- It is common with hosting providers since there is no compatibility issue to make the application live on the server.
- The simplicity of PHP code means it can run as HTML by changing extension of it.
- No jar, preprocessor, no compiler, and deployment dependency exists.
- You can add PHP anywhere in your code by just using a tag that makes PHP more flexible.

Going by the recent trends, most of the startups as well as big name companies (like Netflix, *The New York Times*, PayPal, LinkedIn, and Uber) are looking for alternatives, such as Node. js, Ruby on Rails, or Python/Django instead of PHP for their tech stack. This is because:

- PHP is relatively slower than the advanced server-side development competitors, like Node.
- PHP is not suitable for making larger applications (it is best suited for e-commerce applications).
- PHP is open source, meaning anyone can access it. If there are bugs in the source code, it can be used by people to explore the weakness of PHP.

9.3 Node.js: Server-Side JavaScript

Node.js is a very powerful JavaScript-based framework/platform built on Google Chrome's JavaScript V8 Engine. It offers a server-side environment, which allows the use of JavaScript on the server. Conventionally, JavaScript has been mainly used on the client side to perform actions on web pages. However, Node.js offers a server-side environment, which allows us to use JavaScript to generate web pages. It has all the power of JavaScript and offers a whole new way of developing dynamic web sites. It is an open source, cross-platform run-time environment for developing I/O intensive web applications like video streaming sites, single-page applications, and other web applications. Since its inception, Node.js has been a popular choice because:

- It is significantly faster than PHP because of the event callback mechanism.
- It is primarily a single-threaded mechanism, but can scale on multi-core systems.
- It has separation of concerns, i.e., separate modules for any operation.
- It uses callback structure to pass logic from one call to another.
- It has less or relatively no chance of occurrence of deadlock mechanism.

When we create web sites with PHP, for example, we associate the language with an HTTP web server, such as Apache or Nginx. Each of them has its own role in the process:

- Apache manages HTTP requests to connect to the server. Its role is more or less to manage the in/out traffic.
- PHP runs the .php file's code and passes the result to Apache, which then sends it to the visitor.

As several visitors can request a page from the server at the same time, Apache is responsible for spreading out the requests and running different threads at the same time. Each thread uses a different processor on the server (or processor core). Node.js doesn't use an HTTP server like Apache. In fact, it's up to us to create the server. Unlike Apache, Node.js is mono-thread. This means that there is only one process and one version of the program that can be used at any one time in its memory. However, it does this efficiently due to the event-oriented nature of Node.js. Figures 9.9 and 9.10 show development of web sites in PHP running with Apache and Node.js, respectively.

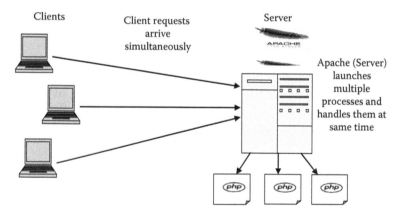

FIGURE 9.9
Creating web sites in PHP and using Apache as server.

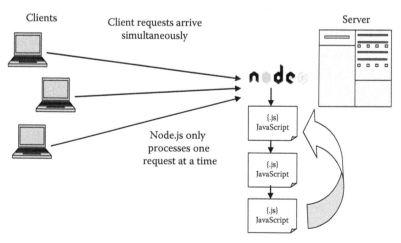

FIGURE 9.10
Creating web sites using Node.js.

Node.js only processes one request at a time. As soon as the first request starts a long operation, it moves on to the next request. As soon as the long request is finished, an event is launched and Node.js continues processing the first request. Node.js is a development environment, which allows for server-side coding in JavaScript. It is not a framework but rather a very low-level environment. There are web-based frameworks, such as Express, which are based on Node.js.

9.3.1 Installing Node.js

Installing Node.js is simple, whether it's on Windows, Mac, or Linux. To install Node.js on Windows, all you need to do is download the installer available on the Node.js web site (Figures 9.11 and 9.12).

Basically, the following 2 programs need to be installed:

- *Node.js*: The Node.js command interpreter, which is used to test JavaScript commands.
- *Node.js command prompt*: A Windows console configured to recognize Node.js, this is where we write Node.js programs.

FIGURE 9.11
The Node.js download page.

FIGURE 9.12
Installing Node.js.

9.3.2 Creating an Application in Node.js

A Node.js app is written in JavaScript under the .js extension. The app is launched with the command node filename.js. A mini web server is created, which sends a "Hi everyone" message in every case, regardless of the page requested. This server is launched on the 8080 port on the last line.

```
1. var http = require('http');
2.
3. var server = http.createServer(function(req, res) {
4. res.writeHead(200);
5. res.end('Hi everyone!');
6. });
7. server.listen(8080);
```

A node.js web application contains the following three parts:

- *Import required modules*: The "require" directive is used to load a Node.js module.
- *Create server*: You have to establish a server which will listen to the client's request similar to Apache HTTP Server.
- *Read request and return response*: The server created in the second step will read an HTTP request made by a client, which can be a browser or console, and return the response.

Let's take a look at the code:

```
var http = require('http');
```

Here, *require* makes a call to a Node.js library. It's the "http" library that allows us to create a web server. There are loads of libraries, most of them can be downloaded using NPM, the Node.js packet manager. The http variable represents the JavaScript object that will let us launch a web server and that is exactly what we're doing here:

```
var server = http.createServer()
```

The createServer() function is contained within the http object and we save this server in the server variable. All this code corresponds to a call to the createServer(). Its settings contain the function to be run when a visitor connects to our web site. Next, we are doing two simple things in the response:

```
res.writeHead(200);

res.end('Hi everyone!');
```

The status code 200 in the heading of the response tells the server everything is ok. Next, we end the response (with *end()*) by sending the message of our choice back to the browser. Here, we don't even send HTML—it is just plain text. Finally, the server is launched and listens to the 8080 port with the instruction:

```
server.listen(8080);
```

Testing the HTTP server: To test the server, we go to the console and type cd desktop on the command prompt. After that, execute main.js to start the server (Figure 9.13).

FIGURE 9.13
Server start.

Now, to make a request to the Node.js server, open your browser and go to the address http://localhost:8080. Connect your own machine to the 8080 port, on which the Node.js program is running (Figure 9.14).

Hi everyone!

FIGURE 9.14
First Node.js code shown in the browser.

Although, Node.js provides an excellent solution, it is not suitable for processor intensive tasks and any CPU-intensive code makes it non-scalable. Choosing between various development technologies depends on many parameters, such as the programmer's abilities, the type of application, development schedule, and other factors. So, it's not about choosing Node.js or PHP. It's about choosing between the two based on project requirements, such as:

- Node is suitable for complex applications that need powerful processing, while PHP is best suited for CMS-based or e-commerce applications.
- Node.js uses JavaScript as the front-end and back-end language, while PHP depends on some front-end framework or language.
- Node.js applications are much faster than PHP.
- PHP has more mature tools and libraries available than Node.js.
- Node.js has more hosting service providers than PHP.
- Node.js applications only run on dedicated host servers, while PHP applications run on shared host servers.

Review Questions

1. What did PHP initially stand for:
   a. Personal home page
   b. Pre-processor homepage
   c. Pretext hypertext processor
   d. Hypertext pre-processor
2. What is the default extension of a PHP file:
   a. .xml
   b. .html
   c. .ph
   d. .php
3. Explain the functionality of the following:
   a. Require()
   b. createServer()
4. Write a program in PHP to:
   a. Concatenate two strings
   b. Display the use of multidimensional arrays
5. Node.js is not a framework, but rather a very low-level environment. Explain its working to justify this.

10

Web Application Frameworks

10.1 Django

Django is a high-level Python web framework that encourages rapid development and clean, pragmatic design. Python uses natural language constructs and makes understanding program structure and flow significantly easier to learn. Django inherits its "batteries included" philosophy from Python. This means that Django implements some common, but complex processes by providing simple tools and wrappers to hide the complexity without compromising power.

Django's "batteries" are located in the *contrib packages*. These consist of *admin* (administration application), *auth* (authentication framework), *contenttypes* (framework for hooking into Django models), *flatpages* (framework for managing special case pages like site policies and terms and conditions of use), *gis* (adds geospatial capabilities to Django), *humanize* (adds template filters to improve readability of data), *messages* (a framework for managing session- and cookie-based messages), *postgres* (postgreSQL database-specific features), *redirects* (manages redirects), *sessions* (framework for managing anonymous sessions), *sites* (allows you to operate multiple web sites from one installation), *sitemaps* (implements sitemap XML files), and *syndication* (framework for generating syndication feeds). The following subsections present a beginner's manual to Django.

10.1.1 The Model-View-Template Architecture of Django

Django closely follows the MVC (Model-View-Controller) pattern. However, it does use its own logic in the implementation. Because the "C" is handled by the framework itself and most of the work in Django happens in models, templates, and views, Django is often referred to as an MVT (Model-View-Template) framework. The MVT architecture is slightly different from the MVC architecture. The main difference is that Django takes care of the controller aspect itself, leaving us with the template. The template is an HTML file mixed with Django Template Language (DTL). The following diagram in Figure 10.1 illustrates how each of the components of the MVT pattern interact with each other to serve a user request.

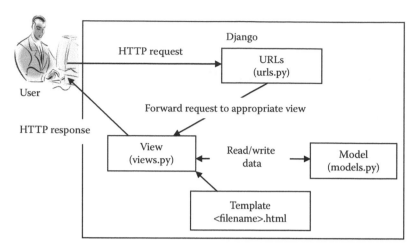

FIGURE 10.1
The MVT architecture of Django.

The developer provides the model. The view and the template then map it to a URL and Django does the magic to serve it to the user. In a traditional data-driven web site, a web application waits for HTTP requests from the web browser (or other client). When a request is received, the application works out what is needed based on the URL and possibly information in POST data or GET data. Depending on what is required it may then read or write information from a database or perform other tasks required to satisfy the request. The application will then return a response to the web browser, often dynamically creating an HTML page for the browser to display by inserting the retrieved data into placeholders in an HTML template. Django web applications typically group the code that handles each of these steps into separate files adopting the MVT development pattern:

- *URLs*: While it is possible to process requests from every single URL via a single function, it is much more maintainable to write a separate view function to handle each resource. A URL mapper is used to redirect HTTP requests to the appropriate view based on the request URL. The URL mapper can also match particular patterns of strings or digits that appear in an URL, and pass these to a view function as data.

- *M stands for Model*: The data access layer contains anything and everything about the data—how to access it, how to validate it, which behaviors it has, and the relationships between the data. Models are Python objects that define the structure of an application's data and provide mechanisms to manage (add, modify, delete) and query records in the database.

- *T stands for Template*: The presentation layer contains presentation-related decisions—how something should be displayed on a web page or other type of document. A template is a text file defining the structure or layout of a file (such as an HTML page) with placeholders used to represent actual content. A view can dynamically create an HTML page using an HTML template, populating it with data from a model. A template can be used to define the structure of any type of file; it doesn't have to be HTML.

- *V stands for View*: The business logic layer contains the logic that accesses the model and defers to the appropriate templates. This works as the bridge between models and templates. A view is a request handler function, which receives HTTP requests and returns HTTP responses. Views access the data needed to satisfy requests via models and delegate the formatting of the response to templates.

10.1.2 Advantages of Django

Django's offers a complete and versatile solution that can be used to to build almost any type of web site (from wikis to social networks), making it a prominent choice for powering web sites. Major sites like Pinterest (a pinboard-style photo sharing site), Bitbucket (a code sharing site), and Instagram (a photo sharing site) are few examples of web sites powered by Django. A few characteristics that make it a popular choice to code web sites are:

- *It has Object-Relational Mapping (ORM) support*: ORM is a technique that enables querying and manipulating data from a database using an object-oriented paradigm. An object-relational mapper is a code library that automates the transfer of data stored in relational database tables into objects that are more commonly used in application code. Django provides a bridge between the data model and the database engine and supports a large set of database systems including MySQL and NoSQL databases. ORMs provide a high-level abstraction upon a relational database that allows a developer to write Python code instead of SQL to create, read, update, and delete data and schemas in a database.

- *It has multilingual support*: Django supports multilingual web sites through its built-in internationalization system.

- *It is a Development Environment*: Django comes with a lightweight web server to facilitate end-to-end application development and testing.

- *It has Framework Support*: Django has built-in support for AJAX, RSS, caching, and other frameworks.

- *It is portable*: Django is written in Python, which runs on many platforms.

- *It is maintainable*: Django code is written using design principles and patterns that encourage the creation of maintainable and reusable code. In particular, it makes use of the "don't repeat yourself" (DRY) principle to avoid unnecessary duplication.

10.1.3 Creating a New Django Project

To create a project using Django, we need to install the following software:

- *Python*: Django is written in 100% pure Python code and the latest Django version requires Python 2.6.5 or higher. Python is a general-purpose interpreted, interactive, object-oriented, and high-level programming language. Python is available on a wide variety of platforms, including Linux and Mac OS X. The most up-to-date and current source code, binaries, documentation, news is available on the official Python web site (www.python.org).

- *Django*: Django is a high-level Python web framework that enables rapid development of secure and maintainable web sites. It follows the "batteries included" philosophy and provides almost everything developers might want to do "out of the box." Django design principles include: loose coupling, less coding, don't repeat yourself, fast development, and clean design. The latest version of Django can be downloaded from www.djangoproject.com/download.

- *Database system*: Django supports both SQL and NoSQL databases, including PostgreSQL, MySQL, SQLite, Oracle, MongoDB, and GoogleAppEngine Datastore.
- *Web server*: Django comes with a lightweight web server for developing and testing applications. This server is pre-configured to work with Django and, more importantly, it restarts whenever you modify the code. However, Django also supports Apache and other popular web servers, such as Lighttpd.

Thus, to create a sample application in Django, we follow the following steps:

- Create a new Django project.
- Run the development server.
- Create a Django application.
- Tell the Django project about the new application by adding it to the *INSTALLED_APPS* tuple in the project's *settings.py* file.
- Add a mapping to the application in the *urls.py* file to direct incoming URL strings to views.
- Run the server to display the response.

Let us now create our first Django application, which will display Hello World.

1. *Create a project*: First, we create a HelloWorld project as follows:

```
$ django-admin.py startproject HelloWorld
$ cd HelloWorld
$ ls
HelloWorld   manage.py
```

This newly created HelloWorld project has two elements: the manage.py file and the HelloWorld folder. The manage.py file is kind of the local django-admin for interacting with your project via command line. The HelloWorld folder is the actual python package of your project and contains the following four files:

a. **__init__.py:** An empty file that tells Python that this directory should be considered a Python package.

b. **settings.py:** Settings and configuration for this Django project.

c. **urls.py:** The URL declarations for this Django project. Essentially a table of contents of our Django-powered site. This is a file to hold the URLs of our web site, such as http://localhost/HelloWorldApp. In order to use /HelloWorldApp in our HelloWorld project, we have to mention it in urls.py.

d. **wsgi.py:** An entry-point for WSGI (web server gateway interface) compatible web servers to serve our project. This file handles our requests and responses to and from the Django development server.

2. *Run the development server*: Inside the HelloWorld project directory, we now run the development server as follows:

```
$ python manage.py runserver
```

This would result in the following:

```
Validating models...

0 errors found
...
Django version 1.6.11, using settings 'HelloWorld.settings'
Starting development server at http://127.0.0.1:8000/
Quit the server with CONTROL-C.
```

Open a browser and enter "http://127.0.0.1:8000/" into the URL box. We get the default page (Figure 10.2).

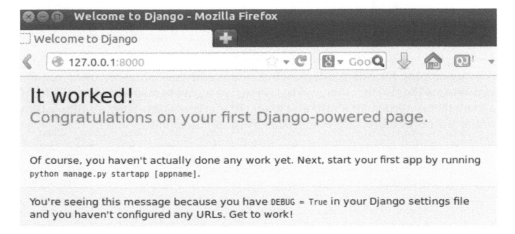

FIGURE 10.2
Django default page.

3. *Create the application*: To create a Hello World app (inside the HelloWorld project directory), we need to run the following command:

```
$ django-admin startapp HelloWorldApp
$ ls
HelloWorld  HelloWorldApp  manage.py
```

The django-admin startapp creates the following files:

a. **__init__.py:** Indicates our app as a Python package.
b. **models.py:** Holds our database information.
c. **views.py:** Functions to hold requests and logic.
d. **tests.py:** For testing.

4. *Add application to the project*: Edit settings.py under the HelloWorld project directory to add the application HelloWorldApp as shown here:

```
# Application definition

INSTALLED_APPS = (
  'django.contrib.admin',
  'django.contrib.auth',
  'django.contrib.contenttypes',
  'django.contrib.sessions',
  'django.contrib.messages',
  'django.contrib.staticfiles',
  'HelloWorldApp',
)
```

5. *View request mapping*: To know what view to send a particular request, Django uses a mapping file called urls.py, which maps addresses to views using regular expressions (RegEx). In other words, Django has a way to map a requested URL to a view that is needed for a response via regular expressions. Thus, editing urls.py under the project directory enables this mapping, as follows:

```
from django.conf.urls import patterns, include, url
from HelloWorldApp.views import foo

#from django.contrib import admin
#admin.autodiscover()

urlpatterns = patterns('',
  # Examples:
  # url(r'^$', 'HelloWorld.views.home', name='home'),
  # url(r'^blog/', include('blog.urls')),

  #url(r'^admin/', include(admin.site.urls)),
  url(r'HelloWorldApp/$', foo),
)
```

In the commented lines, we have ^$. Since the caret character (^) means the start and the dollar sign ($) means the end, ^$ indicates we got nothing. The *r* in "url(r...)" is not a part of RegEx—it is Python indicating "raw" to prevent any character in RegEx from being parsed in Python's way. In other words, it tells Python that a string is "raw" and that nothing in the string should be escaped.

The url() is a function call that builds URL patterns. It takes five arguments, most of which are optional:

```
url(regex, view, kwargs=None, name=None, prefix='')
```

The foo is the Python import string to get to a view.

6. *Create views*: Edit the views.py file under the app directory, as follows:

```
# Create your views here.
from django.http import HttpResponse
def foo(request):
  return HttpResponse("Hello World!")
```

This views.py file takes a request object and returns a response object. We first import the HttpResponse object from the django.http module. Each view exists within the views.py file as a series of individual functions. In our case, we only created one view, called foo. Each view takes in at least one argument—an HttpRequest object—which also lives in the django.http module. Each view must return an HttpResponse object. A simple HttpResponse object takes a string parameter representing the content of the page we wish to send to the client that is requesting the view.

7. *Run the server*:

```
$ python manage.py runserver
```

Type http://localhost:8000/HelloWorldApp/ and we get the successful "Hello World!" (Figure 10.3).

Hello World!

FIGURE 10.3
"Hello World" in Django.

10.2 Ruby on Rails

Ruby on Rails (RoR) is an open-source, full-stack framework written in Ruby for developing database-backed web applications. Full stack implies it includes everything: a simple web server to test your apps, a database layer, a testing framework, and an MVC-based design. It uses the Model-View-Controller architecture pattern to organize application programming. A model in a Ruby on Rails framework maps to a table in a database. A controller is the component of Rails that responds to external requests from the web server to the application and responds to the external request by determining which view file to render. A view in the default configuration of Rails is an .erb file. It is typically converted to output HTML at runtime.

The Rails framework was extracted from real-world web applications. Thus, it is an easy-to-use and cohesive framework that's rich in functionality. All layers in Rails are built to work together and use a single language from top to bottom. Everything in Rails (templates to control flow to business logic) is written in Ruby, except for its configuration files, which are YAML. To understand the framework, you should have knowledge of how to code using Ruby and knowledge of database engines.

Ruby is a dynamic, general-purpose object-oriented programming language that combines syntax inspired by Perl (also influenced by Eiffel and Lisp). In Ruby, everything is an object. Ruby is an interpreted language and supports multiple programming paradigms, including functional, object-oriented, imperative, and reflective. It has a dynamic type system and automatic memory management.

10.2.1 The Model-View-Controller Architecture of Ruby on Rails

Ruby on Rails follows a Model-View-Controller architecture. The MVC design pattern separates the component parts of an application:

- Model encapsulates data that the application manipulates and the domain-specific logic. It responds to queries, exposes application functionality, and notifies views of changes. Models are classes that talk to the database. You find, create, and save models so you don't have to write SQL. Rails has a class to handle the magic of saving to a database when a model is updated. It maintains the relationship between the objects and the database and handles validation, association, transactions, and more. This subsystem is implemented in *ActiveRecord library*, which provides an interface and binding between the tables in a relational database and the Ruby program code that manipulates database records. Ruby method names are automatically generated from the field names of database tables.

- View is a rendering of the model into the user interface. It is a presentation of data in a particular format, triggered by a controller's decision to present the data. It requests updates from models, sends user gestures to the controller, and allows the controller to select the view. Views display the output, usually HTML. This subsystem is implemented in *ActionView library*, which is an Embedded Ruby (ERB)-based system for defining presentation templates for data presentation. Every web connection to a Rails application results in the displaying of a view.

- Controller defines the application behavior. It responds to events from the interface and causes actions to be performed on the model (i.e., it maps user actions to model updates). It also selects views for response. Controllers take user input (like a URL) and decide what to do (show a page, order an item, post a comment, etc.). This subsystem is implemented in *ActionController*, which is a data negotiator sitting between ActiveRecord (the database interface) and ActionView (the presentation engine).

The MVC pattern allows rapid change and evolution of the user interface and controller separate from the data model (Figure 10.4).

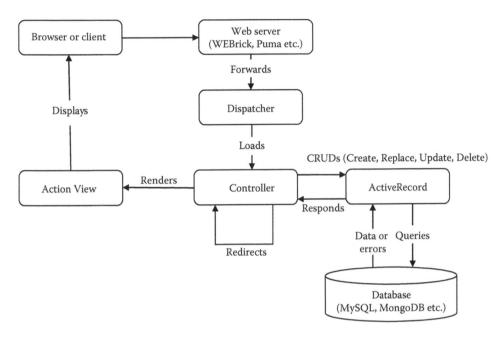

FIGURE 10.4
The MVC architecture of RoR.

Rails enforces the MVC structure for your application as follows:

- *ActiveRecord*: The ActiveRecord library is the model support in Rails. It provides the Object-Relational Mapping in Rails. Rails (model) classes provide a set of class-level methods that perform table-level operations where tables map to classes, rows to objects, and columns to object attributes. Each record object has CRUD (create, read, update, and delete) methods for database access and adds attributes automatically based on the columns in the database. ActiveRecord minimizes the amount of configuration that developers perform. Table 10.1 lists out the differences between a SQL and an ActiveRecord model.

TABLE 10.1

SQL versus ActiveRecord

SQL	ActiveRecord
Relational	Object-oriented
Table	Class
Row	Object
Columns	Attributes
Table level operations	Class methods
Row level operations	Object methods
CREATE TABLE people (id INT(11) NOT NULL auto_increment, name VARCHAR(100), PRIMARY KEY (id)) „	class Person < ActiveRecord::Base; end Person.create(:name => "Rachel Green") rachel = Person.find_by_name("Rachel Green") rachel.name = "Ross Geller" rachel.save

- *Action Pack*: The controller supplies data to the view and the controller receives events from the pages generated by the views. Action Pack is a single gem that bundles both views and controllers. It contains Action Controller, Action View, and Action Dispatch (the VC part of MVC).

  - *Action Controller*: This component manages the controllers in a Rails application. The Action Controller framework processes incoming requests to a Rails application, extracts parameters, and dispatches them to the intended action. Services provided by Action Controller include session management, template rendering, and redirect management.

  - *Action View*: This manages the views of your Rails application. It can create both HTML and XML output by default. Action View manages rendering templates, including nested and partial templates, and includes built-in AJAX support. It creates either all or part of a page to be displayed in a browser. Dynamic content is generated by templates. The most common template scheme to embed the code is *rhtml*, which embeds snippets of Ruby code within the view's HTML. Another template scheme is *rxml*, which is used to construct XML documents using Ruby code. A third template scheme is *rjs*, which lets you create JavaScript fragments on the server that can then be executed in the browser.

  - *Action Dispatch:* This handles routing of web requests and dispatches them as you want, either to your application or to another Rails application.

Apart from these components, Rails includes other components, as shown in Figure 10.5.

- *Action Mailer*: This is a framework for building e-mail services. You can use Action Mailer to receive and process incoming messages and send simple plain text or complex multipart messages based on flexible templates.

- *Active Model*: This provides a defined interface between the Action Pack gem services and Object-Relationship Mapping gems, such as Active Record. Active Model allows Rails to utilize other ORM frameworks in place of Active Record if your application needs this.

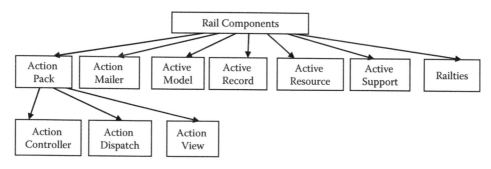

FIGURE 10.5
Rail components.

- *Active Resource*: This provides a framework for managing the connection between business objects and RESTful web services. It provides a way to map web-based resources to local objects with CRUD semantics.
- *Active Support*: This is an extensive collection of utility classes and standard Ruby library extensions that are used in Rails, both by the core code and by applications.
- *Railties*: This is the core Rails code that builds new Rails applications and glues the various frameworks and plug-ins together in any Rails application.

10.2.2 Creating a New Rails Project

To create a project using Ruby on Rails, we need to install the following software:

- *Ruby*: A programming language similar to Python and Perl. It is dynamically typed, interpreted, and can be modified at run time. It has dozens of shortcuts that make it very clean—methods are rarely over 10 lines. It has good RegEx support and works well for shell scripting.
- *Rails*: Rails is a gem, or a Ruby library. Some gems let you use the Win32 API while others handle networking. Rails helps make web applications, providing classes for saving to the database, handling URLs, and displaying HTML (along with a web server, maintenance tasks, a debugging console, and much more). Although Rails is "just another gem," it is the killer library that brought Ruby into the limelight.
- *Database system*: By default, Rails uses sqlite3, but you may want to install MySQL, PostgreSQL, or another database solution.
- *Web server*: WEBrick and Puma Web Server come with Ruby. WEBrick is single threaded, single process. This means that if two requests come in at the same time, the second request must wait for the first to finish. Alternatively, Puma provides a modern concurrent web server.

To create a sample application in Rails, we follow the following steps:

- Use the Rails command to create the basic framework of the application.
- Start the web server and create a database server to hold your data, configuring the application to know where your database is located and the login credentials for it.
- Create Rails Active Records (Models), which are the business objects you'll be working with in your controllers.
- Generate migrations, which simplify creating and maintaining database tables and columns.
- Write controller code to make the application real-time.
- Create views to present your data in user interfaces.

Now let's create our first Rails application, which will "Hi World!"

As described earlier, to develop a web application using Ruby on Rails, we need to install Ruby, the Rails framework, a web server, and a database system. So we will start with these steps:

1. *Install Rails:*

---

1) Open up a command line prompt (On macOS open Terminal.app, on Windows choose "Run" from your Start menu) and type 'cmd.exe'
2) A dollar sign $ should be run in the command line.
3) Verify that you have a current version of Ruby installed

```
$ ruby -v
ruby 2.3.1p112
```

4) On Windows, if you installed Rails through Rails Installer, you already have SQLite installed. To verify:

```
$ sqlite3 --version
```

5) To install Rails, use the gem install command provided by RubyGems and then verify it:

```
$ gem install rails
```

```
$ rails --version
```

6) It will display "Rails 5.1.0" and so the Rails has been successfully installed and we are ready to continue.

---

2. *Start the server:* To do this, go to the parent directory of the Rails application and enter the following command:

```
$ bin/rails server
```

This will fire up Puma and produce the output shown in Figure 10.6:

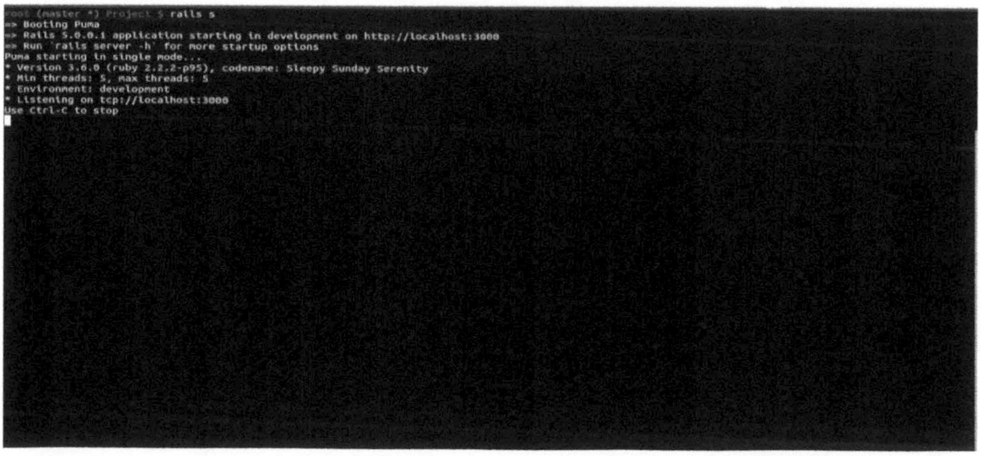

FIGURE 10.6
Output from Puma.

FIGURE 10.7
Page in Rails.

When you open a browser window and navigate to http://localhost:3000, the page shown in Figure 10.7 will be generated.

3. *Create the app*: To create your first Rails application, pop open a shell window and navigate to create your application in the directory structure. In our example, we'll be creating our application in a directory called *project*. In that directory, use the Rails command to create an application called *sample*:

```
root>cd project>rails samplecreate
create app/controllers
create app/helpers
create app/models
: : :
create log/development.log
create log/test.log
project>
```

The command has created a directory named sample. This directory has a number of auto-generated files and subdirectories that make up the structure of a Rails application:

```
project>cd sample
sample>ls-p
README        components/doc/   public/    tmp/
Rakefile      config/           lib/       vendor/
app/          db/               log/       test/
```

All these have a distinct role to play, but the most important ones are:

- **app**
  - *controllers*: Sits between client and database.
  - *helpers*: Module with common Ruby code.
  - *models*: Code to interface with the database.
  - *views*: Web pages containing HTML and ERB.
  - *db*: Contains database.
    - *migration*: Methods to change the database.
- **script**
  - *console*: Interactive console window for Ruby code.
  - *dbconsole*: Interactive console window for the database.
  - *generate*: Methods to generate scaffolding and migrations.
  - *server*: Activates server to be used with localhost.

To write a simple Hi World! application, we need code for a controller and a view. We don't need code for a model because we're not dealing with any data. Let's start with the controller.

We use a generator script to create a new controller for our project. The *generate* command is used from the script subdirectory of the sample application we created. So, to create a controller called display, we make sure we're in the sample directory and run the script, passing in the name of the controller we want to create:

```
sample>ruby script/generate controller Display
                exists   app/controllers/
                exists   app/helpers/
                create   app/views/say
                exists   test/functional/
                create   app/controllers/say_controller.rb
    create test/functional/say_controller_test.rb create app/helpers/say_helper.rb
```

DisplayController is an empty class that inherits from ApplicationController, so it automatically gets all the default controller behavior.

Now let's add an action called *hi* to our display controller. This means we will be creating a method called *hi* in the class DisplayController. The controller class and the action method have been created and now to complete our Hi World! application, we create a template. By default, Rails looks for templates in the file with the same name as the action it is handling. This means we need to create a file called hi.rhtml in the directory app/views/display. Adding basic HTML:

```
<html>
<head>
  <title>Greetings from Rails!</title> </head>
<body>
  <h1>Hi World!</h1> </body>
</html>
```

Hi World!

FIGURE 10.8
"Hi World" in Rails.

Save the file hi.rhtml and refresh your browser window to see the friendly greeting (Figure 10.8).

10.2.3 Strengths of Ruby on Rails

- *Advocates agile web development*: Agile web development techniques and RoR technology are a great fit for one another. While agile development is all about embracing changes, handling database changes is never an easy task. However, RoR not only gives developers a respite from building databases from scratch, it also adapts to changes very easily. This is a valuable asset when making multiple iterations to your product and in the ultimate quest for achieving customer satisfaction.

- *Convention over configuration*: Developers focus on "what" they're doing rather than "how" they're doing. Most web development frameworks for .NET or Java force you to write pages of configuration code. If you follow suggested naming conventions, Rails doesn't need much configuration. In fact, you can often cut your total configuration code by a factor of five or more over similar Java frameworks just by following common conventions.

- *Meta-programming*: Ruby is one of the best languages for meta-programming, and Rails uses this capability well. Meta-programming techniques use programs to write programs. Other frameworks use extensive code generation, which gives users a one-time productivity boost, but customization scripts let the user add customization code in only a small number of carefully selected points.

- *Don't repeat yourself*: DRY is a principle of software development that states that "every piece of knowledge must have a single, unambiguous, authoritative representation within a system." By not writing the same information over and over again, our code is more maintainable, more extensible, and less buggy.

- *Scaffolding*: Developers often create temporary code in the early stages of development to help get an application up quickly and see how major components work together. Rails automatically creates much of the scaffolding, enabling a faster way to build an application prototype.

- *Test-driven development*: Rails embraces test-driven development. Unit testing for testing individual pieces of code, functional testing for testing how individual pieces of code interact, and integration testing for testing the whole system.

Still, although RoR has much going for it, there are areas where it is losing ground, especially due to its slow runtime, boot speed, and difficult learning curve.

Review Questions

1. Describe the architecture of the Django framework.
2. How is a project created in Django?
3. Explain how you can set up the database in Django?
4. Give an example of writing a view in Django?
5. What do the Django templates consist of?
6. How does Ruby on Rails use the Model-View-Controller framework?
7. Along with ActiveRecord, what other modules make up Rails?
8. What are some advantages of using Ruby on Rails?
9. Explain the role of the subdirectories app/controllers and app/helpers in Rails.

11

Web Databases

11.1 Web Database

A web database is a database that can be queried and/or updated through the World Wide Web. It is a system for storing information that can then be accessed via a web site. For example, an online community may have a database that stores the usernames, passwords, and other details of all its members.

Database technology concerns about adopting the right database model and breaking the "one model fits all" approach to handle data. Each database system implements a model to logically structure the data that is being managed. Models must meet the needs of varied types of data (from data that is not changing in structure and is moderately growing at a manageable pace to data that is scaling enormously and changing rapidly). To meet the technology requirements popular databases are categorized into two variants: relational (SQL) and non-relational (NoSQL) databases. These differ in the way data is represented, structured, and stored. Relational databases are structured and require schemas to be defined before adding any data. For example, a phonebook that stores data about customers, such as phone numbers, first and last name, city, and state. A non-relational database is document-oriented and distributed with no predefined schema. For example, a file folder that holds everything from a person's address and phone number to their Facebook profile and online shopping preferences. It is important to select the appropriate data model while keeping in mind the pros and cons of each type if you want to develop consistent systems.

11.2 Structured Query Language: Relational Databases

Developed by IBM in the 1970s, a SQL database (or a relational database) consists of two or more tables with columns and rows providing a stringent, structured way of storing data. Each row represents an entry, and each column sorts a very specific type of information. The relationship between tables and field types is referred to as a schema and must be clearly defined before any information can be added.

Structured Query Language (SQL) is a programming language used by database architects to design relational databases. In a SQL database like MySQL, Sybase, Oracle, or IBM DM2, SQL executes queries, retrieves data, and edits data by updating, deleting, or creating new records. SQL is a lightweight, declarative language that does a lot of heavy lifting for the relational database, acting like a database's version of a server-side script. Some examples of popular SQL databases are:

- *MySQL*: The most popular open source database, excellent for CMS and blogs
- *Oracle*: An object-relational DBMS (database management system) written in C++. Oracle has also released an Oracle NoSQL database
- *IBM DB2*: A family of database server products from IBM built to handle advanced "big data" analytics
- *Microsoft SQL Server*: A Microsoft-developed DBMS for enterprise-level databases that supports both SQL and NoSQL architectures
- *Microsoft Azure*: A cloud computing platform that supports any operating system and lets you store, compute, and scale data in one place
- *MariaDB*: An enhanced, drop-in version of MySQL
- *PostgreSQL*: An enterprise-level, object-relational DBMS that uses procedural languages like Perl and Python, in addition to SQL-level code

11.3 NoSQL Databases: Non-relational and Distributed Data

Modern application developers transact with massive volumes of new, rapidly changing data types, including structured, semi-structured, unstructured, and polymorphic data. Developing a clearly defined, well-organized schema is impossible for such massive amounts of unstructured data. NoSQL databases offer a schema-less alternative to their traditional counterparts, providing greater flexibility. Thus, instead of tables, NoSQL databases are document-oriented. This way, non-structured data (such as articles, photos, social media data, videos, or content within a blog post) can be stored in a single document. Based on the method of representation of data in databases, NoSQL databases can be categorized as follows:

- *Key-value model*: The least complex NoSQL option, which stores data in a schema-less way that consists of indexed keys and values. Examples include Cassandra, Azure, LevelDB, and Riak.
- *Column store or wide-column store*: Stores data tables as columns rather than rows. This is more than just an inverted table—sectioning out columns allows for excellent scalability and high performance. Examples include HBase, BigTable, and HyperTable.
- *Document database*: Follows the key-value concept and adds more complexity—each document in this type of database has its own data and its own unique key, which is used for retrieval. This is a great option for storing, retrieving, and managing data that is document-oriented but still somewhat structured. Examples include MongoDB and CouchDB.
- *Graph database*: Composed of two elements—a node and a relationship. Each node represents an entity (a person, place, thing, category, or other piece of data) and each relationship represents how two nodes are associated. New business requirements and big-data have made graph model a technology solution as it allows frequent schema changes, manages explosive volume of data, offers real-time query response time, and supports more intelligent data activation requirements. Examples include TigerGraph (formerly GraphSQL), Neo4j, and DataStax.

TABLE 11.1

SQL versus NoSQL

Feature	SQL Databases	NoSQL Databases
Data organization	Stored in a relational model as a table with rows and columns. Rows contain all of the information about one specific entry/entity and columns are all the separate data points. For example, you might have a row about a specific car, in which the columns are Make, Model, Color, and so on.	The term "NoSQL" encompasses a host of databases, each with varied data storage models. The primary ones are: document, graph, key-value, and columnar.
Schema and flexibility	Each record conforms to the fixed schema. The columns must be decided prior to data entry and each row must contain data for each column. This can be amended, but it involves altering the whole database and going offline.	Schemas are dynamic. Information can be added on the fly and each "row" (or equivalent) does not have to contain data for each "column."
Scalability	Scaling is vertical. This implies the more data, the bigger the server, thus making it expensive. It is possible to scale an RDBMS across multiple servers, but this is a difficult and time-consuming process.	Scaling is horizontal, distributed across servers. These servers are cost-effective (cheap commodity hardware or cloud-based).
Data manipulation	Specific language using Select, Insert, and Update statements (e.g., SELECT fields FROM table WHERE).	Through object-oriented APIs.
Suitability	• Ensure ACID compliance (atomicity, consistency, isolation, and durability). • Data is structured, consistent, and unchanging.	• Store large volumes of data that often have little to no structure. • Rapid (Agile) development. • Make the most of cloud computing and storage. • ACID compliance varies between technologies, but many NoSQL solutions sacrifice it for performance, flexibility, and scalability.
Examples	MySQL, PostgreSQL, Microsoft SQL Server, Oracle Database.	MongoDB, Cassandra, HBase, Neo4j.
Development model	Mix of open source (e.g., PostgreSQL, MySQL) and closed source (e.g., Oracle Database).	Open source.

Table 11.1 lists the differences between SQL and NoSQL databases.

11.4 Understanding Popular Databases

As a primer to the most commonly used databases, we explain a few in the following sections. The discussion is limited to understanding the most popular MySQL (relational), MongoDB (non-relational), and Neo4j (non-relational).

- *MySQL* is a popular open-source relational database management system developed, distributed, and supported by Oracle Corporation. It stores data in tables and uses structured query language (SQL) for database access. In MySQL, the database schema is pre-defined based on the requirements and set up rules to govern the relationships between fields in your tables. Related information may be stored in separate tables but associated with the use of joins. In this way, data duplication is minimized.

- *MongoDB* is an open source database developed by MongoDB, Inc. It stores data in JSON-like documents that can vary in structure. Related information is stored together for fast query access through the MongoDB query language. MongoDB uses dynamic schemas, which allow the creation of records without first defining the structure, such as the fields or the types of their values. Moreover, the structure of records (which we call documents) can be changed by simply adding new fields or deleting existing ones. This data model gives an ability to represent hierarchical relationships, store arrays, and support other more complex structures easily. Documents in a collection are not required to have an identical set of fields and de-normalization of data is common. MongoDB was designed with high availability and scalability in mind and it includes out-of-the-box replication and auto-sharding (a method for distributing data across multiple machines).

- *Neo4j* offers a free, open source Community edition, which is a high-performance, fully ACID-transactional database. The primary advantage of Neo4j is its lightning fast ability to do very complex queries with unlimited depth and weighted connections. You should definitely store graphs like Users and relationships like Friendship or Subscriber inside Neo4j.

Let's consider a case study of a simplified professor rating system to demonstrate these databases. This example is based on the data storage structure, relationships, and querying. The idea is to understand the representation know-how of data storage for a system for a selected database, akin to www.ratemyprofessor.com where we would track users, professors, and which professors a user has reviewed. (*Rate My Professor is a popular college professor reviews and ratings source based on student feedback*.).

11.4.1 Data Storage Structure

This section looks at the details on the way user data is stored in each of these databases.

- *MySQL*: In MySQL database, data is stored as rows in a table. Each table stores a specific category of data (e.g., users or professors) and has a predefined list of properties for every element in that table (i.e., columns). In our application, users have properties like ID, first name, and last name. We also have an optional parameter: Middle name (some of our users enter it and some don't). Because all data elements in a table must have the same properties, we enter null wherever we don't have a middle name.

UserID	First Name	Middle Name	Last Name
1	Alice	Mary	John
2	Bob	*Null*	Martin
3	Robert	*Null*	William
4	Charlotte	Lee	Pang

- *MongoDB*: Every data element in MongoDB is stored in a JSON-style object called a document. Similar types of documents are held within a collection, much the same way MySQL uses rows and tables. In our system, we'll create user documents and store those in a user's collection. For developers, this object-oriented design should feel very intuitive, as it allows you to use simple dot notation to access properties (user.firstName === "Alice"). A major benefit of MongoDB over MySQL is a flexible data structure. Everything is stored as an object, which allows us to add or remove properties on the fly. Since only some users have a middle name, we can add that property to individual documents without affecting the collection as a whole. Another advantage is the ability to nest arrays and objects within documents. As in the following example, we've added an address property with an object for its value. That object stores both the street and city, allowing us to store all related data in one place within the document:

```
{
_id:UserId,
firstName: Alice,
lastName: John,
address: {
          street: Downtown
          city: Los Angeles
          }
}
```

- *Neo4j*: The Neo4j equivalent of a MySQL row or a MongoDB document is a node. Like MongoDB, nodes do not have set schema and properties can be added or removed as needed. In this example, our user node has a system assigned ID, a firstName, and a lastName. We can query these using dot notation (user.first-Name). We can add new properties or update existing ones in a similar fashion (SET user.middleName = "Mary"). Grouping types of data in Neo4j is done a bit differently than in MySQL and MongoDB (Figure 11.1).

FIGURE 11.1
Neo4j node and label.

You'll see in the top left that this node has a Label of User. Labels are the tool we use to group similar types of data. For simplicity, think of a Label as the Neo4j equivalent of a table or collection, but understand that there is no actual central storage of similar types of nodes—a Label is more like a node property than the name of a table that exists elsewhere. Another major difference is that nodes should contain very little data. We get the majority of the information about a specific node from its relationships to other nodes, which we'll discuss a bit more in the next section.

11.4.2 Relationships

Once we have our data, the next step is to make connections between the users and the professors they are reviewing.

- *MySQL*: A typical way might be to add a new column in the user table for each professor and store the user's review in that cell. But in this case, the user table will expand both vertically (as new users are added) and horizontally (as new professors are added). Moreover, as a new column will be applied to every user in the table, the majority of these fields will be null for most users, thus increasing the space complexity. A join table can be employed for storing relationships between two different tables. In our system, we already have a user table and a professor table, so we'll create a user/professor join table that maps these two tables together (Figure 11.2).

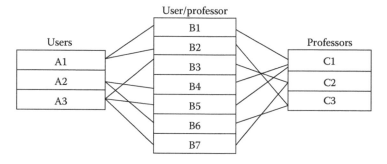

FIGURE 11.2
MySQL join.

The join user/professor table stores the following four things:
- *UserId*: The unique ID of the user from the user table
- *ProfessorId*: The unique ID of the professor from the professor table
- *Rating*: A rating that the user provides
- *Review*: An optional text review provided by the user (this field will be null if not entered). This table (see Table 11.2) is only responsible for storing relationships and does not store any user or professor specific data. Instead, the ID references to a row in another table are stored so that we can find the supporting data we need.

TABLE 11.2

Sample SQL Entries

UserID	ProfessorID	Rating	Review
1	99	LOVED	//text
1	98	HATED	//text
2	99	LOVED	//text
3	97	JUST OKAY	*Null*
3	98	LOVED	*Null*
3	99	HATED	*Null*

- *MongoDB*: To store relationships in MongoDB, the data is nested within the document. Every user will have a property called *ratings*, which will store an array of objects. Each of these objects will hold an individual professor review, just like a row in a MySQL join table. This structure offers the following benefits: First off, since it's already stored within the user document, we just need to keep track of the professor_id, the user rating, and the optional review. Secondly, we only need to add the review property to the database if it has been added by the user, giving us additional flexibility.

```
{
_id:UserId,
firstName: Alice,
lastName: John,
ratings: [
        {
           professorId:
professor_id,
           rating: LOVED
        }, {
           professorId:
professor_id,
           rating: HATED
        }
     ]
}
```

- *Neo4j*: In Neo4j, relationships are represented as lines that connect two different nodes (Figure 11.3). These relationships can be unidirectional or bidirectional and can even contain properties specific to that relationship. Moreover, the relationships, just like Nodes, have a type that gives information about the connection between two nodes. We don't need to create a property on the user called rating because the name of the relationship gives us that information. If the user writes a review, we can store it directly on the relationship itself, keeping the data within nodes trim. The biggest benefit of using this storage structure is the ease of querying across the entire database, which we'll cover in the next section.

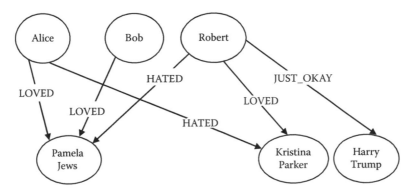

FIGURE 11.3
Neo4j relationships.

11.4.3 Querying

To extract meaningful information from these rows/documents/nodes and respective join tables/nested arrays/relationships, a proper querying protocol needs to be established. In this section, we demonstrate the use and results of the following two queries that are input to the varied storage structures:

- Which professors did a specific user love?
- Which users have reviewed a specific professor?

In the following examples, we'll specifically query for the user Alice and the Professor Pamela Jews, but the query structure is what we're really looking at.

- **MySQL: Get all professors that a specific user loved**

```
SELECT user.*, professor.*
FROM user, professor, joinTable
WHERE user.firstName = 'Alice'
AND user.id = joinTable.userId
AND professor.id = joinTable.professorId
AND joinTable.rating = 'LOVED'
```

Firstly, we need to formulate a query to extract the information we want. This is done using the keyword SELECT. An asterisk (*) tells the system to return all properties from that table. Thus, in the first line we capture all properties from any user and any professor that match with the WHERE clause. Next, the FROM keyword is used to locate where to look for this data. Finally, the WHERE statement helps to filter down the results we want. The first WHERE statement makes sure to extract the appropriate user. The next two lines are then used to match the data in the join table (which only contains references) to the detailed data that is stored in either the user table or the professor table. The last line is used to make sure we only extract the appropriate lines in the join table.

- **MySQL: Get all users that reviewed a specific professor**

```
SELECT user.*, professor.*
FROM user, professor, joinTable
WHERE professor.name = 'Pamela Jews'
AND user.id = joinTable.userId
AND professor.id = joinTable.professorId
```

- **MongoDB: Get all professors that a specific user loved**

```
db.users.aggregate(
{ $match: {firstName: Alice} },
{ $unwind: '$ratings' },
{ $match: { $ratings.rating : LOVED } } )
```

Let's examine each part of the query first individually and then completely. Most queries for MongoDB start with db, which signifies the current database in use. The next part is the collection we want to proceed into, which in this case is the user collection. Normally, *.find()* or *.findAll()* is used to extract specific documents that match our query, but since we want to satisfy multiple requirements, we need to use the *.aggregate()* function to string together multiple queries. A series of objects, each containing key/value pairs of the actions we want, are passed to the *aggregate*. Keys that start with a $ are the MongoDB native functions that are used.

Thus, the following steps create the complete query:

```
1. Go to the db
2. Find the users collection
3. Run the following queries in order
4. Match and return the user document that has a firstName of 'Alice'
5. Find the ratings property within that user's document and return only the
   values of that property
6. Match and return the objects within the previously returned value where rating
   equals LOVED
```

- **MongoDB: Get all users that reviewed a specific professor**

```
??????
```

The answer to this query is not easy with the current data storage structure. We have alternatives to answer this query, but each one has a drawback.

- *Alternative 1*: We could iterate over every single user in the user collection, then iterate through every single object in the rating array and return only users that have a rating object for the given professor. But, if we scale the database to a size similar to that of Rate My Professor with 100 million users, it is going to take too long for a query to run an instance, thus making this alternative a complex, time-consuming, expensive, and non-feasible approach.

- *Alternative 2*: Another option would be to duplicate the data in our professor collection. This would mean creating a ratings property in the professor document and whenever a user creates a new review, we add a userId/review object to professor.ratings and a professorId/review object to the user.ratings array, and then use an aggregate function.

- *Alternative 3*: A third alternative would be to create the MongoDB equivalent of a join table. We would create a new collection that stores rating documents with the same information that was in our MySQL join table. This option might be faster than the previous one because it only contains the data we're looking for, but we'll likely need to do subsequent lookups if we need more than just the user or professorID.

  There isn't a strong recommendation of which of these options to choose as it really depends on the scale of your database and how often you're querying for the data. However, the practical aspect suggests that MongoDB isn't designed for these types of multidirectional relationships and should be avoided for such type of applications.

- **Neo4j: Get all professors that a specific user loved**

Neo4j is designed to find patterns. It scans the database and quickly finds the nodes and relationships that match the pattern queried. Cypher is the query language that Neo4j uses and is designed to answer semantically related queries.

```
MATCH (u:User {firstName:'Alice'})-[rel:LOVED]->(prof:Professor)
RETURN prof
```

Each component of the query is explained in the following:

1. *MATCH*: Find the following pattern.
2. *(u: User {firstName:'Alice'})*: Using parentheses tells Neo4j that we are looking for a node. We then give this node a name that is specific to this query (u). This name isn't stored anywhere on the node; it is just used for reference and any later use in the query. We then provide the Label and finally pass a query object for the parameters we want this node to match.
3. *-[rel:LOVED]->*: Look for any LOVED relationships that start at the user node and point to another node.
4. *(prof:Professor)*: The node that the relationship points to must be a professor.
5. *RETURN res*: Returns any professor nodes you find that match this pattern.

This query returns an array of objects, where each object is a different professor node that matches this pattern. If we want just the professor name, we can use dot notation and RETURN prof.name. If we wanted to view the user entered review, we could RETURN rel.review since Neo4j allows us to store data on the relationship itself.

- **Neo4j: Get all users that reviewed a specific professor**

```
MATCH (u:User)-[rel]->(prof:Professor) {name: 'Pamela Jews'})
RETURN u
```

The query is very similar to the previous search query. We just modified the query objects to match what we're looking for and removed the relationship type restriction. Now it finds any user with any relationship to the specified professor. If we want to know the user and their rating of the professor, we can update the last bit to RETURN u, type(rel).

MySQL was released 18 years ago and is currently the 2nd most popular relational database. It is very robust and trusted by some of the world's biggest organizations. MongoDB is gaining popularity in the tech community because it uses objects, a common construct across all programming languages. It is extremely convenient that related data is stored in a single document and there is no need to join tables because everything is in one place. However, it is difficult with complex queries. To answer chained queries (match this and this and this), though the easiest solution is to duplicate data, but using it as a technical solution it's a trade-off. Neo4j, though not technically a relational database, is fantastic for any project where the relationship between data elements is just as important as the data itself. Neo4j automatically indexes popular nodes so your queries will actually get faster the more times they run. Moreover, Neo4j answers semantic queries. Facebook uses a graph database to allow you to write things like "Show me professors in India that my friends liked." While this query would be tough in MySQL or MongoDB, it is very easy in Neo4j. Table 11.3 summarizes the key features of each of these database types.

TABLE 11.3

Summary of Popular Web Databases

Name	MySQL	MongoDB	Neo4j
Database model	Relational DBMS	Document Store	Graph DBMS
Initial release	1995	2009	2007
License	Open Source	Open Source	Open Source
Implementation language	C and C++	C++	Java, Scala
Data scheme	Yes	Schema-free	Schema-free
SQL	Yes	No	No
APIs and other access methods	ADO.NET JDBC ODBC	Proprietary protocol using JSON	Cypher query language Java API Neo4j-OGM RESTful HTTP API Spring Data Neo4j
Supported programming languages	Ada C C# C++ D Delphi Eiffel Erlang Haskell Java JavaScript (Node.js) Objective-C OCaml Perl PHP Python Ruby Scheme Tcl	ActionScript C C# C++ Clojure ColdFusion D Dart Delphi Erlang Go Groovy Haskell Java JavaScript Lisp Lua MatLab Perl PHP PowerShell Prolog Python R Ruby Scala Smalltalk	.NET Clojure Elixir Go Groovy Haskell Java JavaScript Perl PHP Python Ruby Scala
Server-side scripts	Yes	JavaScript	Yes
Triggers	Yes	No	Yes
Foreign keys	Yes	No	Yes
Transaction concepts	ACID	No	ACID
Concurrency	Yes	Yes	Yes
Durability	Yes	Yes	Yes
Best used	Robust, known applications with clean objectives.	If you need dynamic queries. If you prefer to define indexes, not map/reduce functions. If you need good performance on a big database.	For graph-style, rich or complex, interconnected data. For example, searching routes in social relations, public transport links, road maps, or network topologies.
Web site	www.mysql.com	www.mongodb.com	neo4j.com

Review Questions

1. Databases are the collection of programs that allow users to create, maintain, update, and delete databases.

   a. True

   b. False

2. MongoDB is supported by which of the following?

   a. Python

   b. Perl

   c. PHP

   d. All of the above

3. Neo4j is an open source NoSQL database that has been implemented in Java.

   a. True

   b. False

4. Why is MongoDB referred to as a schema-less design?

5. Differentiate between the following:

   a. SQL and NoSQL

   b. MongoDB and MySQL

   c. MongoDB and Neo4j

6. Explain the role of building blocks like nodes, properties, and labels in Neo4j.

7. Illustrate the functionality of the following for SQL with the help of examples:

   a. Where clause

   b. Select clause

   c. AND clause

8. What does $match, .find(), .findAll(), and .aggregate() do in MongoDB.

9. Explain the basic query language structure of SQL, Mongodb, and Neo4j.

10. Give an example of when to use MongoDB rather than MySQL.

Section IV

Web Research

12

Research Trends on the Web

12.1 Contextual Information Retrieval

The field of information retrieval (IR) has become extremely important in recent years due to the intriguing challenges presented in tapping the Internet and the Web as an inexhaustible source of information. The success of web search engines is a testimony to this fact. The sheer amount of web pages and the exponential growth of the Web suggest that users are becoming more and more dependent on search engines ranking schemes to discover information relevant to their needs.

However, the "one size fits all" model of web search may limit diversity, competition, and functionality. Users typically expect to find information in the top-ranked results and more often than not they only look at the document snippets in the first few result pages and then they give up or reformulate the query. This can introduce a significant bias to their information finding process and calls for ranking schemes that take into account not only the overall page quality and relevance to the query, but also the match with a user's real intent when formulating the query. New search services that incorporate context and further incorporation of context into existing search services could increase the retrieval effectiveness and help mitigate any negative effects of biases in access to information on the Web.

12.1.1 Contextual Retrieval on the Web

Contextual retrieval is defined as "combining search technologies and knowledge about query and user context into a single framework in order to provide the most appropriate answer for the user's information needs" (Bhatia and Kumar 2010). Contextual IR intends to optimize the retrieval accuracy by involving two related steps: appropriately defining the context of user information needs, commonly called search context, and then adapting the search by taking it into account in the information selection process.

12.1.2 The Multifaceted Concept of Context in Information Retrieval

One of the primary questions here is: Which facets of context should be considered in the retrieval process? Figure 12.1 depicts the five context specific dimensions:

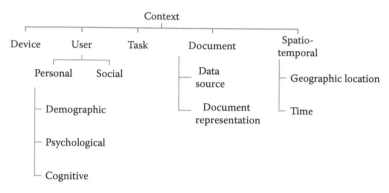

FIGURE 12.1
The multifaceted concept of context.

An information retrieval system is context-aware if it exploits context data in order to deliver relevant information to the user. Contextual IR (CIR) aims at delivering the right information to the user, in response to his query, within the right context. Figure 12.2 presents the basic architecture of a context-aware or contextual IR system.

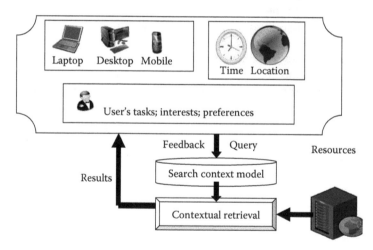

FIGURE 12.2
The contextual IR framework.

Previous work in the area of CIR has focused on three main themes: user profile modeling, query expansion, and relevance.

- *User profile modeling*: Focuses on exploiting the sources of evidence that more precisely include approaches to build the user profile that allows learning the user's context by implicitly inferring the information from the user's behavior and from external or local context sources.

- *Query expansion*: The query expansion approaches attempt to expand the original search query by adding further, new, or related terms. These additional terms are inserted into an existing query, either by the user (interactive query expansion,

IQE) or by the retrieval system (automatic query expansion, AQE), with the intent to increase the accuracy of the search.

- *Relevance feedback*: The notion of relevance feedback (RF) is to take into account the results that are initially returned in response to the input query and provide a means for automatically reformulating a query to more accurately reflect a user's interests.

12.1.3 Research Trends: Context in Information Retrieval

Contextual IR aims at delivering the right information to the user in response to his query, within the right context. Though numerous approaches that employ contextual user profiles, concept-based query formulation, and relevance filtration and relevance feedback/ suggestion already exist, some fundamental challenges still remain, making this area a dynamic field of study. Some key challenges include:

- How can algorithms be extended or developed to facilitate the use of context?
- Does the user need to be actively involved to make use of the context?
- Where should the context information come from?
- How might the effectiveness of such methods be tested in extended evaluation frameworks?

12.2 Web Mining

Information-intensive applications insist that we transcend from typical document retrieval to "knowledge" discovery. A conventional discovery framework encompasses novel methods for automated discovery of targeted knowledge drawn from a gamut of renowned research areas, such as data mining, information retrieval, natural language processing, artificial intelligence, machine learning, and statistics. The important taxonomy is illustrated in the following:

- *Data mining*: Defined as "the non-trivial extraction of implicit, previously unknown, and potentially useful information from large data sets or databases." It is used to identify and extract novel, valid, interesting, understandable patterns from a structured data collection. Data mining refers to extracting or mining knowledge from large amounts of data. It is also referred to as "knowledge mining."
- *Knowledge discovery in databases*: The process of finding novel, interesting, and useful patterns in data. Data mining is often considered as an essential step in the process of discovering knowledge in databases. Data mining and knowledge discovery in databases (KDD) are, therefore, often treated as synonymous.
- *Information retrieval*: A typical information retrieval task is to retrieve the amount of information a user needs in a specific situation for solving his current problem. Web IR can be defined as the application of theories and methodologies from IR

to the World Wide Web. It is about dealing with the technical and practical challenges of implementing information retrieval on the Web.

- *Information extraction*: Information extraction (IE) can make information retrieval more precise as it works at a finer-grain level to transform a collection of relevant documents retrieved using IR into information that can be effortlessly comprehended and analyzed by extracting relevant information from the retrieved documents. IE may include named entity recognition (NER) and relation extraction as subtasks. Suitably, IE can be employed to improve the indexing part of the IR process.

- *Web mining*: Refers to the use of data mining techniques to automatically retrieve, extract, and evaluate (generalize/analyze) information for knowledge discovery from web documents and services. The digital revolution and the phenomenal growth of the Web have generated enormous amounts of data, fostering the need for exploiting intelligent algorithms to uncover valuable knowledge. Due to the heterogeneous, semi-structured, distributed, time-varying, and multi-dimensional facets of web data, automated discovery of targeted knowledge is a challenging task.

Data mining, knowledge discovery in databases, information retrieval, information extraction, and web mining all have explicit diverse objectives. All of these complement each other to ascertain a worthy knowledge discovery framework, and none of these is intended to be a substitute for the others. Web mining includes information retrieval and information extraction as subtasks to preprocess textual data for applying data mining algorithms facilitating useful pattern discovery. Alternatively, web mining can increase the precision of the IR system and present retrieval results in a better organized way.

Figure 12.3 shows web mining as an extension of the data mining process. The major components of web mining consist of the information retrieval module to retrieve relevant documents, the information extraction module for selecting distinctive data from the retrieved documents and transforming them into a formal representation, the generalization module that mostly uses data mining approaches for automatic discovery of patterns across multiple web documents, and the analysis module.

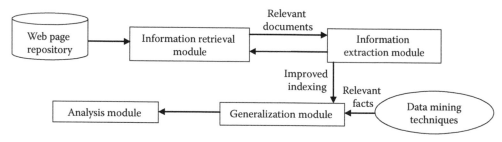

FIGURE 12.3
The web mining process.

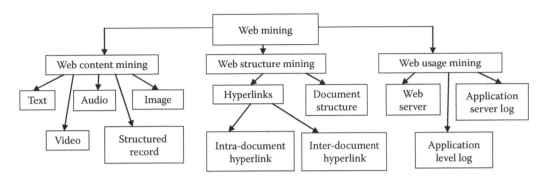

FIGURE 12.4
Web mining taxonomy.

The diversity of information on the Web leads to three broad categories of web mining: Web Content Mining, Web Structure Mining and Web Usage Mining. The web mining taxonomy can be viewed in Figure 12.4.

12.2.1 Sentiment Analysis on Web Data

Text mining is a type of web content mining that entails the process of extraction of knowledge from text. It is also known as text data mining (TDM) and knowledge discovery in textual databases (KDT) and is formally defined as the process of compiling, organizing, and analyzing large document collections to support the delivery of targeted types of information to analysts and decision makers. The generic strategy for text mining includes steps such as preprocessing (eliminating stop-words, stemming, etc.), feature selection using various statistical or semantic approaches, and modeling using appropriate data mining algorithms (classification, clustering, or regression techniques) to predict a model with valid interpretation and viable performance.

Classification or clustering algorithms are two key data mining approaches that have been used significantly in research for mining textual data to discover knowledge. Classification is a supervised learning technique used to assign a predefined tag to an instance on the basis of features, thus requiring training data. Alternatively, clustering is an unsupervised technique that does not require training data and is used to group similar instances on the basis of features.

Sentiment analysis is typically a classification task and regarded as one of the most popular text mining applications on the Web. Sentiment analysis or opinion mining is the computational study of opinions, attitudes, and emotions towards an entity. It segregates the sentiments into the basic polarity of negatives and positives, or otherwise neutral.

The words opinion, sentiment, view, and belief are used interchangeably, but there are subtle differences between them:

- *Opinion*: A conclusion thought out yet open to dispute ("each expert seemed to have a different opinion")
- *View*: Subjective opinion ("very assertive in stating his views")
- *Belief*: Deliberate acceptance and intellectual assent ("a firm belief in her party's platform")
- *Sentiment*: A settled opinion reflective of one's feelings ("her feminist sentiments are well known")

Social media generates a high volume of varied data at a high velocity, thus leading to the "bigness" in data. People choose to express and voice their emotions and opinions over major social media channels, such as blogs, review web sites, posts, comments, and micro-blogs. A persistent need to leverage this big social data for analytics has been identified by both researchers and practitioners.

Practical applications of sentiment analysis on social media include applications in business (marketing intelligence, product and service benchmarking), applications as subcomponent technology (recommendation systems, summarization, question answering), and applications in government intelligence (politics, public participation for improved planning).

12.2.2 Sentiment Analysis Approaches

Sentiment analysis approaches can be broadly divided into the following types:

- *Lexicon-based*: These are based on sentiment thesaurus, which is a collection of known and precompiled sentiment terms. The two main approaches for compilation of opinion lexicon are dictionary-based and corpus-based. In the dictionary-based approach, a small set of opinion words with their orientation is created manually and is enhanced by searching synonyms and antonyms. The corpus-based approach uses statistical or semantic methods for finding sentiment polarity and determining emotional affinity of words.
- *Machine learning-based*: These use supervised and unsupervised machine learning algorithms to find out the polarity orientation in the text.
- *Hybrid*: These combine machine learning and lexicon-based approaches.
- *Concept-based*: These are based on huge a knowledge base and analyze the conceptual information associated to natural language opinion behind the multi-word expressions. Semantic analysis is performed by the use of web ontologies or semantic networks.

12.2.3 Research Trends: Sentiment Analysis

Sentiment analysis is a research direction that drives the cutting-edge SMAC (social media, mobile, analytics, and cloud) paradigm by transforming text into a knowledge-base. The challenging aspects of using social media for sentiment analysis stem from the domains of natural language processing (NLP), text analytics, and computational linguistics.

Some challenges identified in the field are:

- Improved and optimized techniques for feature selection due to the high-dimensional, unstructured social media content
- Issues with natural language processing related to fixed text length, spelling variation (short forms like gr8 for great, gud for good), use of colloquial words and slang, multilingual usage of content in the same tweets or posts, emoticons, negation handling, and word sense disambiguation
- Fine grain sentiment analysis accounting for sarcasm, irony, rumor, aspect, and emotion detection
- Mash-up language sentiment analysis, such as Hinglish (Hindi+English)
- Use of sentiment analysis as a sub-component technology in businesses for customer relationship management and for recommendation systems

Review Questions

1. Answer the following:
   a. _____ aims at delivering the right information to the user, in response to his query, within the right context.
   b. _____ is the non-trivial extraction of implicit, previously unknown, and potentially useful information from large data sets or databases.
   c. _____ defines a settled opinion reflective of one's feelings.
   d. Sentiment analysis is typically a _____ task.
2. What do you understand by IR? How does context play a role to define Contextual IR?
3. Explain the relationship between data mining, web mining, and text mining.
4. What is web mining? Explain its process and types.
5. Explain the various approaches used for sentiment analysis.

Appendix A: HTML Examples

Procedure

1. Type the HTML code into Notepad or another editor, such as Dreamweaver or Visual Studio, using proper syntax and values for each tag.
2. Save the document using .htm or .html as the file extension. The file will be saved at the specified location as a web page to be viewed in your default web browser.
3. Go to the location of the web page and open it. The formatted web page will have the effect of tags but will not show the tag names.

Example A.1: A Web Page with HTML Describing Your Department Using Paragraph and List Tags

Tags Used

Tag Name	Description
<p>	Used to create paragraphs
<ol>	Used to create ordered lists
<ul>	Used to create unordered lists
<li>	Used for defining elements on ordered and unordered lists

Sample Code

```
<html>
    <head>
        <title>CSE Department</title>
    </head>
    <body>
        <h2>Department of Computer Science and Engineering</h2>
        <p>
            The quality of life has improved significantly with the advent
            of computers. PCs, laptops, the Internet, and teleconferencing
            have become household commodities. Hence, the career prospects
            the young generation has are bright in the various fields of
            technology, including networking, software engineering, and web
            designing. The department has developed state-of-the-art
            laboratories in the various fields of computer engineering—
            Computer Architecture Lab, Network Lab, Web Designing Lab,
            Image Processing and Multimedia Lab, Database Management and
            Data Mining Lab, Computation and Programming Lab, Operating
```

```
        System Lab, Artificial Intelligence Lab, Software Design Lab,
        and Software Testing Lab. These labs are equipped with the
        latest configuration PCs and are completely networked with the
        latest software.
    </p>
    <p>
        The Department of Computer Science and Engineering comprises
        the following branches:
    </p>
    <ul>
        <li>Computer Engineering</li>
        <li>Software Engineering</li>
        <li>Information Technology</li>
    </ul>
    <p>
        With the advancing world, everything is being automated in this
        era of computers. Computers are present in nearly every part of
        the world. They are in banks, railway stations, airports, and
        hospitals. So, it is necessary to impart technical education
        about computers. The Department of Computer Science and
        Engineering does just that. Students are taught basic as well
        as advanced level engineering concepts that are essential and
        ready to be applied in this world.
    </p>
  </body>
</html>
```

Output

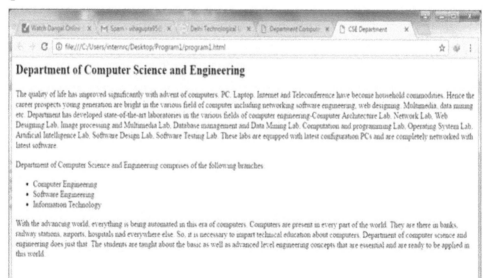

Example A.2: **Design a Single Page Web Site for a University Containing a Description of the Courses Offered. It Should Also Contain Some General Information About the University, Such as its History, Campus info, and Unique Features. The Page Should Use Color, with Each Section Having a different Color**

Tags Used

Tag Name	Description
<style>	Defines style information
<table>	Creates a table
<div>	Creates a block
<marquee>	Scrolling text
<tr>	Defines a table row
<td>	Defines table data

Sample Code

```
<html>
    <head>
        <title>
            Delhi Technological University
        </title>
        <style>
            body {
                background-color: #DCDCDC;
                max-width: 800px;
                margin: auto;
                font-size: 18;
            }
            table{
                background-color: #CCCCCC;
                width: 100%;
                padding: 10;
            }
            .notice{
                float: right;
                padding:10px;
                padding-left: 30px;
                border: 2px solid black;
                margin: 10 10 10 10;
                width: 250px;
            }
            .text{
                float: left;
                width: 410px;
                padding:10px;
                padding-left: 30px;
            }
```

```css
.menu{
    padding-right: 10;
    padding-left: 10;
    background-color: #696969;
    color: white;
    border: 2px solid #CDCDCD;
    display: inline-block;
}
.block{
    padding:10px;
    margin: 10 10 10 10;
    background-color: #808080;
    color: white;
}
div.menu:hover {
    background-color: black;
}
.dropdown{
    position: relative;
    display: inline-block;
}
.dropdown-content{
    display: none;
    position: absolute;
    background-color: #A9A9A9;
    box-shadow: 0px 8px 16px 0px rgba(0,0,0,0.2);
    min-width: 120px;
    padding: 12px 16px
    padding-left: 10px;
    z-index: 1;
}
.dropdown:hover
.dropdown-content{
    display: block;
}
</style>
</head>
<body>
    <img src="C:\Users\internrc\Desktop\DTU Logo.png" style="float:
    left; width: 100px; padding: 10;" >
    <h1 style="padding-top: 20; text-align: center;"><b>Delhi
    Technological University</b></h1>
    <h4 style="text-align: center;" >
        <i>(Formerly Delhi College of Engineering)</i>
    </h4>
    <table>
        <tr>
        <td>About Us</td>
        <td>
        <div class="dropdown">
        Departments
        <div class="dropdown-content">
            <p>Electrical</p>
            <p>Computer</p>
```

```html
            <p>Mechanical</p>
            <p>Civil</p>
            <p>Environmental</p>
        </div>
        </div>
        </td>
        <td>Faculty</td>
        <td>Academics</td>
        <td>Facilities</td>
        <td>Admissions</td>
        <td>Research</td>
        </tr>
</table>
<div class="notice">
    <h2>Important Notices</h2>
    <marquee direction= "up"; scrollamount=3>
        <p>Examination Registration Form</p>
        <br>
        <p>B.Tech ODD Semester Result </p>
        <br>
        <p>Supplementary examination Datesheet Circular</p>
        <br>
        <p>Notice Regarding upcoming holidays</p>
    </marquee>
</div>

        <div class="text">
    <hr>
    <h3 style="text-align: center;">Our Vision</h3>
    <p;>
        <i>"DTU to be a leading world class technology university
        playing its role as a key node in national and global
        knowledge network thus empowering India with the wings of
        knowledge and power of innovations "</i>
    </p>
    <br><hr>
    <h3 style="text-align: center;">
        Our Mission
    </h3>
    <p>
        <i>" Promote the engineering spirit of product development
        through effective integration of design engineering and
        rapid prototyping "</i>
    </p>
    <br><hr>
</div>
<div style="clear: left;"></div>
<br><br><br>
<div class="block">
<h3>History</h3>
<p>Delhi College of Engineering, (initially established with the
name - Delhi Polytechnic) came into existence in the year 1941 to
cater to the needs of Indian industries for trained technical
manpower with practical experience and sound theoretical
knowledge. From July 2009, the DCE has become Delhi Technological
```

```
University vide Delhi act 6 of 2009.The erstwhile DCE has
functioned from its historic Kashmere Gate Campus for almost 55
years and has shifted in 1996 to its lush green sprawling campus
of 164 Acres at Bawana Road, adjoining Sector-17, Rohini, Delhi-
42.</p>
</div>

<div class="block">
<h3>Departments</h3>
<p>The university caters to a wide range of departments:
<li>Computer Science</li>
<li>Civil</li>
<li>Biotech</li>
<li>Mechanical</li>
<li>Environmental</li>
<li>Electrical</li>
<li>Applied Physics</li>
</p>
</div>

<div class="block">
<h3>Facilities</h3>
<p>The huge campus offers a plethora of facilities to its
students. 7 housing hostels surround the college, along with a
central library, gymnasium, health center, bank, and guest
house.</p>
</div>
<div class="menu" ><p>Log In</p></div>
<div class="menu"><p>Training and Placements</p></div>
<div class="menu"><p>Hostels</p></div>
<div class="menu"><p>DTU Times</p></div>
<div class="menu"><p>Central Library</p></div>
<div class="menu"><p>Computer Center</p></div>
</body>
</html>
```

Output

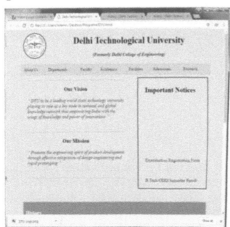
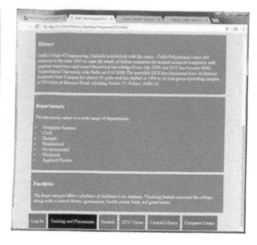

Appendix B: A Recipe Web Site Project Using Django and Neo4j—Kitchen Ninja

Introduction

Do you feel too lazy to go to the market to buy food ingredients and would rather make a new recipe out of the ones in your refrigerator?
Then this is just the web site for you!

Kitchen Ninja is a web application that allows the user to search for recipes based on ingredients provided by the user as a search query. This application uses Django as a framework and Neo4j as its database. Front-end is coded is in HTML, CSS, and JavaScript.

Django is a high-level Python web framework that encourages rapid development and clean, pragmatic design. Built by experienced developers, it takes care of much of the hassle of web development so you can focus on writing your app without needing to reinvent the wheel. It's free and open source.

Neo4j is a highly scalable native graph database that leverages data relationships as first-class entities, helping enterprises to build intelligent applications to meet today's evolving data challenges.

Front-End

The front end was mainly coded in HTML, CSS, and JavaScript.

Workflow

The home page (firstpage.html) of the web site is divided into four sections:

1. The first section greets the user with an image and a captivating slogan. It also contains a SEARCH button, which allows selection of ingredients. There are also various tabs on the top right corner to allow navigation through the page.

2. The second section guides the user to steer through the web site.

3. We also allow the user to select recipes by category. The third section specifies some categories of recipes; clicking on one directs the user to recipes from that particular category. It also contains a "more" button, which takes the user to the complete set of categories.

4. The fourth section provides details about the team member with the link to their github, Facebook, and LinkedIn profiles.

Search Functionality

As the user begins typing an ingredient name, suggestions are auto-populated so the user can select from the suggestions and a tag corresponding to that ingredient is created. In a similar fashion, the user can select multiple ingredients, all of which appear as tags. Tags can also be discarded. The user can then proceed and a page containing recipes corresponding to the selected ingredients is displayed. The recipes also contain the number of ingredients matched from the query. The recipes are displayed in descending order of matched ingredients.

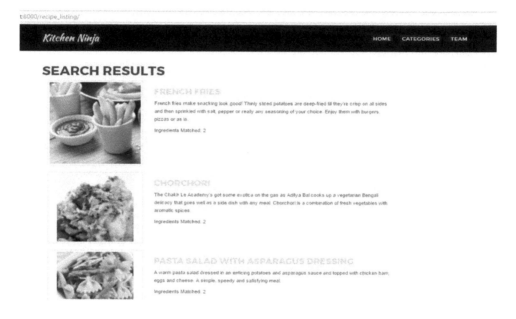

The user can then click a search result to view the detailed recipe page.

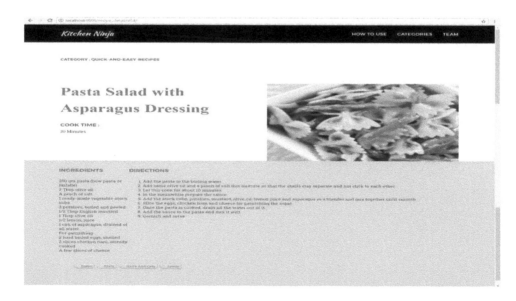

Categories

The recipes are segregated into various categories such as kids recipes, chicken recipes, vegetarian recipes, and so on. The user can select a particular category to view all the recipes belonging to that category.

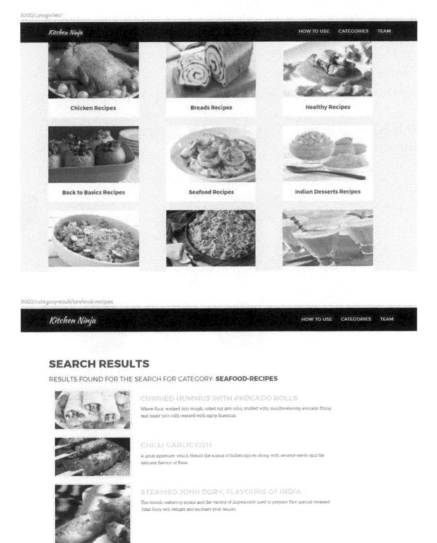

***

Back-End

The back end was coded in Django, a python web framework. We used Neo4j, a graph database, to store our dataset. The interlinking between the two was done using neomodel.

Neo4j

Neo4j stores data as nodes. Relationships between data are shown through edges connecting these nodes. A graph database was chosen for the project as it focuses on relationships as much as it focuses on the data. Since our data model consisted of highly connected elements, Neo4j was an ideal choice. Our model consisted of two types of nodes:

- Recipe nodes (Grey nodes)
- Ingredient nodes (Black nodes)

The relationship between these two types of nodes was labeled as "Child".
  Recipe → (child) → Ingredient

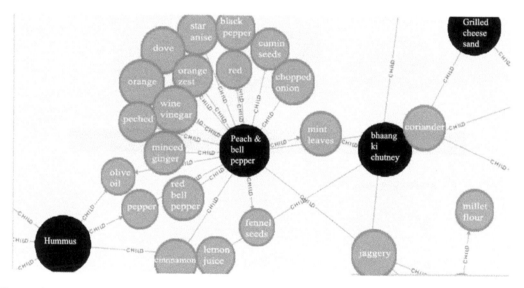

The graph representation of the dataset. Grey nodes are Recipe nodes and the black nodes are the Ingredient nodes. The edges are marked as "child."

Django

The project was implemented as a Django app.

The directory structure of the Kitchen Ninja App. (It is denoted as cook_ninja in this figure.)

Steps in creation of the back-end functionalities:

1. *Integrating neomodel into the project*: After installing neomodel, the following code was added to the settings.py file to set the connection URL.

```
from neomodel import config
config.DATABASE_URL = 'bolt://username:password@localhost:7687'
```

2. *Dataset models*: models.py contains the definition of the model. Recipe and Ingredient nodes have been defined here along with their attributes and relationships.

```python
class Recipe(StructuredNode):
    name = StringProperty()
    index = IntegerProperty()
    method = ArrayProperty()
    image_path = StringProperty()
    image_url = StringProperty()
    description = StringProperty()
    category = StringProperty()
    ingredients = ArrayProperty()
    cook_time = StringProperty()
    tags = ArrayProperty()

    ingredient = RelationshipTo('Ingredient','CHILD')

class Ingredient(StructuredNode):
    name = StringProperty()

    recipe = RelationshipFrom('Recipe','CHILD')
```

Models.py File

3. *Homepage*: The homepage consists of a search box where the user can enter the ingredients. The function index is used for the homepage.

```
def index(request):
    request.session['ingredient_list'] = []
    return render(request, 'recipe_app/index.html')
```

A session variable named "ingredient_list" is maintained. This is a list consisting of the ingredients entered by the user.

The search box displays a drop down list recommending ingredients depending on the text entered by the user. We used jQuery autocomplete for this purpose. Whenever a user enters something (character by character), jQuery autocomplete fetches a list for the entered query at the url "/api/get_ingredients," which is mapped to the function "get_ingredients" in views.py.

```
$(function() {
  $("#tag_list1").autocomplete({
    source: "/api/get_ingredients/",
    minLength: 2,
  });
});
```

In the function get_ingredients, the query is the same as the one entered by the user in the search box, as fetched from the AJAX call (jQuery autocomplete). Using this query, results are returned from the Neo4j database as shown, with a limit of 10 items.

```
def get_ingredients(request):
    if request.is_ajax():
        q = request.GET.get('term', '')
        query = 'match(i:Ingredient) where i.name contains (q) return(i) order by length(i.name) limit 10;'
        ingredients, meta = db.cypher_query(query, params={"q":q})
        # ingredients = sorted(Ingredient.nodes.filter(name__icontains = q)[:10], key=lambda o:len(o.name))
        # print ingredients
        results = []
        id = 0
        for ingredient in ingredients:
            ingredient_json = {}
            ingredient_json['id'] = id
            id += 1
            ingredient_json['label'] = ingredient[0].properties['name']
            ingredient_json['value'] = ingredient[0].properties['name']
            results.append(ingredient_json)
        data = json.dumps(results)
    else:
        data = 'fail'
    mimetype = 'application/json'

    return HttpResponse(data, mimetype)
```

Tags are created as the user selects the ingredients one by one, for which the function createTag is used as shown. As a new tag is created, the ingredient is pushed into an array *ing*. We will use this array to store the ingredients entered by the user. This array will help us in querying our database as shown in the following.

```
function createTag(text) {

    if (text != '') {

        var tag = $('<div class="tags">' + text + '<a class="delete"></a></div>');

        ing.push(text);
        tag.insertAfter($('#tag_list1'), $('#tag_list1'));

        $('#tag_list1').val('');
    }
```

When the user selects all the ingredients and clicks on submit, 2 actions take place:

a. A post request is sent to the url "/selected_ingredients" via AJAX. This post request contains array *ing*.

```
$('#submit_button').on('click', function() {

    $.ajax({
            type: 'POST',
            url: "/selected_ingredients/",
            data: {'ingredients[]': ing},
    });
```

b. The list retrieved from the post request is stored in the session variable *ingredient_list*.

```
def selected_ingredients(request):
    ingredient_list = request.POST.getlist('ingredients[]')
    # print ingredient_list
    request.session['ingredient_list'] = ingredient_list
    # print request.session['ingredient_list']
    # response = {'status': 1, 'message': _("Ok")}
    # return HttpResponse(json.dumps(response), content_type='application/json')
    # return redirect(reverse('recipe_app:recipe_listing'))
    return HttpResponse('success')
```

The form gets submitted on url "recipe_listing" as specified in the action attribute of the form.

```
<form action="/recipe_listing" id="search_form">
```

4. *Implementing the ingredient search functionality:* In the recipe_listing function, a query is executed to match recipes with the selected ingredients in the ingredient_list, which is obtained from the session variable. The results are stored in a list called "recipes" and the response is sent in the form of recipe_listing.html along with "recipes."

```
def recipe_listing(request):
    # ingredient_list_sample = ["fennel","sugar","mustard oil"]
    ingredient_list = request.session.get('ingredient_list')

    query = """ match(r:Recipe)-[:CHILD]->(i:Ingredient)
        where i.name in {ingredient_list}
        RETURN count(*) as degree,r as recipe
        ORDER BY degree DESC
        LIMIT 3"""

    results, meta = db.cypher_query(query, params={"ingredient_list":ingredient_list})

    recipes = []
    for r in results:
        recipes.append({'no_matched' : r[0], 'name' : r[1].properties['name'],
            'image_path' : r[1].properties['image_path'] , 'id' : r[1].properties['index'],
            'description' : r[1].properties['description']})

    return render(request, 'recipe_app/recipe_listing.html', {"recipes" : recipes })
```

5. *Search according to category:* When the user selects a category from the homepage, the category name is used to query the database and all the recipe nodes whose category attribute matches the category name are returned.

```
def categoryresult(request, name):
    recipes = Recipe.nodes.filter(category = name)[:10]
    return render(request, 'recipe_app/categoryresult.html',
```

6. *Recipe detail:* When the recipes are listed, either by category or after being searched via ingredients, the user can click on a recipe to view all its details. The recipe ID is used to query the database and all the attributes of that particular recipe node are returned.

```
def recipe_detail(request, id):
    recipe = Recipe.nodes.filter(index=id)[0]
    # print recipe.cook_time
    # print recipe
    return render(request, 'recipe_app/recipe_detail.html', {"recipe" : recipe})
```

References

T. Berners-Lee, J. Hendler, O. Lassila. The semantic web. *Scientific American*, 2001, 284(5), 34–43.

M.P.S. Bhatia, A. Kumar. Paradigm shifts: From pre-web information systems to recent web-based contextual information retrieval. *Webology*, June 2010, 7(1).

M. Kajewski. Emerging technologies changing our service delivery models. *The Electronic Library*, 2007, 25(4), 420–429.

B. Schwartz. Google's search knows about over 130 trillion pages: In less than four years, Google's search knowledge of pages have grown by more than 100 trillion new pages. 2016. https://searchengineland.com/googles-search-indexes-hits-130-trillion-pages-documents-263378.

Bibliography

J. Allan. Challenges in information retrieval and language modeling *Report of a Workshop Held at the Center for Intelligent Information Retrieval*, University of Massachusetts, Amherst, MA, 2002.

M.P.S. Bhatia, A. Kumar. Contextual paradigm for ad-hoc retrieval of user-centric web-data *IET Software*, August 2009, 3(4), 264–275.

M.P.S. Bhatia, A. Kumar. Information retrieval & machine learning: Supporting Technologies for web mining research and practice. *Webology*, 2008, 5(2), 5.

M.P.S. Bhatia, A. Kumar. A primer on the web information retrieval paradigm. *Journal of Theoretical and Applied Information Technology (JATIT)*, July 2008, 4(7), 657–662.

R. Kuhlen. Information and pragmatic value-adding: Language games and information science. *Computers and the Humanities*, 1991, 25, 93–101.

A. Kumar, V. Dabas, P. Hooda. Text classification algorithms for mining unstructured data: A SWOT analysis. *International Journal of Information Technology*, Springer, 2017, 1–11, doi: 10.1007/s41870-017-0072-1.

A. Kumar, T. Sebastian. Sentiment analysis: A perspective on its past, present and future. *International Journal of Intelligent Systems and Applications (IJISA)*, September 2012, 4(10), 1–14; MECS Publisher.

B. Liu. *Sentiment Analysis and Subjectivity. Handbook of Natural Language Processing*, Second ed., CRC Press, *New York, 2010*.

T. O'Reilly. Web 2.0 Compact Definition: Trying Again (O'Reilly Media, Sebastopol), http://radar.oreilly.com/archives/2006/12/web_20_compact.html, 2007.

B. Pang, L. Lee. Opinion mining and sentiment analysis. *Foundations and Trends in Information Retrieval*, 2008, 2(1–2), 1–135.

Websites

AngularJS: angularjs.org
Bootstrap: getbootstrap.com
Django: www.djangoproject.com
Internet Engineering Task force: www.ietf.org
Internet Live Statistics: www.InternetLiveStats.com
Node.js: nodejs.org
PHP: php.net
Python: www.python.org
Ruby on Rails: rubyonrails.org
World Wide Web Consortium: www.w3c.com

Suggested Readings

Bootstrap: Responsive Web Development, 1/E, Jake Spurlock, O'Reilly Media, Sebastopol, CA, 2013.
The Definitive Guide to MongoDB: The NoSQL Database for Cloud and Desktop Computing, 1/E, Eelco Plugge, Apress, New York City, New York, 2010.
Graph Databases: The Definitive Book on Graph Databases, Ian Robinson, Jim Webber and Emil Eifrem, O'Reilly Media, Sebastopol, CA, 2015.
HTML and CSS: Design and Build Websites, 1/E, Jon Duckett, John Wiley & Sons, Hoboken, NJ, 2011.
JavaScript: The Good Parts, 1/E, Douglas Crockford, O'Reilly Media, Sebastopol, CA, 2008.
Learning Angular JS, Brad Dayley, Addison Wesley, Boston, MA, 2014.
Learning PHP, MySQL and JavaScript: With jQuery, CSS & HTML5, 4/E, Robin Nixon O'Reilly Media, Sebastopol, CA, 2014.
Mastering Node.js, Sandro Pasquali, Packt Publishing Limited, Mumbai, MH, 2013.
MySQL in a Nutshell, A Desktop Quick Reference, 2/E, Russell Dyer, O'Reilly Media, Sebastopol, CA, 2009.
Node.js, MongoDB and AngularJS Web Development, Brad Dayley, Addison Wesley, Boston, MA, 2014.
Programming Ruby 1.9 & 2.0 (4th edition) The Pragmatic Programmers' Guide, 4/E, Dave Thomas, with Chad Fowler and Andy Hunt, Pragmatic Bookshelf, 2013.
TCP/IP Protocol Suite, 3/E, Forouzan, Tata McGraw-Hill Education, 2005.
Two Scoops of Django: Best Practices for Django 1.8, 3/E, Audrey Roy Greenfeld, Lightning Source Inc, La Vergne, TN, 2015.
Web Design and Development Black Book: The Ultimate Reference for Advanced Web Designers, Scott Jarol, Marisa Pena, Coriolis Group, 1997.

Index

Note: Page numbers in italic and bold refer to figures and tables respectively.